MAR   2000

PUEBLO PROFILES

PUEBLO PROFILES

Cultural Identity through Centuries of Change

Joe S. Sando

Foreword by **Regis Pecos**
Afterword by **Alfonso Ortiz**

Clear Light Publishers
Santa Fe, New Mexico

Dedication

To the Pueblo People

Copyright © 1998 by Joe S. Sando

Clear Light Publishers, 823 Don Diego, Santa Fe, New Mexico 87501
WEB: www.clearlightbooks.com

First Edition
10 9 8 7 6 5 4 3 2 1

Library of Congress Cataloging-in-Publication Data

Sando, Joe S., 1923 –
    Pueblo profiles: cultural identity through centuries of change /
Joe S. Sando; foreword by Regis Pecos; afterword by Alfonso Ortiz.
        p.   cm.
        ISBN 0-940666-39-1: $24.95 — ISBN 0-940666-40-5 (pbk.): $14.95
        1. Pueblo Indians—Biography.   2. Pueblo Indians—History.
    3. Pueblo Indians—Ethnic identity.   I. Title.
    E99.P9S188   1998
    978'.004975—dc20   94-17268
                                                                                        CIP
PHOTO AND ILLUSTRATION CREDITS:
    Pueblo Cultural Center, archival collection, pages 22, 40, 50, 56, 64, 70, 78,
        106, 113, 127, 168, 226, 236, 240, 262
    © by Marcia Keegan, pages 131, 138, 142, 150, 156, 164, 177, 186, 188, 190,
        197, 200, 213, 216, 222, 233, 246, 249, 253, 271, 280, 283, 286, 292
    Courtesy Bethel Agency, New York, pages 92, 147
    Felix Vigil, page 30
    George Toya, page 2

Cover Photo: C. C. Naranjo, Santa Clara Feast Day. Photograph © Marcia Keegan.
Cover and Book Design by Marcia Keegan
Typographical Design/Production by V. S. Elliott

Contents

Foreword
by Regis Pecos

As we come to the end of the twentieth century, *Pueblo Profiles* reminds us of the enormous responsibility our children will bear in continuing the struggle of our survival.

After nearly five hundred years of being subjected to the worst policies ever conceived to destroy a people, we still have a land base to call our homelands, we still have our native religion, which is the heart of our sense of spirituality and worldview, we still have our language that affords us the means by which we are able to maintain the seeds of our values, traditions, and customs, we still have traditional forms of governance, a system which underlines the highest standard of individual commitment to family and community, and we still have the strength of family which maintains the vitality and a sense of community. *Pueblo Profiles* is not a tribute to individuals, but a tribute and a testament to all those within our respective communities that is reflected by and through these individuals. Who we are today is the result of family and our respective communities. A Pueblo word *Ske'wa* is the Pueblo word my grandfather always used to describe what must be our mission in our individual lives. He often said that we must give equal value to all those things that make us who we are, our language, our religion, our songs and dances, and we must give equal value to those skills necessary to protect all that we cherish, all that we have inherited that enriches our lives from all of the external forces that will never cease to influence us. How profound and visionary these words are. As long as there are these seeds of words to plant and as long as we nurture them, we shall never perish as a people. *Pueblo Profiles* is thus a beautiful testament of a long and beautiful history of a people who have never been willing to compromise a way of life so that children yet unborn might enjoy inheriting those seeds and a world that affords them the opportunity to experience all that enriches our lives. No one can ever take away from us all that has been passed on to us generation by generation by word of mouth by our forefathers except ourselves when we fail individually to live up to the highest levels of commitment to the principles of family and community.

REGIS PECOS
Executive Director for the
New Mexico Office of Indian Affairs

Preface and Acknowledgments

Of the persons that I have written about, I know most personally and have been aware of their experiences and successes over the years. I have worked with John C. Rainer and Domingo Montoya. I have served on committees and boards with Dr. Ortiz, Jerry Montoya, Agnes Dill, James Hena, Benny Atencio, and Pablita Velarde. Frank Tenorio and Joe H. Herrera I had known since our high school days together. George Rivera and Peter Pino were my students at either the Institute of American Indian Arts (IAIA), or University of New Mexico. I interviewed the relatives of Sotero Ortiz, Alcario Montoya, and Miguel Trujillo. Pablo Abeita I had known since my childhood—one of his sons is my godfather who gave me his name.

In the early 1970s, when I was doing research for my first book, *The Pueblo Indians,* I went to the National Archives in Washington, D.C. While I was on the east coast I stopped at Bethesda, Maryland to visit and interview Dr. George Blue Spruce. From there I went to Princeton, New Jersey to interview Dr. Alfonso Ortiz. I met with them on various occasions after they returned to New Mexico and obtained more information necessary for their stories.

I knew Popovi Da in high school and later met with him on two occasions. The first time was to write about him in my first book. I talked to his mother, Maria Martinez, at that time and I went back later to see her before Popovi Da died.

I wish to thank all the Pueblo Indians I interviewed for their cooperation. Special recognition for their assistance goes to my private editor and wife, Louisa, who buoys my spirit with affectionate support, and the final editor, Sara Held, another strong supporter and advisor. Lastly, for making this publication more meaningful, thanks to the two photographers, E. "Swede" Sholer and Marcia Keegan. "Tsa mo no pah" to the illustrators, Felix Vigil and George Toya.

PAA PEH/JOE S. SANDO

Introduction

Throughout the history of Indian education American Indian students have heard the litany that George Washington is the father of their country. Washington and other American folk heroes and icons who have been studied in the classroom have little meaning for Indian children. The truth is that Indian students' backgrounds are in many ways foreign to the mainstream American way of life. In the communities where these Indian students grow up there are other personalities to whom they can relate.

Not much has been written about Pueblo Indian culture and history in the past. Since Indian students often cannot relate to the mainstream history and culture presented in the classroom, these students quickly lose interest and are more apt to drop out of school. By reading a book such as this, about successful people with whom Indian students relate and can identify, it is hoped that they may be motivated to pursue their education and set their goals high.

This book is also meant for non-Indian students and general readers who may wish to learn about Pueblo Indians and their contribution to their communities and their country. Reading about individuals helps to eliminate stereotypes, misconceptions and distortions. The reader will also learn about continuing issues like Indian sovereignty, land and water rights, government-to-government relations of the tribes, and relations with the federal government. I have attempted to give the reader a sense of each individual's personal experience as a Pueblo Indian and to show how these people have utilized contact with mainstream society to the benefit of their own communities and retained their Indian identity throughout the process.

The book begins with the story of the Pueblo Revolt, told through the life of Popé, the war captain of San Juan Pueblo. For the first time the story of the revolt of 1680 is told from the perspective of pueblo legacy, tradition, and common law. Most of the published information about Popé and the Pueblo Revolt has been negative up to this time. Popé has been maligned and vilified, but then what Indian leader of the past has not? Drawing on my pueblo background, I have used numerous fragments of oral history to fill in the Spanish account in order to tell about this great event in a way that brings balance and does justice to the Indian perspective. It also will give the reader some of the historical reasons why the pueblos have been able to maintain their culture while most other tribes have lost much of theirs.

Writers have described pueblo societies as peaceful. It has been conventional wisdom to view the pueblos as peaceful farmers who, when pressed, defended against the common enemy. The truth is the pueblos always had warrior societies much like those found among the Toltec, Maya, and Aztec, down to body paint. The logical conclusion to be drawn from the facts and circumstances leading to the revolt is that it was a holy war for the pueblos. At stake, along with the need to fight to free themselves from the Spanish system of economic exploitation, was the need to preserve sacred religious practices, including the kachina dances. The deliberate destruction by the Spanish of pueblo religious institutions was more than enough to turn the natives against the representatives of the cross, the sword, and the Crown. Pueblo language and religion were considered an obstacle to Native absorption into the Spanish Empire as loyal hardworking subjects of the Crown.

The story of the struggle to regain the sacred Taos Blue Lake is presented to give the reader an understanding of the importance of land and sovereignty to Indian people.

The book includes brief biographies of more than one person from some pueblos. I wished to write about at least one from each of the nineteen pueblos of New Mexico, since each has its uniqueness and each has contributed to Pueblo Indian culture and experience in its own way. I have not attempted to write an encyclopedia or a comprehensive "Who's Who of Pueblo Life." In a book of limited scope it is of course not possible to include all the people who have made significant contributions to Pueblo life and history, and some I have written about in detail elsewhere.[1]

Although I have told their stories before, I include the "Troika"—Ortiz, Abeita, and Montoya—because of their importance to pueblo history early in the twentieth century. They successfully opposed Indian Commissioner Charles Burke in 1926, when he was crusading against the All Pueblo Council for operating without Bureau of Indian Affairs (BIA) sanction and against the pueblos for practicing their ancient culture. The work of these leaders laid the foundation for many of the advances the pueblos have achieved since that time.

Miguel Trujillo, another important figure in pueblo history, effected a significant change by opening the door to political participation so that Indians in Arizona and New Mexico could have the right to vote in state and national elections. He waged a personal battle against national political forces at a time when others declined to support him.

Robert Lewis, the long-time governor of Zuni Pueblo, was a strong person who brought many improvements and changes to his community.

All of the people whose stories are told in this book have made important contributions in their communities and in specific fields of endeavor, from administration and politics to economic development, from the arts to education and medicine. All have desired to give something back to their heritage and the communities that fostered them. None of them began life with the advantages that are so often the stepping stones to success. This book is a testament to the determination, endurance, and creativity that have enabled Pueblo Indians to preserve their identity within the dominant culture while moving with the times and achieving success on their own terms.

Certain Pueblo Indian artists, such as the potter Maria Martinez, have become world famous themselves and at the same time instrumental in gaining recognition for Indian artists in general at a time when Indian works of art were considered, at best, collectible craft items. Among the younger generation, several artists, including sculptors George Rivera and writer/educator Greg Cajete, are contributing to the preservation and development of the arts in Pueblo Indian communities.

NOTES

1. See Joe S. Sando, *Pueblo Nations: Eight Centuries of Pueblo Indian History* (Santa Fe, N.M.: Clear Light Publishers, 1992).

PART I

Resistance
and Revolt

Drawing of Pueblo runners by George Toya.

CHAPTER 1

Popé and the Pueblo Revolt

The story is one familiar to all Americans. A group of frontier farmers, traders, and hunters living on the edge of the wilderness were oppressed by an autocratic foreign government which ruled by decree, taxed them unjustly, gave them no voice in governmental decision making, and denied them freedom to worship as they chose. It was a system to which they had been subjected for years; during this time uncorrected grievances and hostile, even cruel, treatment at the hands of the representatives of a monarchy housed in luxurious palaces across the Atlantic Ocean had forced them to a point of no return. They had to drive the Europeans out of their country even though they lacked the empire's arms and military might. So the men gathered clandestinely in their villages to plot an uprising and select their best men as leaders. This was done in great secrecy, mindful of the possibility of information leaking to the enemy; some of the family members of the revolutionaries were in the foreigners' camp, working for and sympathizing with the ruling order.

Finally, the time came, and messengers sped to notify the people that the insurrection had begun and that all men and boys capable of fighting were needed. Underarmed, considered inferior by the bureaucrats and royally appointed officials, the frontiersmen nevertheless prevailed and won their freedom to live and worship as they pleased and to govern themselves.

These were, however, not the farmers and villagers of Concord and Lexington fame. These were the Pueblo Indians of New Mexico, who in 1680, nearly a century before the more celebrated revolution of 1776, staged the first successful American revolution against a foreign colonial power, Spain.[1] Their leader was not a patrician planter. He was a man of the people, an Indian about fifty years old whose world was bounded largely by the pueblos up and down the Rio Grande and a few others situated farther off the river and El Camino Real (The Royal Road),

3

which paralleled it, an avenue for bringing supplies into New Mexico and exporting Native products to the seat of empire.

The leader of the 1680 Pueblo Revolt was, as best as can be determined, born in the village of Oke Owinge (San Juan Pueblo). Early in life, he probably was given the name Po-pay or Po-pyn ("ripe squash").[2] Later, the Spaniards wrote the name as Pope (pronounced Popé) and often referred to him as El Pope. Growing up in Oke Owinge, there was nothing to set him apart from his companions. That would come later, in his maturity.

Since revolutions do not explode spontaneously without cause, before looking at the Pueblo Revolt in detail it is important to examine the history of both Popé's people and their Spanish conquerors in order to place the Pueblo Revolt of 1680 in historical context.

The story began on a May day in 1539 when a black man "unlocked for the world the gateway to the Southwest of the future United States."[3] This man, named Estevanico, was the first man of Old World origin to reach the American Southwest—present-day New Mexico and Arizona— and make contact with the people. Yet, because he was a Moor, a black from Azamore, Morocco, his feat was credited to the leader of his party, a padre who was not present at the encounter. Fray Marcos de Niza, the leader, had been designated by Spanish officialdom to explore the territory of the so-called Seven Cities of Cíbola. But de Niza failed officially to make contact with the Natives and merely observed Hawikuh— supposedly one of those Seven Cities of Cíbola—from a distance, returning to Mexico to make a questionable report of his findings. The expedition, however, generated this saying among the Pueblo Indians: "The first white man we saw was a black man."

Hawikuh was one of the "Seven Cities of Cíbola," which became the object of the Spaniards' search when they came to verify the stories of the four survivors of a shipwreck that took place in 1528 near present-day Galveston, Texas, during the abortive attempt of the Spaniard Pánfilo de Narváez to settle Florida. From an estimated total of two hundred and fifty in the company, only four survived.[4] The survivors journeyed westward toward Mexico and were captured by hostile Natives. In time they escaped, only to be captured by other Natives before they reached Mexico. In telling stories of their adventure, they included tales of riches to the north. Thus, the myth of the mysterious Seven Cities of Cíbola was created.

Subsequent to the de Niza trek into the Southwest, a series of expeditions of Spanish fortune-seekers and clerics invaded the pueblo country. From the beginning, these adventurers showed little concern for the Indians and less inclination to understand their ways. This behavior set the stage for the eventual uprising.

The 1680 Pueblo Revolt was born of several causes, several persistent

Spanish practices that ensured the enmity of the conquered. One was the harassment and persecution of Pueblo people who followed traditional religious practices. The Spaniards were determined to stamp out the "pagan" forms of worship and replace them with Christianity. Cruel exploitation of Indian labor and resources through the *encomienda* and *repartimiento* systems kept the anger of the pueblos smoldering.

Through the system of encomienda, the Spanish forced the involuntary donation of part of the crops of certain pueblo families every year to support the Spanish missions, military forces, and civil institutions. It was superficially akin to the system of tithing, but the amount the Natives were forced to contribute was well above what they could afford. For the Spanish, Indian tribute was considered necessary to support the institutions of the privileged ruling class.

The institution of repartimiento was somewhat similar; however, instead of tribute, Indians were forced to work in Spanish households and fields. They were required to perform a substantial amount of labor each year. The encomienda and repartimiento systems had their origins in the feudal practices of the Spanish Crown; these consisted in part of granting Spanish knights manorial rights over the peasants on lands regained from the Moors during the centuries of the Spanish *Reconquista*, which ended with the expulsion of the Moors in 1492, coincidentally the year Columbus arrived in the New World.

As harsh and humiliating as the systems of forced work and payment were, the continual religious persecution during the years from about 1598 to 1680 was even more galling to the Indian people and evoked more resistance. However, despite relentless pressure from the conquerors, the Pueblo people held tenaciously to their traditional religion; it was of paramount importance to them since it was their way of communicating with their Creator and deities. This religion had served them well from time immemorial, providing the faith they needed to survive the vicissitudes of life.

Into this life of subjugation Popé was born, around 1630. But, as the Pueblo Indians say, his future already was decided at the place of his origin—heaven, non-Indians call it. There is no reason to believe he did not grow up like any other Pueblo Indian boy of his time, strictly following the rules and rhythms of the community. Religion was inextricably woven into the pattern of pueblo life. Even during periods of intensive work—such as hoeing and irrigating, harvesting, drying and storing food or medicinal herbs for later use—religious observances were not neglected. When ceremonies demanded, other members of the extended families took care of seasonal business while certain men stayed in the *kiva* (ceremonial chamber) to pray for rain.

In accordance with tradition, as a young man Popé undoubtedly went to the river certain mornings to take a ceremonial bath to make himself strong both physically and mentally. Each morning he threw corn pollen to the east to the rising sun, towards Cikumu and Sipofenae, and asked the deities for a good life and blessings for his people. For the pueblos, the ideal was life in harmony with all creation.

As he grew towards maturity, Popé would have begun to take part in the tribe's Cloud and Turtle Dances, as well as the animal dances of the winter months. As the years progressed, he evidently began to serve as an assistant to the war captain, helping supervise the dances held by the tribe.

The next step for Popé was appointment by the village leaders as war captain, assuming all the responsibilities connected with that position. At this time he would have become more intensely aware of the pressures on the Tewa people from the Spanish colonial government and missionaries. Originally, when the first Spanish settlers under Don Juan de Oñate came to the colony in 1598, the Tewas had not been inimical and, in fact, had given the newcomers land to share. The Spaniards, without interference, established their first capital at Yunge Owinge (Mockingbird Place Village) directly across the river from Popé's home village of Oke. Although the capital was moved to Santa Fe by 1610, some Spaniards remained in the area.

Popé, like the other Tewa leaders, was well aware that many Spaniards were telling his people not to perform their traditional, centuries-old religious dances because they were "idolatrous." Instead, the Europeans said, the Pueblo people were to go to the Spanish houses of worship, which in many cases their forced labor had helped to build, to listen to the padres. This pressure to abandon their religious practices was resolutely, if passively, resisted by the pueblos. How could they simply relinquish the religion that was not just a weekly exercise but interwoven into every part of their daily lives, including much fasting and sacrifice on behalf of the world they knew? Their religious beliefs formed their worldview; their entire year was crowded with religious activities that maintained their peaceful attitude and outlook. The Spaniards were asking them to give up all this for something they did not understand and which did not sustain them.

Part of Popé's education in this new and confusing world was learning that the Spanish, giving nothing in return, came to Tewa families and took food and wood as assigned them by the governor in Santa Fe (encomienda). Beyond that, Tewa men and women were forced to work (repartimiento) for Spanish settlers while the Spanish men were away on duty as citizen-soldiers or as professional soldiers exploring the high plains or fighting raiding nomadic tribes of the Llano Estacado to the east.

Popé also discovered that some war chiefs, captains, and religious leaders were harassed in various ways by the Spaniards. A Tewa *estufa* (kiva) was filled with sand so the people could not hold their nightly dances. Although this was a sacrilege to the Indians, the Spaniards viewed the destruction of kivas as a mandate from God, considering such desecration not only legitimate but praiseworthy.

Early in the history of the New World, there was protracted debate in the highest political and religious circles in Spain about whether Indians were, indeed, humans and had immortal souls as Europeans did. Having finally concluded that Indians did have souls, the Spaniards considered it their duty to bring Christian salvation to these "heathens." One of the ironies of the Spanish attitude was their accusation that the Natives conducted devil worship. In fact, the pueblos had no concept of Satan; however, ironically the devil was a part of the Spanish belief system.

It was against this background of long-festering grievances that Popé and other Tewa war captains began discussing what might be done. The harmony of their lives had been seriously threatened. When their indigenous religion had been suppressed, it meant that the natural order of life was disrupted. All forms of creation, they believed, depended on one another—rocks, trees, flowers, birds, animals. These, in turn, relied for their existence on the clouds, snow, rain, lightning, and wind. In their religious ceremonies, the pueblos called on the Creator to perpetuate the natural order of life so that mankind might live. It was their conviction that mankind's purpose in life was to adore, thank, and praise the Creator for the continuation of life and harmony within his creation. The pueblo people did this by fasting in their kivas, sacrificing, offering prayer feathers, and dancing.

Thus, Popé and his contemporaries considered the suppression of their religion a threat to pueblo culture in its totality. This belief was confirmed by a severe drought that occurred about this time which the Indians interpreted as a sign of the disruption of the natural order because of Spanish hostility toward their religion.

Regarding the Spanish, the pueblo tribes near Santa Fe observed that the lay government was constantly struggling with the Franciscan padres concerning who had ultimate authority over the Indians and who should collect tribute and labor from the Natives. It appeared at the time that the balance of power favored the Franciscans.

During the final decades of the seventeenth century, Popé and the other Tewa leaders met periodically to discuss the galling problem of repression by a series of inconsistent but usually self-serving Spanish civil and ecclesiastical rulers. How long were they to put up with the persecution and exploitation they suffered? The consensus was that something had to be done. But what? The situation of the tribes was grave. Their religious freedom was increasingly impinged upon, their right of conscience was seriously threatened, their personal security was endangered by the encomienda system; life itself was in danger.

At one of the northern Tewa leaders' conferences, it was decided to invite the Tanos of Tanogeh to join them for discussion of the Spanish oppression. (The Tanos of Tanogeh, or southern Tewas, included the people at Galisteo, San Cristobal, San Lazaro, and Pecos.) In addition, the invitation was extended to leaders of pueblos at San Marcos and La Cieneguilla de Cochiti, although the Cieneguilla Indians were not Tewa speakers.

Among this new group, records show, was Juan of Galisteo, a servant around Santa Fe often called Juan El Tano. Others might well have been Antonio Bolsas and Cristobal Yope of San Lazaro and, from La Cieneguilla de Cochiti, the great Keresan leader Antonio Malacate.[5]

In addition to Popé, some of the northern Tewa leaders at the early gatherings most likely included men such as Francisco El Ollito and Nicolas de la Cruz Jonva, both of Po-sogeh (San Ildefonso); Domingo Naranjo, a half-black from Ka-'p-geh (Santa Clara); and Diego Xenome of Nampe (Nambé). Leaders from Cuyamungue and Jacona seldom were mentioned by Spaniards in their documents, but their warriors also took part in the fight for pueblo emancipation.

Much as historians of today might wish the pueblos in the 1600s had had a written language, it actually was fortunate that they did not. The pueblo way of life was passed to succeeding generations by the oral tradition, what they called "remembering by the eyes and ears." These remembrances could not be seized or burned like the written word. Even the closest surveillance by the Spaniards could not control this form of communication. In fact, the oral tradition gave the pueblos the ability to trick the Spaniards. During those trying times, the Indians learned to conform outwardly to the religion of the Spaniards while keeping alive their own faith inwardly. Consequently, few Spaniards realized until too late that conversion by the sword had been a dismal failure in seventeeth-century New Mexico.

Agitation among the tribes against Spanish rule continued to quietly grow in the pueblos. More and more leaders, mostly war chiefs and war captains, were invited by the Tewas to their meetings to discuss what could be done. Among them were such men as Luis Conixu of Walatowa (Jemez); El Saca from Teotho (Taos); and Luis Tupatu from We-lai (Picuris). The latter was often listed by the Spaniards as El Picuris. Malacate was generally identified by the Spaniards as the interpreter for all the Keresans in Rio Abajo. Another Spanish-speaking Keresan was the half-breed from Khe-wa (Santo Domingo), Alonzo Catiti, whose brother, Pedro Marquez, was firmly on the side of the Spanish settlers.

The revolutionary conspirators generally avoided those pueblo leaders, called *governadores,* who had been given office by the Spaniards when they had established their system of village government in 1620.

Because they owed their authority to the Spanish, many of these officials were considered suspect by Popé and his colleagues. In fact, at one point, Popé moved his operations because of his own son-in-law, who was the governor of Oke.

After several meetings among the Indian leaders, it soon became clear that Popé stood out as the most outspoken and knowledgeable among them. More and more frequently, it was his voice that was given the most weight. One leader perhaps said to another that the man from Oke Owinge had "the cunning of the fox and the heart of the bear." At the same time, according to tradition, it was said that Popé was not arrogant but instead was always willing to learn, consider advice, and to explain his decisions. In view of the uncertainty of the future, the pueblos wanted a common leader who would evidence calmness and wisdom, be reliable, and exert a leadership to be respected. They began to see these traits in Popé.

The first plan of the pueblo leaders, as they gathered more frequently to explore ideas about how to approach the Spaniards, was to deliver a reasonable ultimatum presenting their ideas for changing the system to respect pueblo customs and traditions. But as time went on and discussions grew more focused, it became evident to men like Popé, Luis Tupatu, Antonio Malacate, and Alonzo Catiti, who understood and could speak some Spanish, that negotiation was useless and that the Spaniards must be expelled before they could be safe in their homes and religion.

Unfortunately, the oral tradition that is the source of information about the Indian view of the Pueblo Revolt of 1680 has perpetuated little detail about the conduct of the planning meetings. Nevertheless, there is enough known about incidents of that period, as well as about ancient Pueblo Indian traditional council procedure, to buttress the following imaginative re-creation of the tense times prior to the rebellion:

Men from the different pueblos gathered in a large meeting room lit only by the glow of dying embers in the fireplace behind the door. A small round opening was visible on the wall next to the fireplace, but the mica in it permitted only the sunlight in; no one could see through it. Next to another wall by the entry door a pair of three-pronged juniper posts stood implanted in the dirt floor, each holding an *olla* (clay jar) full of water and a gourd ladle for drinking.

Members of the host council had seated themselves along the wall under the mica window and near the fireplace to absorb the fire's warmth. Nearby was a pile of cornhusks and tobacco; lying in the fireplace, ends glowing, were three sunflower stems. Aides would pass them around to light cornhusk cigarettes. The faces of the delegates were hard to make out in the gloom, but quiet talk in many dialects could be heard.

Shu-fa from Nafiat (Sandia Pueblo) made his way to the front by the fire-place and began to speak:

"We have suffered since the first time the 'wearers of the metal' arrived, our grandfathers have said to us. They told us that one of the foreign men asked a Tiwa man to hold his horse; then the man proceeded to attack the Tiwa's wife. [The event Shu-fa described occurred during Francisco Vásquez de Coronado's initial expedition into present-day New Mexico.] This incident cost us many lives, and many of our people fled to the mountains in fear while there was still much snow. Our warriors fought back with bows and arrows. In the end they tied prayer feathers to the twin war gods, Maseway and Oyoyeway, hoping some day the intruders would be repaid by our war gods. And we know that they were, since they experienced much bad luck."

No sooner did Shu-fa sit down than another man arose to speak—Francisco Jutu, the interpreter:

"My people, in times past, have been of great assistance to these invaders. We have acted as guides, and our warriors have served them faithfully. But the Spaniards have no feelings for human beings. For many generations our people have been trading with the Jicarillas and the Faraones. They have been our friends. Yet when the Spaniards went beyond our village and into the *llano* (plains) they met some of our friends and slaughtered them because they refused to be sold into slavery. This happened under the violent and greedy governor Luis de Rosas.[6] We don't care about his problems with the Franciscans, but the Apaches were our friends. Since this incident, they have lost faith in us and have accused our people of being tools of the Spaniards." Visibly shaken by anger, the speaker sat down. He was handed a cornhusk cigarette and began to smoke and calm down.

Luis Conixu from Walatowa (Jemez Pueblo) then walked to the center of the room. Most of the men present remembered the details of his complaints. He, too, was angry.

"I do not have to go far back in time to remind you, since most of you remember, that we lost twenty-nine of our men when the governor, Fernando de Arguello Caravajal [1644–1647], accused our leaders of working with the Apaches and Navajos and hanged them as traitors. But that was not the end. The next governor, Hernando de Ugarte [1649–1653], killed nine more of our men from Walatowa, Nafiat, and Alameda when he discovered that our people were going to let the Apaches take the royal herd while the *Castyilash* [Spanish] were busy with religious activities during their Holy Week. Many of our people were sold into slavery for ten years."

After he finished speaking, a Tewa man, Nicolas Jonva, began to address the assemblage: "Talking about recent times, Governor Juan de

Trevino [1675–1677], arrested forty-seven of our people and sentenced four of them to be hanged. Trevino claimed that the four men had bewitched the guardian of Po-sogeh, Fray Andrés Duran, along with his brother, the brother's wife, and the interpreter of Po-sogeh. Francisco Guitar,[7] a collaborator with the Spanish, had identified the so-called sorcerers to Francisco Xavier. He was trying to be on the side of the Kwan-Ku [Spanish], and he told them what he knew. Xavier and his men went to the villages, broke into the houses of the accused men, and took away many religious articles, herbs, and medicine. Popé, you were one of the men arrested, maybe you can tell what happened to you."

Popé rose to his feet, gathered his robe around him, and started to speak: "As most of you know, following the Fray Andrés affair, forty-seven of us from different villages were rounded up and arrested. We were taken to Santa Fe for trial. Four were condemned to die; they were taken to their own villages and hanged in front of their people as an example. One man was hanged at Walatowa (Jemez), one at Koots-cha (San Felipe) and the third at Nampe (Nambé). The fourth man hanged himself before he could be taken to his village. Forty-three of us were condemned to lashings and imprisonment. I was one of those humiliated by being whipped publicly, and I shall never forget that. But while we were in prison, as you all know, our leaders got together and went to Santa Fe in a group to confront Trevino. Our people came prepared to fight if the governor did not release us. That saved us because, having seen the number of our warriors, Diego López Sombrano and our protector, Capitan Francisco Garcia, interceded for us. So Trevino told our leaders: 'Wait a while, children; I will give them to you and pardon them on condition that you forsake idolatry and iniquity.'"[8]

Popé paused, then continued.

"We were released, and the governor gave our people some woolen blankets. Because of this treatment and all the other things that we have heard our brothers discuss, I am for telling the Spaniards to leave our country or suffer the consequences."

With this, Popé quietly took his seat once more. These were strong words that reflected the feelings of most of the men present.

The delegates were seated in groups according to the languages they spoke. After each speaker concluded, the different dialect groups huddled to interpret what had been said. It was a slow process, but every man was eager to know what everyone was saying about this important matter.

Some of the men knew the Spanish language—mostly Tewas, since the Spaniards had settled on their lands many years earlier. They also knew the Spanish officials in Santa Fe and the *alcaldes* (district leaders) in the provinces. The delegates told the council how many priests were in their villages. The man from Ka-'p-geh announced that there were thirty-two padres in the entire province. Popé stated that there must be between two thousand and three thousand Castilians altogether, but he was not sure because he had heard that the majority lived in Rio Abajo to the south.

The men assigned to monitor the night skies called out that morning was approaching; it was time for the council to end. The representatives quickly prepared to leave, feeling that much had been accomplished. Although no action had been planned, many issues had been raised to consider before they gathered again. Popé set the next meeting for Tetsugeh (Tesuque), the date to be dictated by the urgency of the circumstances. The men left by ones and twos, as clandestinely as they had gathered.

Meanwhile, in the Spanish settlements, nothing had changed. Life for the Spanish colonists continued to be dictated by frontier necessity and the small number of officials who governed in Santa Fe. The settlers lived in fear of the governor's power and the equally strong-willed and dictatorial church authorities. Always at issue with these two ruling groups were the social and economic control of the Pueblo Indians. Both ruling factions in the Spanish community recognized the growing danger of an Indian uprising. In the face of persistent rumors as well as overt signs of revolt in some of the villages, neither church nor state was willing to admit to mistakes or assume any share of the blame for the Indian condition.

The governor and churchmen would have been wise to recall the words of Fray Diego de Mercado. As the friar watched the troop of people going through the town of Tula, Mexico, when Don Juan de Oñate was preparing his expedition to settle New Mexico in 1597–1598, he observed:

> God certainly does have great riches in these remote parts of New Mexico, but the present settlers are not to enjoy them, for God is not keeping these for them; so it has been, for all the first people have died without enjoying them, and amidst great suffering, because they have always come with these desires and greediness for riches, which is the reason they went there to settle, and they spent their fortune.[9]

The pueblo leaders continued to communicate; soon messengers were sent out by the Tewa leaders while the other villagers worked as usual in their cornfields. Subsequently, one evening delegates began arriving secretively at the prearranged meeting place in Tetsugeh. The moon was well up in the sky when the grand council resumed its deliberations in a semidarkened room.

There was a short prayer by the host *opi*, or war chief, before the work of the meeting began. One of the messengers announced that the southern Tiwa village of Tuei (Isleta) had returned to the law of the Spanish God and pledged obedience to the Spanish king. This raised serious doubts about the wisdom of inviting those Tiwas to any meetings.

By midnight, representatives of the majority of the northern villages had arrived. After more talk by delegates about the oppressiveness of the hated Spaniards, it became apparent that the pueblos had no other choice than to make a show of force.

However, before this discussion went further, a Hemish man, Luis Conixu, got up to say: "Before we go too far we must decide on a general leader. Whatever course the Great Spirit leads us to follow, I must remind you that our elders have always advised us to pick our leaders wisely if we are to succeed. Leadership is the soul of all human endeavor. It was the flame that enabled my people to stand up against the Uta-ong and the K'elatosh [Navajos]. If the flame burns low, the Castyilash will take advantage of us. It is in it that we should place our trust. We should also trust in our people's moral courage, and in our irrepressible determination to hold onto our religion and beliefs. We must drive all the Castyilash's purposes to a conclusion and move on past all hazards and dangers with ceaseless concentration of intent that is aware of no obstacles. It will be the power of leadership that must and will direct us through our temporary hard times, but into a greater and blessed future. My council at Walatowa advised me to tell you that good leadership alone will be the decisive and concluding force in this great struggle between faiths of sunshine and darkness. This much I say with the thoughts given me by Maseway, Dabesh." And he left the floor.

A Tewa man then took the floor.

"As you know by now, we Tewas have been involved for some time. And in our meetings we have all agreed without acting on it that our brother, Popé, from Oke is the leader that we are looking for. Of course, there is Luis Tupatu and Antonio Malacate, and they would also make excellent leaders, except that they have not been involved as long as Popé has."

This prompted the host war chief to say:

"As my brother from Ka-'p-geh has indicated, we have studied our brother Popé and agree that he would be an excellent choice. Since we have many more things to discuss, why don't we make this selection of a leader short by agreeing on Popé?"

There was a brief discussion among the delegates before a man from either Tamaya (Santa Ana) or Tsia (Zia) spoke out: "If our brothers who have been involved in this difficult problem for some time are able to identify a leader, let us all stand behind them and agree on their man."

Following a discussion among the delegations, spokesmen for all the groups announced that their delegates had agreed with what had just been said. All looked toward Popé.

The chosen leader rose slowly and somberly approached the middle of the floor. He thanked the delegates for choosing him and then asked for a roll call of the villages to assess the forces that might be brought against the Spaniards. After the tally, Popé and Tupatu talked about villages that might be considered friendly to the Spanish, among them the Tiwas of Tuei. In addition, a leader they did not name from Taos and Governor Juan de Ye of Pecos[10] were identified as friends of the conquerors.

Having considered the decision to oust the Spaniards, Tupatu presented his thoughts to the assemblage: "It appears to me that all the delegates have reached a conclusion, and that is to tell the Spaniards to get out. I, for one, told my council at We-lai before I left that we cannot stand the Kwanama treatment of us any longer. At this meeting we have agreed to remove the Spaniards. So it is a matter of deciding when to begin. Let us hear from you, Antonio [referring to Malacate]."

Malacate responded, "I have a heavy heart. As you know, we still are not all agreed on the sacred mission as I see it unfolding at this meeting. You know some of the villages are not all with us. I question Alonzo Catiti of Keewa (Santo Domingo) mainly because his own flesh and blood, his brother Pedro Marquez, is a leader on the other side. So who knows where Catiti stands? If we can get his full cooperation and commitment, then we can proceed with the plan. If we knew that we were all in accord, we could set the day and begin to prepare for it. This night will soon be over, and we must work fast."

Popé nodded in agreement and offered this suggestion: "At an earlier meeting at my village, someone reported that this is the year the supply caravan arrives from Chihuahua. I say we should strike before the Kwan-Ku get more powder, new swords, and shields."

This prompted a Tsia delegate to speak up.

"If you are wondering about the date to drive out the Casteras, I say we start on the fifteenth of August, since that is the date of our Spanish feast day in my village, and many padres and Casteras will be there."

Tupatu suggested another day. "Our Spanish feast day is on the tenth; why can't we start ours on that day? We also will have many padres and Spanish from Rio Arriba on that day."

Popé broke into the discussion.

"Those are good suggestions, but it must all start on the same day. I say begin on the thirteenth, but if something happens before then let the situation take its course. Let us have a show of approval."

Popé's recommendation touched off intense debate among the delegates until one man waved his arm in the air for quiet and then said: "Yes, we here," and he pointed to the men around him, "are agreed, but all those who do not agree may say so."

No one spoke. The most successful revolt in America by Natives against colonial intruders was thus set in motion.

As dawn approached, Malacate took the floor to admonish his companions: "Remember to tell the warriors that we are not bloodthirsty; our sole goal is to get the Casteras to leave our country and let us return to the ways of our grandfathers. We will ask them to leave and if they will leave let them go peacefully. It is only if they absolutely refuse that we must use force. Is that clear?"

The delegate from Tsia jumped up to add: "We must not forget to wash our hands upon rising from bed, take corn pollen in one hand and feathers in the other, and offer them to the twin war gods at dawn each day. Prayer feathers should also be offered to the deities of the sacred mountains from Waynema to Shipapu."

And another of the councilors was quick to remind his fellows: "All of us, including the warriors, should bathe before sunrise at the rivers and streams to cleanse us for the sacred struggle."

There was quiet while the pueblo leaders pondered the significance of what had been said. Then one of them brought up the question of how those people who were not present at the meeting might learn the date of the revolt without the Spanish also finding out.

It was the man from Ka-'p-geh (Santa Clara), Domingo Naranjo, who suggested the ingenious answer. He said that narrow strips of tanned deer hide with a number of knots tied in them should be carried to each of the conspiring villages, with the number of knots corresponding to the number of days remaining before the start of the uprising. The day the last knot was untied would be the day it would commence.

Agreement to this excellent idea was followed by the host war chief's offer to send two of his aides as messengers with the knotted strips to the villages. The young men he chose were Nicolas Catua and Pedro Omtua. Pieces of the war plan were falling into place just as the false dawn was starting to light the eastern sky.

Popé tossed the remains of a tobacco-stuffed cornhusk into the fire and spoke once more.

"This is not the way of our people; however, we have been forced to the blinded path, and we can find no alternative. Our people do not approve of wars. But when such times do come upon us, the war chiefs can call us to defend our lands. Our people also exercise unlimited obedience to these leaders, who act under the religious leaders. It is the great duty of the people to abide by the decisions of these leaders. I can see no other possibility of escaping from the hand of the oppressor, and the deities know we have tried. I am fearful that the way we have just chosen will have to be the way. It is true that we respect the Kwan-Kus' superior weapon power, but we also despise their unpolished manners. We know their weaknesses and we must take advantage of them.

"And one last note; most of us know of the three most hated 'blue eyes.' They should not be spared; wherever they are they should be located and dealt with. For those of you who may not know them, they are Francisco Xavier, Luis de Quintana, and Diego López Sombrano. And I say to you, brothers, go to your *owinges* [homes] and await further word. *Sengi di ho!"* [Goodbye].

With these words, Popé sat down. To conclude the meeting, the host war chief said a few prayers, calling upon the deities, and especially the twin war gods, to guide the people and the warriors along the chosen path until the conflict was over.

The delegates left this council with heavy hearts, for they knew that war was inevitable. And yet the meeting—the most serious one ever held by the pueblos since the Spaniards had arrived so many years earlier— infused the delegates with determination. They returned to their home villages on foot. They were not allowed to use horses that had been brought by the Spaniards; nor were they permitted to use Spanish guns.

The plan set at Tetsugeh was put into action on the morning of August 8, 1680, when the two young men designated to be messengers left Tetsugeh headed for Tanogeh (Tano villages). The two must have made their first contact at La Cienega and then continued east, along the Galisteo Basin. The messengers' presence was noted at Galisteo first as the villagers told their padre, Juan Bernal. Immediately Bernal sent word to Governor Antonio de Otermín in Santa Fe.

The presence of the messengers was also divulged to the clergy at Pecos. The Christian Indians told their pastor Fray Fernando de Velasco that the two messengers had gone to the home of the war chief, Diego Umbiro. They concluded that the two had come to announce the general uprising of Pueblo people that had been rumored for some weeks. Velasco scribbled a hasty message to Otermín, dispatching it with the cooperative Pecos governor Juan de Ye. Thus, by August 9 Otermín had received communications concerning the rumored uprising from three sources— Taos, Galisteo, and Pecos. Consequently, Otermín sent his *maestro de campo* (field officer), Francisco Gomez Robledo, with a company of horsemen to find and arrest the messengers of war. The Spanish troopers found their quarry on the second day in Tanogeh, south of Santa Fe, and took the youths to the governor for interrogation, placing them under house arrest in the capital.

Word of the arrest spread rapidly through Tewa country. Tempers flared. Tension heightened. A Spaniard, Cristobal de Herrera, was killed by angry Natives at the home of the two messengers. The Tetsugeh pastor, Fray Juan Pio, decided to spend the night in Santa Fe to ensure his own safety. The uprising was exposed. What would be the next step?

The following morning Padre Pio, in the company of a soldier named Pedro Hidalgo, returned to Tetsugeh to say mass. But when the two men reached the village they found it deserted. Eventually, Padre Pio tracked the villagers down into a ravine in the nearby hills. The men were all armed with bows and arrows, lances and shields, their faces painted red.

The priest approached them and asked: "What is this, my children, are you mad? Do not disturb yourselves; I will help you and will die a thousand deaths for you."[11] Going down into a ravine where the main body of armed men was gathered, he asked them to return to the village, where he would say mass for them.

The Spanish soldier, meanwhile, was stationed on a nearby knoll ready to intercept anyone who might pass that way. He looked over toward the gully where the Indians were and was startled to see a man known to be the *tyse oke* (war chief) of Tetsugeh walk out of the ravine holding a shield which Hidalgo knew the priest had carried. A little later he saw the interpreter for the village, Nicolas, emerge from the same location spattered with blood. Hildalgo was aghast, but before he could do anything, a group of villagers rushed at him, caught his horse by the bridle, and proceeded to take away his sword and hat. Fearing for his life, Hidalgo jammed his spurs into his horse's flanks and was able to escape, even though several pueblo men hung onto his saddle and were dragged for some distance as they tried in vain to hold him. A volley of arrows fell short of the fleeing Spaniard, and he raced into Santa Fe, arriving at seven o'clock in the morning to report the fearful events he had witnessed. Although he did not know it at the time, Hidalgo was the herald of the first successful Native American revolt against outsiders.

After eighty-two years of silent submission and resentment, the Pueblo people had had enough. Their pent-up hatred for the Spanish soldiers, suppressed for so long, had been released. The capture of the two young messengers from Tetsugeh touched off a bloodbath throughout pueblo territory. For years the Spaniards had piously justified every action they had taken against the Indians, no matter how harsh or cruel. Now they were reaping the bitter harvest of the encomienda and repartimiento systems, the destruction of pueblo religious buildings and suppression of their religious practices, and the forceful imposition of a new religion on the Indian villagers.

Meanwhile at Santa Clara Pueblo, two soldiers had been killed while six other men had escaped. After learning of the calamities, Luis de Quintana, mayor of LaCanada (Española), gathered as many of the settlers as possible at his house to defend them if necessary. Fortunately, two messengers from the Taos area, Nicolas Lucero and Antonio Gomez, who had been ordered by their alcalde (mayor) to carry the news from the Taos district to Otermín, had stopped at LaCanada. Otermín was unaware that the uprising had gone beyond Tetsugeh. Thus, he ordered Francisco Gomez, with an escort of soldiers, to scout the Tewa country.

The report Otermín received was that the Tewas of Santa Clara, San

Juan, San Ildefonso, Nambé, and Pojoaque Pueblos were all gathered at Santa Clara. To add to the anguish, it was reported that the warriors from Walatowa (Jemez) had come over the mountains to join the Tewas against the Spaniards after the Jemez people had concluded their assault of the Spaniards in their area. Other Tewas from Cuyamungue, Jacona, and Tetsugeh were gathered at the latter pueblo. Since many of the settlers had not learned of the Indians' plan they were caught completely off-guard by the sudden revolt. Two days later, on the twelfth, Otermín became aware of the seriousness of the situation. The countryside was in absolute chaos. The next day he ordered the settlers from LaCanada, Los Cerrillos, and other nearby settlements to come to Santa Fe to defend themselves.

A prophecy by another Spaniard, Fray Juan de Escalona, had come to pass. Nearly a decade earlier, Escalona had been praying during the Ave Maria at a convent not far from Puebla, Mexico, where he was the superior. When the prayer was ended, all of the other religious stood up except the superior, who remained kneeling in prayer. After a time, the other clerics were startled to hear Fray Escalona suddenly cry out: *"Beati primi! Beati primi!"* ("Blessed are the first!")[12]

When the superior's ecstasy was ended, his colleagues asked him what the words had meant, but Escalona refused to speak. The next day when Escalona was going to confession, his confessor begged him earnestly, under the protection of confession, to reveal the meaning of the words. Escalona replied: "Under the condition, my dear Father, that as long as I live no one will know about this, I will tell you." The confessor gave his word.

This is what Escalona said: "Yesterday afternoon, when we were praying the Ave Maria, God revealed to me all the riches and worldly possessions that he is keeping in the interior land of New Mexico to the north and that some religious of my Father, Saint Francis, are to explore it. And as the first ones who will enter there, they are to be martyred. These religious appeared before me and I saw them suffer martyrdom with so much courage and spirit, I said, *'Beati primi! Beati primi!'* It was revealed to me that after that land is sprinkled with the blood of these martyrs, the Spanish will go there to enjoy the many riches that exist."

The Pueblo Revolt had begun the instant Padre Pio was killed. Now messengers started out immediately for the north, the west, and the south, carrying the word of rebellion. As they received the signal, other messengers from each of the various villages sped on their way to inform neighboring pueblos. Each time the messengers arrived at the home of a war chief, that official would climb to the highest rooftop in the village and give the dreaded war cry—a fearful sound instantly understood by all the villagers. They had heard the cry many times before when raiding tribes had come sweeping in from the plains, the hills, and the mountains.

After hearing the war cry, as was customary, the men and older boys quickly collected their weapons and reported to the leaders of their war societies. Each pueblo tribe differed slightly in this regard, but most had war societies headed by a war chief or a bow chief.

In each case, one group of warriors went to the padre's residence while others hurried to the homes of the alcalde and other Spanish officials stationed in the villages. The Europeans were ordered to leave. The numbers of Indians were overwhelming, and the tribes were enraged. Some of the most dedicated priests who had hoped to remain to save souls refused to leave. The war cry sounded again and they were martyred. Some of the other Spaniards tried to defend themselves and save their ranchos. They met the same fate as the padres.

From Taos to Isleta the whole region, with the exception of Santa Fe, was devastated and depopulated. The settlements and haciendas of the Spanish settlers had been robbed of household goods, the houses destroyed by fire, and the animals in the fields taken. The aim of the pueblos had been to totally expel the Spaniards.

Meanwhile, Otermín gave instructions to have the survivors of the jurisdiction of Santa Fe assemble in the *casas reales* (royal houses) so that offensive and defensive plans against the enemy might be adopted—plans that had been made following the arrival of Hidalgo from Tetsugeh (the present Tesuque), where he had witnessed the slaying of Padre Pio. At the same time all the royal arquebuses, swords, daggers, shields, and munitions of the town were taken out to supply the servants who were not armed. Sentinels were placed around the villa, while a squad of soldiers was stationed in the church to guard the holy sacraments and other sacred objects. Later, with all the refugees from around Santa Fe now gathered at the *casas reales,* the Spaniards numbered about one thousand, of whom less than one hundred were men capable of fighting.

Meanwhile, the pueblo warriors were on a mission: to persuade the Spaniards that they must leave or be killed. Twenty-one of the thirty-three Franciscan friars in pueblo country had been killed as were some four hundred of the more resistant Spaniards. The Spanish churches and other centers of religious activity were naturally targets of the rebellious Indians, who had seen their own holy places desecrated, one of the chief reasons for the revolt.

Despite all their fury, the pueblos refrained from rape and mutilation, for such outrages were prohibited according to the rules of the war societies. Although taking a scalp from an Apache or a Navajo was sometimes done ceremonially as part of the initiation of a war chief, the pueblos did not take scalps routinely. In addition, the purpose of this uprising was to rid their country of the outsiders. The fact that sexual misbehavior was frowned on by the war gods was underscored by a story passed down through generations of pueblo oral tradition. According to this story, a young warrior, overcome by the sight of a Spanish woman, fondled her breast. A few days later the hand that had touched the woman was kicked by a burro.

As the revolt continued, it took the outlying pueblos from three to four days to oust the Spaniards and destroy their houses of worship. By Tuesday, August 13, the tribes closest to Santa Fe invaded the capital—tribes from Pecos, Galisteo, San Cristobal, and San Lazaro, as well as warriors from the Keresan villages of San Marcos and La Cieneguilla de Cochiti. Numbering some five hundred, they were led by Juan el Tano, who, having worked around Santa Fe, was fluent in Spanish. El Tano's fate had changed radically. On the day the revolt began, El Tano had been sent by his Spanish bosses to his home village of Galisteo to deliver a letter to the local mayor, José Nieto; now he was returning to the capital as a leader of the Native emancipators.

In the meantime, two other Indians who were servants of Spaniards had been sent to Nieto with another letter. On their way, they saw the warriors, their faces painted for war, moving on Santa Fe and rushed back to the capital to report what they had seen. Alarmed, the authorities sent out a reconnaissance patrol, which reported seeing El Tano on horseback, leading a column of warriors; he was armed like a Spaniard with arquebus, sword, dagger, and leather jacket and was wearing a sash of red taffeta, which the patrol recognized as being from the convent of Galisteo.

When he entered the capital city, El Tano was persuaded to come to the plaza to parley with Governor Otermín. Rather than being intimidated by the Spanish official, he presented Otermín with an ultimatum: get out or perish. The Indian leader told Otermín he had been elected captain of his force and that the pueblos were bringing two crosses, one white, the other red—white for peace, red for war. If the Spaniards chose the white cross, El Tano said, their lives would be spared, and they could depart peacefully from pueblo territory; however, if they chose red, they would die. When Otermín asked El Tano how the Indians expected to live without the Christian religion, the latter laughed in his face and crossed the Agua Fria River to Analco, (site of the present-day State Capitol) to consult with his followers.

Within a short time, however, El Tano returned to the plaza to meet again with the governor and to deliver the demand from his people that all the Apache men and women whom the Spaniards had captured in war be turned over to the pueblos. He also ordered that his own wife and children, whom El Tano had left in Santa Fe, be given to him. If these things were not done, El Tano warned, the Indians would declare war immediately.

Otermín stalled. He said there were no Apaches in Santa Fe since that tribe was at war with the Spaniards as well as the pueblos. El Tano countered by telling Otermín that time was running out; more pueblo warriors would be arriving soon, and together they would destroy the Spaniards.

Meanwhile, back across the river, El Tano's followers had begun to pillage the abandoned houses of the Mexican Indians at Analco and had set fire to the Chapel of San Miguel. Otermín pleaded with El Tano to stop his men, but when El Tano approached them, he was met with the peal of bells, the blare of trumpets, and the loud cries of war. Then the Indians began streaming across the river.

Otermín called on his soldiers to attack and was forced to join them as they engaged the Indians. The battle raged for most of the day. At one juncture, when the Spanish thought they had overcome the rebels, Tewa and Jemez warriors approached from the north to join the battle. Finally at nightfall the fighting diminished, and the Indians withdrew to the eastern hills for the night. The next day, August 14, the warriors returned to the villa, but the day passed without further combat. On August 15th there were some light skirmishes, mainly efforts by the Spaniards to prevent burning and sacking of houses farther from the center of town.

On August 16, the Spanish arms and military training began to pay off since the Indian warriors were not accustomed to this type of fighting. However, to aid the Indians, more reinforcements came from Teotho (Taos) and We-lai (Picuris). Soon the Keresans from Rio Abajo, led by Alonzo Catiti of Santo Domingo, also arrived on the scene at the ravaged villa. According to Otermín's report, 2,500 warriors laid siege to Santa Fe.[13] The pueblo warriors entrenched themselves in houses and at the entrances to all streets. They cut off the water supply from the arroyo as well as that in the irrigation canal in front of the casa reales, and although the Spanish soldiers fought to protect it they failed. Indian warriors succeeded in burning the church and setting fire to the doors of the fortified towers of the royal palace. As the siege continued, the Spanish became acutely aware of the peril they faced from a lack of water for both humans and livestock.

By this time, the opposing forces were within talking distance of one another. At one point, a group of warriors met some Spanish soldiers on horseback, and when the Spanish officer in charge tried to speak to them, they shouted him down.

"This man talks a great deal," one Indian cried. "You know he needs a whole day in which to talk. But it is already too late."

After a while, the officer with the help of his chaplain, attempted to make peace. In an effort to persuade him to submit to them, the Spaniards focused on the Keresan leader, Alonzo Catiti, since he was a "coyote" (half Spanish, half Indian) and his brother, Captain Pedro Marquez, was a Christian fighting for the Spanish Crown.

Catiti was told that his sins were many and he was thus condemned. To this he answered: "Is what you are telling me true and will you pardon me before God and Santa Maria and in the name of the King?"

The officer replied, "Before the Virgin and her precious Son and in the name of the King, our Lord, I pardon you and all the rest if you will come down and submit."

Mistrustful, Catiti was unwilling to move. Instead, he said, "I am fearful and do not believe you; they have told me here that they must take me to Spain to be severely punished."[14] The negotiations were interrupted by a clamor of warriors advancing to fight, and the Spaniards withdrew. Other encounters that day between groups of Spaniards and Indians led to some discussions of ways to obtain peace but produced no results.

As Saturday morning dawned, the Indians pressed harder, firing arquebuses and arrows and hurling stones at the besieged Europeans. By this time, according to Spanish accounts, the colonists were highly fatigued and very thirsty. Their animals were dying from hunger and lack of water. In this desperate circumstance, the Spaniards chose to make an all-out attempt to win.

With a few mounted men, some infantrymen armed with arquebuses, and some Indian allies armed with bows and arrows, the Castilians made an audacious charge which caught the pueblo warriors off-guard. The Indians fought bravely against the first wave but had to retreat in subsequent attacks. Although some of the Natives fortified themselves in houses, they also fled to the hills when the Spanish started burning the buildings.

Later accounts indicate that in this encounter and others more than three hundred warriors died. Many were trampled under the hooves of Spanish horses. Forty-seven warriors were captured and executed.

Although the Spaniards claimed a minimum number of their force killed and wounded, for them it was a Pyrrhic victory. Santa Fe was laid waste, and nearby fields were barren. There was no food and only a trickle of water. No more of either would be forthcoming from the pueblos. Faced with this dismal scenario, Otermín decided to abandon Santa Fe and leave the pueblo territory.

Thus it was that on Wednesday, August 21, after the governor had interrogated and executed the pueblo prisoners, he distributed provisions from his own stores to his people for the long journey south. Later, he would write that the Spaniards left Santa Fe without a crust of bread or a grain of wheat or corn and with no other provisions for a convoy of a thousand refugees. In fact, the Spanish caravan leaving Santa Fe included four hundred animals—horses, cows, sheep, and goats—and two loaded carts belonging to a private individual.

The pueblo warriors watched from the hills as the hated Spaniards left. There was no more need to attack; the former overlords had heeded their grim ultimatum. After the Spanish had filed away down the river, the exultant warriors gathered in the plaza to hear some of their leaders give victory speeches about the return to a free world and traditional ways. Each speaker thanked the Great Spirit and the twin war gods, Maseway and Oyoyeway, the deities that had rescued the people just as the old men had said they would.

The final speaker was Popé. According to tradition, he said: "Within and around the world, within and around the hills and mountains, within and around the valleys, your authority returns to you. Therefore, return to your people and travel the corn pollen trail again. A trail with no pebbles, no boulders, and no obstructions. Go home and enjoy your families, the birds, the clouds, the mist, the rain, the lightning, the wind, the rivers, the mountains, the trees, and the sky. Remember the words of our leaders upon arriving home, go to the rivers and cleanse yourselves of the recent past. Lastly, don't forget, each morning before our father, the sun, makes his appearance, to take feathers in one hand and corn pollen in the other hand and offer them to the deities in the mountains, in the clouds, in the valleys, to the north, to the west, to the south, to the east, to Sipofinae and to Waynema. *Sengi di ho!*"

With these words, each warrior took his corn pollen pouch from his belt and offered a prayer to the twin war gods for their assistance. After distributing the pollen to the winds, they each brushed themselves with their hands to expunge any ill effects of their experience.

One warrior prayed aloud: "I shall remember with gratitude the great men that I have seen and met here and those no longer with us. Those who have sacrificed so much for the benefit of my people. Let me keep their high cause in my heart and one day in some measure try to repay them for all the benefits I and my people have received by their sacrifice."

It was over. The tyrants had been driven from the lands of the pueblo people. The first American revolution had succeeded. A few days later, after returning to their villages, some of the warriors performed the Bow and Arrow Dance, a victory dance, in honor of both the warriors who returned and those who did not. This dance is still performed in many of the pueblos today.

NOTES

1. "Handbook of North American Indians," Vol. 9, *Southwest* (Washington, D.C.: Smithsonian Institution Press, 1979), 194.

2. Alfonso Ortiz, *El Palacio* 86, (Winter 1980-81): 18–22.

3. John Upton Terrell, *Estevanico the Black* (Los Angeles: Westernlore Press, 1968).

4. Joe S. Sando, *Pueblo Nations: Eight Centuries of Pueblo Indian History* (Santa Fe, N.M.: Clear Light Publishers, 1992), 57.

5. J. Manuel Espinosa, *Crusaders of the Rio Grande* (Chicago: Institute of Jesuit History Publications, 1942), 83–84.

6. John L. Kessell, *Kiva, Cross and Crown* (Washington, D.C.: U. S. Department of the Interior, 1979), 158.

7. Charles W. Hackett, ed., and Chamion C. Shelby, trans. *Revolt of the Pueblo Indians of New Mexico and Otermín's Attempted Reconquest, 1680–1682* (Albuquerque: University of New Mexico Press, 1970), 289–300.

8. Ibid, 301.

9. Fray Geronimo de Zarate y Salmeron, *Relaciones, 1626,* trans. Alicia Ronstadt Milich (Albuquerque, N.M.: Horn and Wallace Press, 1966), 97.

10. Kessell, op. cit., 493.

11. Hackett, op. cit., vol. VIII, 6.

12. Salmeron, op. cit., 100.

13. Hackett, op. cit., vol. VIII, 101.

14. Hacket, op. cit. vol. IX, 294.

CHAPTER 2

Aftermath of the Revolt

During the twelve years of pueblo freedom following the Pueblo Revolt of 1680, Governor Otermín and his successor, Governor Domingo Jironza Petriz de Cruzate, both returned to Pueblo Indian country, each burning several pueblos and scattering the people; most fled to the Hopi country.

Meanwhile, Popé, leader of the revolt, was replaced by Luis Tupatu of Picuris Pueblo, who became the new leader, at least of the northern pueblos. Consequently, Tupatu sent an emissary, Juan Punsilli of Picuris, to El Paso del Norte (present-day El Paso) in July 1683.[1] There are two possible reasons the emissary was sent. One is that there was unrest among the pueblos; the other is that the Apaches and Navajos had begun to raid the pueblo villages after learning that the Spaniards were gone—intent on appropriating the livestock left behind by the Spaniards as well as pueblo field crops.

Once in El Paso del Norte, after presenting gifts to Otermín, Punsilli stated that the new pueblo leader, Don Luis Tupatu, had sent him to negotiate peace with the Spaniards and to say that if they should again return to New Mexico, Don Luis Tupatu would aid them in their entry, provided they came peacefully and did not kill the people or burn their homes.

Meanwhile, a new governor was appointed by the viceroy. On February 22, 1691, Governor Diego de Vargas assumed command of the dispirited Spanish New Mexico colony in exile. Due to poverty, misery, and the fear of Indian attack, it had drawn many New Mexico refugee families to desert. Nevertheless, on August 14, 1692 de Vargas and his troops left to reclaim the pueblo country, knowing that the new pueblo leader would be on his side.

He enlisted one hundred Indian allies headed by war captain José Padilla of Senucu, his lieutenant Juan de Valencia, and war captain Diego de Luna of Socorro, all of the Piro tribes.

On August 16, 1691, they left at 2 P.M. with their horses, mules, live-stock, and their food supplies in two ox carts and wagons pulled by mules. After arriving in pueblo country, de Vargas made a detailed plan. He and his allies set out for Santa Fe on September 10, bypassing many pueblos, which were abandoned because when Otermín had come in 1681 and Cruzate in 1689 they burned Isleta, Sandia, and Zia Pueblos.

On Friday, September 12, the small army planned to lay seige to La Cieneguilla, the village of Antonio Malacate, a revolt leader of the Kere-sans. However, Malacate told de Vargas that he was old and just wanted to be left alone. Consequently, the army went on to recapture Santa Fe. As they approached the village, everyone was to cry out five times in unison, "Glory to the Blessed Sacrament of the Altar." The Natives would be asked to submit peacefully; no one would fire a shot until de Vargas so ordered. Should it be necessary to attack, de Vargas would give the signal by unsheathing his sword.

At 4 A.M. the Spaniards reached the walled city of Santa Fe. It is said that Padre Francisco de Corvera said mass at that early hour and gave ab-solution to the men in case they were killed in battle. The planned cry in praise of the blessed sacrament was made, but the enemy had already sounded the alarm, and as daylight approached, Indian warriors could be seen in great numbers. Soon men, women, and children swarmed to the rooftops to observe the confrontation.

Interpreter Pedro Hidalgo tried to talk calmly to the pueblo leader Antoni Bolsas. And at this opportune moment, more Spanish arrived with food supplies. De Vargas had two cannons placed in position with a squad of soldiers and Indian allies. The Indian warriors began to be less defiant.

By 11 A.M., de Vargas began to prepare for battle with forty Spanish soldiers and fifty Indian allies stationed at strategic points. Boxes of powder were prepared for quick use. At 1 P.M. three armed Indians ap-peared on horseback. Fortunately for the Spaniards, one of the three was Tesuque Governor Domingo Romero, who unlike the others, was friendly and submissive. Still, de Vargas planned to attack.

The pueblos told de Vargas that they did not want to build the Spaniards' churches and houses. In addition, they wanted to know if the three most hated Spaniards—Francisco Xavier, Luis de Quintana, and Diego Sambrano—were in the returning group. These three men had whipped their servants before the 1680 Pueblo Revolt. De Vargas assured the Indians that the three men were not returning.

After a night of readiness for battle, the next day, September 14, de Vargas dressed in gala finery instead of wearing armor. He entered the Indian-occupied area, where a cross had been planted in the patio. De Vargas fell to one knee and kissed the cross. The pueblos watching evidently were impressed since they came down from the rooftops and mixed with the Spaniards. Then de Vargas asked the pueblos to become vassals of the Spanish king and be good Christians—requests that were granted, with Governor Domingo Romero and Antonio Bolsas speaking for the pueblos.

Consequently, de Vargas formally took possession of Santa Fe. The royal standard was raised three times, and each time de Vargas cried out: "Long live our king, Carlos the Second! May God spare him! King of Spain and of all this New World, and of the realm and provinces of New Mexico, and of these subjects newly won and conquered." Each time his men answered, "May he live many years and rule happily." In joy, they tossed their hats into the air, while the missionaries fell to their knees and thanked God for their good fortune. The Indians were then blessed with holy water, followed by an *alabado*, "praise to God." At noon Domingo Romero notified de Vargas that all the Tewas and Tanos had promised their allegiance. And it was learned that the Indian leader Luis Tupatu would arrive the next day.

Pueblo legend offers a different version of the reconquest of New Mexico. According to legend some pueblos journeyed to El Paso del Norte to confer with de Vargas. Thus, when the Spaniards returned in 1693, the pueblos, under Bartolome de Ojeda of Zia Pueblo, traveled a few days ahead of the conquistadors to pave the way for a peaceful reconquest. The pueblo men carried letters and rosaries. The letters read:

> *Jesus and Mary. My son and beloved Brother. This is to notify you that I am near and about to enter your city. I am very desirous to greet you and all those sons to whom you will make known my message. Tell everyone that the friars and all the Spaniards and many others who they do not know are coming with their wives and children and that consequently they should be very happy for they will live happily with the Blessed Virgin, our Lady and Mother, and with God. My son, may he spare you many seasons. As a sign of my love, I send you a rosary.*
>
>

Don Diego de Vargas
Zapata Lujan Ponce de Leon[2]

After arriving in Santa Fe, "El Picuris" Tupatu was made governor of the northern region and was given a horse with a saddle. With Indian friends, who included Felipe Chistoe of Pecos and the people of San Felipe, Santa Ana and Zia Pueblos, all under Ojeda, the Spaniards made successful headway.

Despite this, the Indians attempted two other revolts in 1694 and 1696—the latter being the more meaningful. During this last revolt, five missionaries and twenty-one soldiers were killed. The last battle took place at Embudo on the Taos road on July 23, 1696. The rebel leader was Lucas Naranjo, the war captain from Santa Clara Pueblo, brother of Joseph Naranjo, an interpreter, both sons of Domingo Naranjo. Lucas Naranjo was shot in the Adam's apple by a Spaniard, Antonio Cisneros of Santa Fe. When Naranjo fell, he was decapitated, his head carried to de Vargas in Santa Fe.[3]

After this defeat, many Rio Grande Pueblos fled to the Hopi country, and some Jemez Indians went to their former homeland along Cañon Largo, where the Navajos were now their neighbors. In addition, a group of Keresans from La Cieneguilla, Cochiti, and Santo Domingo fled to Acoma. The Acomas let them settle at neighboring Kocima, the Enchanted Mesa, north of present-day Sky City (about 50 miles west of Albuquerque). Governor de Vargas with his Zia friend Ojeda tried to persuade them to return to their Rio Grande villages, but they refused.

In 1697, Governor de Vargas was replaced by Pedro Rodriguez Cubero, who, with the aid of the pro-Spanish, part-Indian Joseph Naranjo, was able to coax the Keresans to return home. However, they traveled only as far as a huge lake, which they evidently felt a connection to since they asked the governor if they could settle there. Thus, San José de Laguna Pueblo was established July 2, 1698.

The people of Picuris fled to Cuartolejo, to live with the Jicarilla Apaches. Cuartolejo was in western Kansas, east of present-day Pueblo, Colorado. Later, Joseph Naranjo assisted the Spanish again, as interpreter, in leading soldiers and a hundred pueblo auxiliaries back to their village of Picuris. There is a painting of this encounter at Cuartolejo between the Indians and Spaniards on a buffalo hide at the Museum of New Mexico, Palace of the Governors, in Santa Fe.

Gradually, peace was restored as many of the Pueblo Indian refugees returned to their homes. By the beginning of the 1700s, the Pueblo Indians and their Spanish neighbors had begun to cooperate in order to defend themselves against raids from other Indian tribes. Living as they did, the two groups called one another *vecinos* (neighbors) and soon became *compadres* as they celebrated christenings, weddings, feast days, and victories over the raiders. The celebration of saints' feast days in both the Indian and the Spanish communities continues today. This is the origin of the unique New Mexico culture, which is a combination of Indian, Spanish, and Anglo cultures. Spanish became the trade language, and the Spanish and Indians adopted each other's tools and farming practices.

From our modern perspective one of the most important consequences of the Pueblo Revolt of 1680 that expelled the Spaniards is that when the Spaniards returned, the hated practices of encomienda and repartimiento and the suppression of Native religion did not occur again in New Mexico. Although the pueblos accepted Roman Catholicism from the Spaniards, they secretly maintained their Native religion, which they still practice today. However, the most important result of the 1680 Pueblo Revolt is that the Pueblo Indians are the last of North America's original Natives to retain the great majority of their languages and Native religious practices, as compared to those tribes that were suppressed by the British, the French, or the Russians. The 1980 census first called attention to this fact. Thus, because of the brave leaders and warriors who faced the Spaniards and their superior arms in 1680, the Pueblo Indians of today enjoy America's oldest culture.

NOTES

1. Punsilli, Juan, Testimony of, State Records Center and Archives, Santa Fe, N.M., roll 21, frs. 115–22.

2. Sando, op. cit., 71.

3. J. Manuel Espinosa, *The Pueblo Revolt of 1696 and the Franciscan Missions in New Mexico* (Norman: University of Oklahoma Press, 1988), 278.

An early Council meeting room. Drawing by Felix R. Vigil.

PART II

Gaining a Foothold in the Twentieth Century

CHAPTER 3

Sotero Ortiz
San Juan Pueblo

From 1870 to 1920 American Indians experienced unprecedented persecution. They endured, nevertheless, through governmental attempts to annihilate them through military action, starve them into submission, and destroy their cultural identity by removing them from ancient homelands and binding them with repressive laws. Despite these harsh measures, the "problem" of the Indians remained, and the U.S. government began to come to terms.

The federal government was compelled to recognize the Pueblo Indians as Natives with inalienable rights, as a consequence of the *Sandoval* case of 1913,[1] which affirmed that the Pueblo Indians were indeed protected by the Indian Trade and Intercourse Act of 1834. To "recognize" or "not to recognize" the rights of Indians was always a question of ponderous importance to the federal government. Pueblo-United States relations have been the subject of litigation, congressional legislation, and congressional hearings since 1848 when this country acquired the territory of the Southwest. For the Indians, the struggle for recognition, land, and political rights had become a way of life.

As a result of the *Sandoval* case, the Pueblo Indians became entitled to benefits under the earlier Indian legislation of 1834. One such law was the Indian Trade and Intercourse Act. The other was the Indian Service Act. The first act required that traders with Indians be licensed by the government; the second established the Department of Indian Affairs as a government bureau.

Since 1848, when New Mexico became a U. S. territory, the pueblo leadership faced these challenges under a traditional system of government. To deal with these problems under a form of government understood by the non-Indians, the pueblo leaders had reorganized their council of governments and created a statement of purpose.

Into these circumstances was thrust a descendant of the tribal group that had suffered most from the abuses of the Spanish regime, which had resulted in the Pueblo Revolt of 1680. He was Sotero Ortiz of San Juan Pueblo—the first elected chairman of the modern All Pueblo Council. Ortiz was chosen by vote on November 5, 1922, at Santo Domingo Pueblo during the reorganization meeting resulting from the threat of the infamous Bursum Bill, which would have "resolved" land claims in favor of non-Indian squatters who had taken possession of as much as 90 percent of the pueblos' irrigated land.

Ortiz was born at San Juan Pueblo in 1877. His mother was Maria Reyes Atencio of the Summer moiety; his father was José Dolores Ortiz, a Spanish man from a neighboring community. Although his first language was Tewa, his mother's tongue, Ortiz also learned Spanish from his father. He attended the government day school at San Juan Pueblo through the fourth grade, a minimal education that did not prepare him adequately for life in frontier Anglo New Mexico. Nor did he have sufficient knowledge of the English language to make a place for himself in that society.

Following his schooling, Ortiz helped his family with farming. Often he and his father also assisted non-Indian farmers, for which they were paid in cash. With this money they purchased shoes, sugar, and beans for the family. They grew their own wheat and corn, which was prepared for consumption in a variety of ways.

One year when there was a good piñon crop in the hills southeast of Santa Fe, many San Juan Pueblo people, including Ortiz, gathered to harvest the nuts. Soon Ortiz found himself inside an enclosure, where a no trespassing sign had been posted. As he was gathering the piñon nuts, the owner of the property appeared.

"Didn't you read the sign?" the man asked.

Ortiz replied, "Maybe I saw the sign, but I am looking for piñons, and I have no time to read signs."

"Young man," the stranger said, "this is my land, and any piñons on my land I will pick. I'll have to ask you to leave."

"I am not going to leave until I have picked all I can carry," Ortiz responded. "These piñons are for all God's children, and we have a right to pick them wherever we find them. This is the way of my people, and they have been doing this long before you white men came."

The stranger was intrigued by the piñon picker's spirit. "What is your name, and where is your home?" he asked. Ortiz gave the information, and the man then asked if he would like to work for him occasionally.

"I'll have to ask my father," said Ortiz.

The man who had challenged Ortiz's right to pick the piñons was Thomas B. Catron, a lawyer and the greatest land baron in the history of New Mexico. Later that fall, Catron came to San Juan Pueblo and brought

Ortiz to Santa Fe, where the youth did such work as chopping wood and laying adobes to construct a wall around the Catron residence. Since it was a long way back to San Juan, Ortiz would sometimes remain at the Catron home for several days at a time.

Evenings in the Catron home were especially interesting for Ortiz. The lawyer had a good library, and the young man began to read law books, "skipping over the big words," as he later explained. Also available in the library were letters and papers of attorneys from other parts of the state, which Ortiz had an opportunity to examine. As a result of his reading, he became particularly interested in the land problems of the Pueblo Indians in New Mexico.

Whenever Ortiz worked in Santa Fe, he took special pleasure in reading or talking with Catron. Soon he had improved his English sufficiently to be appointed a policeman in his village by the Indian Service. Later, Ortiz served as an interpreter when the governor was selected from the Summer moiety, his own group. Afterwards, as interpreter for his governor he attended the All Pueblo Council meetings at Santo Domingo Pueblo.

It was a long wagon ride to Santo Domingo. Delegates from San Juan started their journey at the break of dawn; the sun would be well up in the sky by the time they reached Pojoaque. Sometimes they met delegates from other Tewa villages as they traveled towards Santa Fe. There were occasions when the delegates went to Lamy, boarding a train that took them more quickly to Santo Domingo. The council meetings would last for three or four days.

Ortiz was quick to learn the procedures of the meetings. Pablo Abeita of Isleta usually chaired the meetings while Ortiz, with Charlie Kie of Laguna, and Alcario Montoya of Cochiti, contributed to most of the discussions, also interpreting to their fellow delegates throughout the meeting. Later, other young men, such as Porfirio Montoya of Santa Ana, Martin Vigil of Tesuque, Jesus Baca of Jemez, and Abel Sanchez of San Ildefonso began to take part in the discussions. These men tried to explain the problems confronting the pueblos to the older delegates and the councilmen.

When the Bursum Bill was introduced, John Collier, a young anthropologist who had become interested in the pueblo land question, came to a meeting to ask the pueblos to organize their council on an official basis, so that politicians in Washington would recognize them as official spokesmen for the pueblos. A special meeting was called for this purpose on November 5, 1922. A statement of purpose was drawn up, and an election of officers was held. It was on this occasion that Ortiz was elected the first chairman of the All Pueblo Council.

At this time it was also decided that a few of the pueblo leaders should appeal directly to the American people in both the East and West, explaining the threat posed to the Indians in New Mexico by the Bursum Bill. They would talk about the need for fund-raising to fight their case in the courts. Collier, who was their guide on their trip to the East, said when they arrived in New York, "Now it is up to you. Speak up and talk like you never have done before."

As chairman, Ortiz knew he would be required to speak, and he protested, "I can't even speak good English. I have never talked to so many white men in my life. What shall I say?"

"You know the history of your people. Tell them how you lost most of your land. Tell them what this Bursum Bill will do to your people," Collier advised.

Pablo Abeita volunteered, "Don't be afraid. Just look over their heads, and you won't even know they are looking at you. What you don't cover, I'll tell them."

Later that evening, in a large auditorium, with the biggest crowd the pueblo men had ever seen, Ortiz spoke. "Ladies and gentlemen," he began. "My name is Sotero Ortiz. I am a Tewa Indian from San Juan Pueblo, New Mexico. We are here tonight to tell you we are in deep trouble. We want to ask for your help. We need money. We need your letters to your congressmen about our problems. We are here to tell you the truth about ourselves, and you should not listen to what someone else says about us."

He was referring to a statement made by the sponsor of the bill, Senator Bursum of New Mexico, who claimed the Pueblo Indians supported the bill.

Ortiz continued, "We do not want this bill. We were never consulted about this bill. Once already our ancestors were overcome by the forces of the kingdom of Spain, in the 1690s. They then gave up their rights to the central part of what is now the state of New Mexico. They were forced to do this. In return, the Spanish government gave us small grants of land. We have become, in time, used to these small confines of land. But, in all the years from that time till now, we have been the victims of continued trespass and intrigue, until there is little left to us of even the original grants of land. Many among us are very poor. Descendants of the soldiers of Spain who fought against our people, and Mexicans from Old Mexico who drifted into our country, have now become so numerous that we feel the time has come when we must stand in our own defense. Otherwise we will lose everything, even the little that remains from the great land that once was ours."

Ortiz was speaking freely now, recovered from his stage fright and discussing his favorite subject. As a result, he made a lasting impression upon his New York audience. He exposed the fact that the pueblos were opposed to the legislation and that Senator Bursum was fraudulently claiming the bill had the Indians' support.

When the pueblos returned from the East, they made plans with Collier for a tour to the West Coast. There the crowds were large and a considerable amount of support was generated. Thus, information finally became available to the American public about the true state of Pueblo Indian affairs.

After protests such as these, the Senate reviewed the proposed legislation again, took another vote, and recalled the Bursum Bill.

Although Ortiz served as an official of the All Pueblo Council for a quarter century, he was never elected to any office in his home village, other than serving as an interpreter. However, he was a willing servant of his people, who were fighting to hold onto their small, already diminished land base. San Juan still has one of the smallest per capita land bases of any pueblo.

In the early years of Ortiz's chairmanship, the council had a running battle with the Indian Service. The service denounced the All Pueblo Council as an unauthorized governing body. Attempts were continually being made to undermine the council. During the early part of his tenure, the superintendent of the Eight Northern Pueblos, a Mr. Crandall, sent out an announcement stating that the old pueblo governments were contrary to American ideals and ordering the pueblos to adopt a new system of government using European-style elections. He gave the example of how, at Taos Pueblo, the governor and all his officers were arrested, brought to Santa Fe, and locked up for having administered mild punishment to an offending pueblo member, thereby exercising their traditional governing ways. The pueblos did not comply with Crandall's order at that time, but since 1934, with the Indian Reorganization Act, some pueblos have begun using the ballot system for elections. In the traditional system of governments, secular leaders were chosen for one-year terms by the religious leaders.

In 1923, the Indian Service attempted to prohibit the pueblos from practicing their religion. They were given one year in which to give it up; the Service threatened to compel the pueblos to comply if they refused to forego practicing their religion voluntarily. However, once again the pueblos did not comply and instead merely practiced their religion more secretly.

During that time, few Indians were able to travel to Washington, even though they would be using their own funds, held for them by the United States. The Indian Service controlled the tribal monies, as well as the funds belonging to the individual "restricted" Indians. In this manner, the service was able to dictate which Indians should go to Washington, when they should go, and, of course, what they should say.

Other problems that Ortiz and his colleagues had to deal with during those years related to stock reduction on certain pueblo reservations, land purchases under the Pueblo Lands Board Act, the organization of individual pueblo governments under the Wheeler-Howard (Indian Reorganization Act) legislation, and the loss of land to squatters. Ortiz's village of San Juan was hard hit by squatters, losing much of its land in this way. Although he was unable to maintain recognition of the traditional San Juan boundaries, Ortiz helped his people to hold onto some of the remaining land by physically removing squatters from the reservation.

During his many years of service to the All Pueblo Council, Ortiz often attempted to persuade the council to replace him as chairman. At the meeting held April 6, 1936, he said:

> *The chairman and secretary and interpreter were not to be appointed for life. When we believed that our term had expired, then I stood up, just as I am now standing, and spoke to you . . . it was our duty to appoint another chairman here, say a new board. Well, then you re-elected us again, and every time we try to bring up the question to retire us, you have been reelecting us, and you know very well for how many years I have been your chairman. I don't know if you have been reelecting us because we have been giving you good service here.*
>
> *You know very well I am not taking this seat because I want it or am asking for it. Because you have asked me to take it, I am still your chairman, and also the two gentlemen on my side. One of them is your secretary, and the other is the interpreter.*

On May 31, 1940, during the All Pueblo Council's regular meeting, Ortiz finally got his wish to step down as chairman. But instead of being retired from office, he was elected to serve as interpreter. He served in this position until October 12, 1946, another six and a half years, for a total of twenty-four years in public service to the Pueblo Indians.

Ortiz lived at San Juan Pueblo most of his life, while farming and doing odd jobs in the off-season for his old friend Thomas Catron. He was married to Maria Reyes Abeita of San Juan, and they had four children: José Manuel, Pasqualita, Rafaelita, and Joe Dolores.

Living until age eighty-six, Ortiz died on July 28, 1963. Until the very end of his life he remained a fighter for his people, a hardworking, gentle pueblo man who strove mightily to improve his knowledge. Like most other Indians who are forced into a position of leadership by the needs of their times, his entire life was spent defending the rights of his people. In the face of such enduring struggles, it is difficult to see the many sides of a man, as his children and grandchildren knew him. Ortiz had too little time for the pleasure and contentment of traditional ways, with their regular rituals and religious observances marking the story of birth, growth, and death. Instead, Ortiz was a dedicated pueblo leader, a great man who devoted his life to struggle, litigation, legislation, the study of law books and legal documents, travel to inform people of matters affecting the pueblos, and conferences for devising strategies for preservation of pueblo land and culture.

NOTES

1. Joe S. Sando, *Pueblo Nations: Eight Centuries of Pueblo Indian History* (Santa Fe, N.M.: Clear Light Publishers, 1992), 114.

CHAPTER 4

Pablo Abeita
Isleta Pueblo

Pablo Abeita[1] was a man who might well have become a governor of New Mexico. In another era, his experience and abilities could have earned him the highest place in the leadership of the state. He spoke Spanish, English, and his own mother tongue of Tiwa fluently. He was the product of three civilizations and was perfectly at home in each of them.

Abeita was born February 10, 1871. His parents were José P. Abeita and Marcelina Lucero. The day before his eighteenth birthday he married Maria Dolores Abeita. They were to have five sons: Juan Rey, José Simon (the author's godfather), Remijio, Ambrosio, and Andrew. In 1889, he was appointed by the governor of his tribe to serve on the All Pueblo Council. From that time on he remained a member of the Isleta Council and held many offices in the village government.

The local Catholic priest enrolled Abeita in a Jesuit school in Old Albuquerque. From there he was transferred to St. Michael's College in Santa Fe. Altogether, he had ten years of formal education, a rare scholarly achievement in territorial New Mexico. After completing his education, he returned to Isleta Pueblo.

During his youth, Abeita worked as a typesetter for the *Albuquerque Morning Democrat,* now the *Albuquerque Journal.* Later, he was a commercial clerk for three years, before entering the Indian Service. Here he served as a resident farmer, as they were called in those days, a post equivalent to an extension agent today.

In 1905, Pablo Abeita took over operation of the family general store at Isleta, his family having been in the trading business for many years. It is said that his grandfather, Ambrosio Abeita, advanced some fifty thousand dollars to the United States government through military officials in the early 1860s, to pay subsistence and forage for federal troops and their animals when New Mexico Territory was invaded by the Confederates. In 1863, while Ambrosio was in Washington, President Abraham Lincoln presented him with field glasses, which Pablo later owned. For Ambrosio's assistance to the government, his estate was reimbursed after his death during the administration of President James A. Garfield.

In 1912, when Isleta Pueblo organized a business council, Pablo Abeita was chosen as its first president. This council came into being because of differences between two factions, the conservatives and the progressives. The business council was part of a progressive pueblo movement supported by the Indian agent. Through the business council, the pueblo was able to restore large areas of land, as well as to triple pueblo funds, in less than three years. By contrast, according to the Indian agent the conservative Isleta Pueblo Council did not have financial success because it was more interested in old tribal ways, ceremonies, and graft.

As president of the Isleta Pueblo Council, Abeita attended the All Pueblo Council meetings. Since he was one of the most articulate and efficient leaders of the time, the council appointed him to conduct the meetings, record the proceedings, write the resolutions, and generally do the clerical work.

During those years, the traditional Indian courts had been abolished, and judges were now being appointed by the federal government's Indian Service. In 1913, Abeita was appointed a judge in the Indian court system by the Indian Service and served in that capacity until 1923. By this time he had become the secretary of the All Pueblo Council, which fought the Indian Service to preserve self-government within the pueblos.

Any strife between the factions of Isleta always culminated in a hearing before the Court of Indian Offenses, which had jurisdiction over all Indian misdemeanor offenses. During his tenure as judge, Abeita was naturally open to the charge of advancing his progressive party and his own personal interests. One case in which Abeita had to act against the rival governing party took place when the people of Isleta were still making their own wines and the United States Liquor Service had not succeeded in discouraging the circulation of such beverages. One night, when many of the conservative Indians were engaged in a dance and drinking wine the Indian agent Phillip T. Lonergan attempted to disperse the group, seizing the ceremonial drum. As a result, his life was threatened by the Tiwas. Lonergan arrested and charged their leader with inciting a riot. The arrested leader demanded counsel at his trial, and a man from Bernalillo defended him. The trial was conducted in accordance with authorized Indian Service legal procedures, Judge Pablo Abeita presiding. The defendant received a sentence of forty days in jail. It was useless for the defendant to appeal to the Indian agent, since the agent himself had prosecuted him.

Among the events of that period was a visit to Isleta by King Albert of

Belgium and his queen in 1919. Although Albuquerque had little to show the royal guests that they had not seen in other southwestern towns, Isleta was an ancient pueblo only thirteen miles away. The plaza of Isleta provided a historic stage for the event while the Franciscan cathedral which had been built by Fray Juan de Salas before 1629, was a perfect backdrop. The entire population of Isleta was present to greet the king and queen; the mission bells, a gift of the Spanish king three hundred years earlier, announced their approach. They were received by the pueblo governor, J. Felipe Abeita, with a speech in his native tongue. As on other official occasions, Pablo Abeita acted as interpreter.

On November 5, 1922, Abeita was elected secretary of the All Pueblo Council. In this capacity, he traveled many times to Washington, D.C., on behalf of his Isleta people and the nineteen pueblos of New Mexico. Abeita used to say that he had met and shaken hands with every United States president from Grover Cleveland to Franklin D. Roosevelt except Calvin Coolidge.

Throughout his life, Abeita dressed in typical Isleta fashion. He wore a tall, white Stetson hat with no crease and a straight brim. His red undershirt was covered by a lace-front white shirt. He always wore a handwoven red pueblo sash as a belt, the fringes hanging at his right side. Abeita had a wry sense of humor. As Marc Simmons wrote in an article about him entitled "Pablo and the President," "Even when criticizing his political foes, he made his points with a quaint sarcasm rather than malicious barbs. And he loved a joke, especially if he could put one over on the Anglos."[2]

Abeita was an able spokesman for the Pueblo people and an avid writer to the newspapers, presenting his views on problems of the day. During the difficult days of the Bursum Bill, Senator Bursum sought to demonstrate that the Indians were to blame for their problems. To this, Abeita said, "My grandfather used to tell me that his grandfather was half Spanish."[3] When friends asked him why he always wore a blanket, he would reply, "I can drop this blanket quicker than I can an overcoat should a bear get after me."[4] In one of his many speeches before a congressional committee, when he referred to Columbus discovering America, Abeita said:

> *Columbus goes back to Europe and claims that he found a New World. What right did Columbus have to make such a claim, or what proofs did he have that it was a New World that he found? This world was not "lost," and may be as old if not older than the one Columbus came from. . . . Imagine what Europe would have been if some Indian sailed eastward in search of the rising sun, and had come into the port of Palos, to proclaim that he had found a New World. . . .*

The white people may say that they did not take all of this country by force, but in some cases had bought it off the Indians. We will not deny that, but look at the bargains they used to get, and remember that Manhattan Island was sold about three hundred and eighty years ago for $24 worth of glass beads. . . . Had it been the other way, and some foolish Irishman had sold the British Isles for $2 worth of tobacco, would that have been a good bargain?

Our principal needs today are that you eject all non-Indian trespassers off our lands. Instead of reimbursing the Indian for what land the non-Indian holds, why not reimburse the non-Indian trespasser and make him get off? He knows that he is holding the land illegally, only you know that he won't vote for you if you don't kick us into submission.[5]

In November 1926, the pueblo leaders were called to Santa Fe for a three-day meeting when representatives of the federal government led by New Mexico territorial governor Hagerman attempted to form a pueblo council that would work under the dictatorship of the United States government. Although many pueblo leaders refused to attend this meeting, a few stalwarts were present. The following exchange was recorded by the council:

PABLO ABEITA: *I said last night that if we were to form a new organization, the new organization would not interfere with the All Pueblo Council. I do not want to give that name to the new organization. You can call the new organization anything you please.*

GOV. HAGERMAN: *I suggest that the name of this organization be "The United States Pueblo Council."*

DR. CHARLES LUMMIS: *I suggest "The United States Junta."*

PABLO ABEITA: *The people in Washington would not know what junta means. We are talking in the American language now and in terms that will be accepted by the authorities in Washington. I think junta is a good word, but the Americans will not know what it is. But I suggest that we put in the word Indian. The "United States Pueblo Indian Council."*

GOV. HAGERMAN: *I believe the suggestion is a very good one.*

PABLO ABEITA: *My friends, may I have a few moments. Of course, this is the third day of the meeting, and in my opinion we have just about started. I think there should be another day if we have the assurance that the sessions will be continued until the business is finished.*

I do not want to take too much of your valuable time telling about the traditional history of the pueblo government of today. I cannot, as I did in 1905, talk for an hour and a half to President Teddy Roosevelt on this interesting subject, but I will try to say a few words explaining our government. This form was given to us, not by the king of Spain, but by the Christian missionaries who were more orderly than the king himself. This is Christian law that we have.

It is from the Spanish that we get the name "governor." We were put on this part of the earth by the Great Spirit, and in the early days we always had among us "a man who leads," or what is now called the government, very much like our own traditional way. Where your president takes the place of our governor, and your councilmen take the place of ours, or rather your Congress. We do not want our governors to be merely scarecrows; we want them to have some authority among their people.

Other tribal governments throughout Indian country had been shaken up, replaced by the European or American system of government, and even forcibly consolidated under the Indian Reorganization Act. But the pueblos were fighting to keep their form of government since they knew that it served them best. At this meeting, men like Abeita had to negotiate carefully to maintain their government and avoid confrontation. Abeita continued:

This seems to be one of the great steps we are able to undertake to serve our people. Consequently, we cannot sign our names to a paper of this sort. This is a very good thing that has just been mentioned. We will have to make our people understand.

I understand that I can write a paper like that, but I would ask if you grant time enough, that we go back home and present this matter before our people. We write up some sort of resolution and then call on our old Pueblo Council, and each pueblo has their own resolutions read and out of them all then make one, in that way it can be more satisfactory. If it was only me, they could finish this business in fifteen minutes, but I have to consider one thousand people at home.

. . .

The fox had circled the snake. Both were wary, but the fox had avoided being bitten. The new group was indeed formed at the meeting, and it was Abeita who then said:

PABLO ABEITA: *Mr. President, since I have agreed with you in all of your talks, I agree that a president be elected, and I present the name of Frank Paisano, who is from Laguna Pueblo.*

GOV. HAGERMAN *(quickly): Friends, you have heard the nomination. The motion has been seconded. All in favor of this motion will signify by rising.*

There was not one negative vote. Paisano was elected president of the

"United States Pueblo Indian Council." Following this piece of railroading by the representatives of the federal government, Abeita rose and said:

> I want to say a few words, since Mr. Hagerman made a remark about the council. We have an organization that we call the All Pueblo Council, and we want to know if this is going to be abolished. I know my people would refuse to discontinue it. We would like to keep the All Pueblo Council. During our Indian meeting last night, I tried my best to make them understand. I told them to think very carefully, and here is another thing: I told them in the Santo Domingo meeting that we don't want outsiders to settle our matters, so what can we do? We cannot let go of our hold on the Indians. Is it not best that we get together?
>
> After the fight between Santo Domingo and San Felipe in 1905, we made a solemn pledge, followed by a solemn pledge by all the pueblos in 1922; we agreed that in the future, if any disagreements should come up between any one of the pueblos, these things should be settled in the council. Also, if there is any trouble, we would all join in and help them. If there should be a plague of grasshoppers, epidemics, or floods, they would help them until they could get along.
>
> If the present council has been called here to do away with this solemn pledge, I might as well go home. I have nothing against John Collier, Mr. Hagerman [governor], or Charley Burke [commissioner of Indian affairs]. I have no doubt that the United States Government means well, but actual facts make us feel the need of conferring with our friends outside the government. We do not want to be deprived of our right to appeal to our friends.[6]

The new organization was formed as a rival of the All Pueblo Council. A budget was established by the federal government. However, during the year, none of the pueblo leaders ever attended a meeting called by the president. Consequently, after a year the new organization was discontinued for lack of attendance. But the All Pueblo Council continued, and Pablo Abeita remained its secretary.

On April 6, 1936, the All Pueblo Council was meeting at Santo Domingo Pueblo. A discussion took place as to the appointment of John Collier as commissioner of Indian affairs. Abeita said at this time:

> I for one did not pull for him because he had been a friend of the pueblo Indians for such a long time that I thought if the doings in the office were going to continue in the same shape and form that they had been for years past, I would probably be the one who would go to Washington and fight Mr. Collier face-to-face, and in all our fights since the time we have known Mr. Collier, he has fought our battles.

After Mr. Collier is appointed commissioner, who is going to fight for us? I thought instead, we are going to fight him. That is one of the reasons why I did not pull for him. When he was appointed commissioner, I think I was the first one who wrote a letter of congratulations to Mr. Collier. I did the same thing when he announced that he was going to appoint Dr. Sophie Aberle to be our superintendent of the United Pueblos Agency.[7]

On the subject of the United States national elections of that time, Abeita said:

I don't care about politics, but I hope that I will be seven feet under the ground when my people start voting. But I hope that Mr. Roosevelt will be reelected so that Mr. Harold Ickes will remain as secretary and Mr. Collier as commissioner. I wrote a little article in the paper the other day about somebody trying to introduce a bill in Congress so that all the federal land would be given back to the states. I said, "Why not do a little better than that—give it back to the original owners?" The government never bought it, and the states never bought it. What land we hold today is land that the white people didn't take away from us.

We have a patent, saying the United States gave us a piece of ground. I don't like to say that statement made in the patent lies, but it looks that way, because I see no reason why the government gave us a piece of land. Where did they get that right? The land was always ours, so I consider the patent doesn't read right; but we were always a peaceable people. We probably had the same sort of government that we have today long before Christopher Columbus had any grandparents. We were civilized, more or less, in the same form of civilization that we are today, when the Europeans were murdering, pillaging, and everything else when they came here and tried to civilize us.

What is civilization? To my way of thinking, civilization is nothing but happiness and contentment. The white person doesn't seem to feel civilized unless he has a million dollars, and then he is not satisfied because the million isn't ten million, and after ten million, the whole world.[8]

In 1940, the state of New Mexico observed the Coronado Quattrocentennial. On May 29, one celebration was held at the old pueblo ruins in Kuaua, the present site of the Coronado Monument across the river from Bernalillo, New Mexico, where Coronado supposedly visited. Abeita was invited by the centennial committee to speak. Among the members of the committee was Senator Clinton Anderson. Although

Abeita's actual speech has not been located, this writer's grandfather, José Manuel Yepa, who was a leader of Jemez Pueblo, was present at the celebration and told his family about the speech given by his friend Abeita. As I recall Grandfather's words, the gist of Abeita's speech was the following:

> *I don't know why you invited me here, because I am not particularly proud to be here to observe this quattrocentennial. After all, you people are honoring those who brought diseases to my country and my people, thereby reducing the Indian population. We have very little land left, but you continue to encroach upon our villages. You strip our trees from the watersheds to produce lumber and floods; you plow up the earth to raise grain crops and sandstorms; and you have turned a large section of land that used to be fertile enough for at least a subsistence economy for Indians, into outright desert.*
>
> *You call us savages for dancing without street clothes on, although our costumes are very pretty, and then you show up at our dances with so little clothing on that we wonder who the real savages are.*

According to another report of the event by Marc Simmons, Abeita also remarked, "I am afraid I will have to contradict some of the things you gentlemen have said. Coronado came by Isleta, and as you who have read his chronicles know, was given food and royally received. He came up the valley, and what did he do? Well, we had better say no more about it, for his record isn't good and you know it."[9]

And still another account of the celebration reported by Marta Weigle and Peter White in their book *The Lore of New Mexico* noted that the crowd broke into the heartiest applause of the afternoon, and did so again at every pause, as the respected Isletan continued a short and cutting debunking of white man's history, which he said was 90 percent wrong.

Seldom mentioned is the fact that Abeita was also an important figure in the religious life of his pueblo. Through all the changes in the civil life of the pueblo, and all the changes in the world outside, the one thing that did not change was Abeita's feeling for his Native religion. Every morning, with his corn pollen sack in hand, he would address the Great Spirit, thank Him for the many blessings, and beseech Him for peace and prosperity for all mankind in the world.

In recognition of his renown, the 1937 *Who's Who in New Mexico* contained a half page devoted to Pablo Abeita. However, those who knew Abeita knew that he was important for being himself, not just for the many offices he held in his lifetime or the honors he was awarded. The Grand Old Man of Isleta Pueblo, Abeita, was truly an important and great Pueblo Indian leader. Since he was erudite and multilingual, he communicated between the pueblo people and non-Indians. He could communicate with legislators in Washington, as well as with businessmen in Albuquerque and Santa Fe. For all these qualities, the people of his pueblo trusted and admired him.

Pablo Abeita died December 17, 1940.

NOTES

1. Joe S. Sando, *Pueblo Nations: Eight Centuries of Pueblo Indian History* (Santa Fe, N.M.: Clear Light Publishers, 1992), 181.

2. Marta Weigle and Peter White, *The Lore of New Mexico* (Albuquerque: University of New Mexico Press, 1988), 156.

3. Leo Crane, *Desert Drums, The Pueblo Indians of New Mexico* (Boston: Little, Brown & Co., 1928), 314.

4. Ibid., 316.

5. Ibid., 317.

6. Weigle and White, op. cit.

7. Weigle and White, op. cit.

8. Weigle and White, op. cit.

9. Weigle and White, op. cit.

CHAPTER 5

José Alcario Montoya
Cochiti Pueblo

Nobility does not necessarily entail wealth or power or family connections. True nobility derives from within a person—from his or her virtues and personality characteristics.

This is particularly true in the Pueblo Indian culture, where for centuries leaders have served their community diligently without expecting monetary compensation. In the distant past, perhaps the *cacique,* or war chief, was supplied with firewood or venison in exchange for services. But in more recent times it has been customary for elected leaders to donate their time to community service while simultaneously working outside their governmental roles to make a living for their families. The attitude that leaders bring to their job is perhaps even more significant. As one studies the pueblo way of life, it becomes increasingly obvious that among the most important characteristics of the large majority of leaders are humility and modesty; a great leader will not advertise or take personal advantage of the position.

Such a leader was José Alcario Montoya of Cochiti Pueblo, who helped his tribe make the difficult transition from the nineteenth to the twentieth century while, despite great pressures, maintaining their traditional ways. Of particular significance was his position as interpreter for the still relatively new All Pueblo Council.

Montoya was born at Cochiti Pueblo in 1877. Like many pueblo men for generations before him, while he was in his teens his parents offered him for initiation into the Koshare Society of his tribe. With all his responsibilities later in his life, he was still able to fulfill his tribal obligations to assist in the activities of the society.

Members of the Koshare Society are the individuals who help dancers during a performance with emergencies such as loose costumes or shoestrings; they also joke and play pranks on the dancers, as well as on the audience, while the dancers are resting. Thus, they have been called clowns. Adolph Bandelier called them "the delight makers" in his book by that name.

Montoya began his formal education at a Spanish language school in his village. After several years there, he continued for a few more years at the Albuquerque Indian School. This school was established in 1880 to educate Pueblo, Apache, and Navajo children since there were no English language schools on the Indian reservations. It was at the Albuquerque Indian School that Indian children often began to learn English between the ages of six and eight, since all classes were taught in English by predominantly Anglo-American teachers.

From the time the Indian schools were established through the 1920s they were modeled on the military system. Students were required to wear uniforms, to participate in drills and inspections, and to march to class and to the dining rooms. In those days Indian education was minimal. It was considered sufficient if students could read and write at the sixth or eighth grade level by the time they graduated. There was also a pronounced separation between Indian students and the Euro-American teachers—who often had little or no regard for Indian traditions. For Indians, education did not become more meaningful until after World War II, when pueblo war veterans were able to obtain college education through the GI Bill. After receiving degrees many of these veterans returned home to teach, becoming role models for the younger generation.

From Albuquerque Indian School Montoya transferred to St. Catherine's in Santa Fe. During his school years, he showed a particular aptitude for languages. By the time he left St. Catherine, Montoya was well prepared to serve his people.

After Montoya's return to Cochiti Pueblo as a young man, one of his first appointments was as sacristan, or deacon, of his village church, San Bonafacio. In this position, he was in charge of the sacristy and ceremonial articles of the Catholic priest. He also was janitor of the church and rang the bells before mass on Sundays.

During his lifetime, Montoya held many significant positions in the government of the Pueblo people. Perhaps the most distinguished position was that of interpreter for the All Pueblo Council, from 1920 on. Before that time, council meetings were not recorded or held consistently at one location. However, with increasing pressure from the non-Indian political system, the pueblos reorganized in 1922 to meet the political challenges of the time.

It was at the reorganization meeting at Santo Domingo Pueblo on November 5, 1922, that José Alcario Montoya was elected official interpreter of the council. The council members' wisdom in making the appointment was evidenced by the long tenure Montoya enjoyed, using his mastery of languages to serve the council until 1940.

In the early days of the All Pueblo Council, the interpreter had to be proficient in English, Spanish, and one of the pueblo languages. At a typical meeting Montoya would interpret first in Spanish to those councilmen who understood that language. Then for the benefit of Keresan speakers Montoya would interpret in Keresan, his own language, and finally, he would explain the responses of the Indians to any guests in English or Spanish or both, as necessary.

Politics being the same everywhere, during his years as interpreter working diligently for the benefit of all Pueblo people, Montoya did not escape controversy and occasional criticism. From time to time, he and other pueblo leaders were misunderstood by factions from the various villages; and now and then a group of progressives wanted to break with traditions, but their strident voices soon abated.

At one point in the early 1920s, a group of progressives became active in Montoya's village of Cochiti, and one of their first initiatives involved a complaint about Montoya and other pueblo leaders. On March 7, 1921, the All Pueblo Council mailed a petition to the United States secretary of the interior to protest Indian Agency interference in pueblo government. A few weeks later, a small group of pueblo leaders, accompanied by Montoya as interpreter, went to Washington, D.C., to express to a congressional committee their complaints about the agency and what they felt was the overreaching authority of the Indian agent.

This action did not sit well with the Cochiti dissidents, who wrote a letter of protest to the Indian agent in Albuquerque, Leo Crane.

In part, the June 10, 1921, letter read:

> . . . for some time past our Governor and some of our councilmen have been holding meetings secretly with other pueblo governors and their councilmen, with the object to form some kind of scheme that will enable them to successfully abolish the Indian judges and policemen, which the Indian Department has appointed . . . in various pueblos wherever men are found who are well qualified for such positions.
>
> There is absolutely nothing whatsoever to make complaints of about the administration of the Indian judges. . . . Whatever these men may have petitioned to the Indian Department at Washington is not true, but a combination made up of false reports to suit themselves the petitioners. . . .
>
> A man by the name of Alcario Montoya has gone on to Washington, D.C., as a delegate representing our pueblo, and we do not know how many more pueblos he may be representing for the same purpose . . . . We others of the council who were not let in on these doings don't want to pay for these sightseeing trips on which our fellows

*stare at beautiful white women until their eyes pop out of their heads.
. . . These men must be placed under a guardian. All pueblo money
must be taken away from them so they can't blow it on damn fool
trips like these. . . .*

*If you ever expect to see us pueblos prosper and be at peace with
one another and attending to our own business, we need to be allowed to make some changes of our old mode of ruling or governing
ourselves and establish new rules as the Indian Department may see
it fit for our government among ourselves in the future.*

                                    We are yours respectfully,
                                    [Signed by six councilmen of Cochiti][1]

This letter was written at about the time the federal government was
taking steps to begin eradicating the traditional pueblo way of life. Pueblo
Indians' freedom of religion was under attack. In fact, in 1923 the government mandated that the pueblos had one year to rid themselves of
their Native religious practices. It was skilled men such as Montoya who,
fortunately, rescued the pueblos from this fate by explaining to various
congressional committees the Indians' true feelings and interpreting for
them the pueblo way of life. Although the Indians had gained some recognition of rights in 1913, they were not considered citizens of the United
States until 1924. Neither were they constituents of any New Mexico
congressional delegation, since they did not win the right to vote until
1948. They were thus at the mercy of whatever Bureau of Indian Affairs
(BIA) official happened to be wielding power.

As a skilled linguist, Montoya made numerous friends all over the
country. Many were people whom he had impressed during his official
trips to Washington, New York, and California. One of his good friends
was Mike Kirk, an Indian trader from Gallup, New Mexico. Twice Kirk
arranged for Montoya to take a tribal dance group to Los Angeles to
perform the pueblo version of the popular Comanche dances for the
Shriners Convention. They also performed in 1927 before another large
group which had witnessed the outstanding Cochiti Buffalo Dance two
years earlier.

Although he received no monetary compensation for his many years
of tribal service, José Alcario Montoya reaped the reward of a long, ful-
filling life. He died March 5, 1966, at the age of eighty-nine and was
buried in the Cochiti Pueblo cemetery, which he had supervised during his
lifetime.

The people who knew Montoya held this unpretentious, noble pueblo
leader in high esteem. He was a great leader; he and his contemporaries
confronted and overcame difficult challenges to the pueblo people regarding important issues of the time. Through his strong will, outstand-

ing character, and consummate skill in interpreting for his people, Montoya was instrumental in making it possible for the pueblo people of today to retain their remaining land base and their unique culture and traditions.

NOTES

1. Letter, from Cochiti files, Southern Pueblos Agency.

Miguel Trujillo and his wife Rochanda Paisano.

CHAPTER 6

Miguel H. Trujillo
Isleta Pueblo

A baby boy was born to José Trujillo and Juanita Jaramillo of Isleta Pueblo on April 30, 1904. This boy, Miguel H. Trujillo, was to play a decisive role in the historic struggle for basic civil rights of the Indians of New Mexico.

According to his daughter, Josephine Waconda, Trujillo was the second child in a family of four children. Their father maintained the family through a farm and garden while their mother occasionally made pottery for sale. The sale of this pottery provided opportunities for pleasurable trips twelve miles to Albuquerque in a horse-drawn wagon. On such excursions, the boys would care for the girls while their mother sold her pottery to tourists at the train depot. The tourists got off the train and took pictures, gave the Indian children candy, gum or small change, and sometimes bought Indian crafts.

According to Trujillo, his father took the garden produce to neighboring Los Lunas by wagon. After he sold some chiles and melons, he would stop at a bar and buy wine. Consequently, on the return trip home he would be intoxicated, and his team of horses, Tim and Jack, would have to bring the wagon home without a driver; this often caused a minor family disagreement. At such times his father's condition and the image of the horses bringing the wagon home empty made a lasting impression on Trujillo. Consequently, as an adult he was always opposed to drinking liquor.

When Trujillo was about seven years old, his father became ill and died, leaving their mother with no means of supporting the family. It was expected that Miguel and his older brother, Manuel, who was called Bob, would work in any kind of job to earn money for basic family needs. As a result, they worked cleaning irrigation ditches, herding sheep and goats, hoeing chile and melon fields, chopping wood, and feeding livestock. Since they were small boys, their combined pay was only equivalent to one man's wages. Sometimes when they herded sheep for a month, they would get a sheep or goat in payment, which was food for the family.

As the two boys reached school age, a major decision had to be made—to let them go to boarding school or have them stay at home and take care of the family. Fortunately, their mother, who had attended a Catholic school in Bernalillo for three years, was aware of the value of education. She decided to let the boys go to school despite the wishes of other relatives.

At the boarding school the mandate was to "Americanize" the Indians. The school program was strictly military; all the students wore uniforms, and a bugle was the main indicator of time. There were dress parades on Sunday afternoons preceded by a thorough cleanup of the living quarters, and preparation of uniforms to be worn at the parade. Speaking in Native languages was forbidden. Any child caught breaking this rule was dressed in traditional prison clothes, black-and-white attire with an iron ball chained to one ankle, and marched around the campus.

However, a positive result for Trujillo in attending this school was that one of his teachers, Mrs. Isis Harrington took an interest in him. He also met her son, Eldred, who became a lifelong friend. Harrington encouraged Trujillo to continue his education, and since the Albuquerque school only had ten grades he went on to the Haskell Indian Institute in Lawrence, Kansas, which he attended for two years. Meanwhile his brother returned to Isleta to help the family. The Haskell Indian Institute was also a military environment, but Trujillo had experience with the system and had no problems but actually benefited from it. He was interested in playing football, but the Plains Indians were much bigger, so he joined the school wrestling team instead. He also played trombone in the school band. During the summer months he remained in Kansas and worked in the beet fields. Of the little money he earned, he mailed part to his mother.

In his senior year Trujillo became interested in teaching and took some courses to earn a teaching certificate. After his graduation in 1925 he began teaching in Yuma, Arizona. It was during this time that his brother was hospitalized at the sanatorium in Laguna with tuberculosis, from which he died within the year. This was a great loss for Trujillo, since he and his brother had been close since childhood. However, he later told his family that he believed the tragedy had made him stronger.

After two years at Yuma, Trujillo transferred to the Tohatchi Indian School on the Navajo Reservation, which was closer to home. While employed there he married Ruchanda Paisano of Laguna Pueblo (shown on page 56 with Trujillo). Their children are Josephine Waconda of Isleta and Dr. Michael H. Trujillo of Bethesda, Maryland, in addition to seven grandchildren and six great-grandchildren. The grandchildren are Patricia W. Abeita, Kareen, John, Jr., and Lawrence from Josephine; and Susan, Catherine, and Rebecca from Michael. The great-grandchildren are Amy,

Catherine, and Maureen from Patricia W. Abeita; Camille from Kareen; Lanora from John, Jr.; and Amanda from Lawrence.

In addition to his contributions to the cause of Indian civil rights in New Mexico, Trujillo was a lifelong advocate of education. He believed that education gave pueblo young people the opportunity to gain their rightful place in society. Josephine related to me that because of her father's guidance, four of his grandchildren have master's degrees from various colleges while two other grandchildren have bachelor's degrees. Josephine did not have to tell me that Trujillo's family members have been achievers. Both his children are extremely successful. Josephine is a graduate nurse with a B.S.N. degree from the University of New Mexico as a Family Nurse Practitioner and is currently director of the Albuquerque area office of the Indian Health Service. Her brother, Dr. Michael Trujillo, is director of the National Indian Health Service with his office in Bethesda, Maryland.

To understand Trujillo's contribution to Indian civil rights, it is necessary to gain understanding of the historical background of his times. Many magazine articles and books have been written about the African-American struggle for civil rights that has earned honored places for Reverend Martin Luther King, Jr., Rosa Parks, and others. But the American media have always relegated American Indians and their struggles to the social periphery, except for famous Indian leaders of the past or the modern Indian leaders of much-publicized confrontations with the United States government. In his effort to gain civil rights for Indians Trujillo confronted bias and prejudice from both Indians and non-Indians who discouraged Indian participation in the larger system of federal politics. At that time Indians had reason to fear losing their sovereignty as well as their lands if they voted. A precedent for this was the way the Hispanic people lost lands due to the American system of taxation. Before the Anglo-Americans arrived in 1846, the Hispanics did not tax unused land. However, under the new American system, all non-Indian lands were taxed in New Mexico. Thus, back taxes often piled up on the Hispanic landowners, forcing them to forfeit their lands when they had to pay the crooked attorneys who represented them in court because they did not have the money to pay taxes. Likewise, the Indians feared that New Mexico State control would result in further loss of land. The Indians' reluctance to vote also stemmed from their unwillingness to be identified with people who had caused them so much sorrow and hardship.

Trujillo was able to use the American legal system as his weapon in the fight for Indian civil rights in New Mexico. This he did while proudly maintaining his Indian identity. On June 14, 1948, Trujillo attempted to register to vote in Los Lunas, near Isleta Pueblo, and was refused by the recorder of Valencia County, Eloy Garley, under the "Indians not taxed" provision of the New Mexico Constitution, which specified that Indians could not vote since they were not taxed. Trujillo and his attorneys, one of whom was Felix S. Cohen, asked the federal district court in New Mexico for an injunction restraining the recorder.

Previous attempts to register Indians to vote had been unsuccessful and were discouraged by the pueblos. Although Trujillo had tried to persuade the All Pueblo Council to unite on the issue, there were still some old-timers on the council who were fearful of losing their lands and their autonomy. Consequently, Trujillo decided to attempt on his own to vote, and he was subsequently arrested and sued the recorder of Valencia County. Some other Indians whose names appeared in court actions withdrew from legal action for fear of reprisal from their own tribal councils.

Furthermore, in New Mexico where the majority party held power by an approximately 8,000 vote margin, not all parties favored enfranchisement of some 20,000 potential Indian voters. However, times were beginning to change. In 1947, the report of the President's Committee on Civil Rights was published, which condemned disenfranchisement of Indians in New Mexico and Arizona, now that Indians were citizens and subject to both federal and state taxes, except for lands in trust status. The committee recommended that New Mexico and Arizona grant suffrage to their Indian citizens.

Often attempts by Indians to gain voting rights attracted much public support because the plaintiffs were veterans of World War II, and this was also the case during Trujillo's hearing. At one point the judge said, "It is perhaps not entirely pertinent to the question here, but we know how these Indians . . . have responded to the need of the country in time of war in a patriotic wholehearted way, both in furnishing manpower in the military forces and in purchase of war bonds . . . why should they be deprived of their rights to vote now because they are favored by the federal government in exempting their lands from taxation?"

In addition to the issue of Indians being World War II veterans, the federal government exerted other forms of pressure on states to give Indians the vote. For example, the federal government threatened to withdraw funds from states that denied Social Security to Indians. In Trujillo's case, a three-judge panel was appointed to rule on the injunction requested by Trujillo and his attorneys. They argued that the state constitutional provision "Indians not taxed" violated the Fifteenth Amendment to the United States Constitution, which states, "The rights of citizens of the United States to vote shall not be denied or abridged by the United States or by any state on account of race, color, or previous condition of servitude." Furthermore, Trujillo's attorneys stated that New Mexico Indians paid a variety of taxes, such as income and sales tax—all taxes except those on trust lands. The attorneys also argued that New Mexico's

Indians were counted in the 1940 congressional apportionment, which resulted in an extra congressman for the state.

Subsequently, on August 3, 1948, the presiding judge delivered the decision for the panel. The court ruled that those portions of the New Mexico Constitution and the statutes (Article 7, Section 1) that denied Indians the right to vote were unconstitutional and void and that the plaintiff and all citizens of Indian blood had the right to vote. As a result of Trujillo's case, after thirty-six years of statehood New Mexico was forced to grant its Indian citizens voting rights in federal, state, and local elections.

During his struggle for Indian voting rights, Trujillo was threatened by the guardian of the Indians, the Bureau of Indian Affairs. His defense of Indians and their cultures at meetings of the All Pueblo Council and elsewhere resulted in pressure from the BIA, which threatened to transfer Trujillo to South Dakota. However, by this time his mother was in poor health, and he toned down his outspoken defense of Indians in order to remain closer to home. Despite this, he was transferred to the Intermountain School in Brigham City, Utah, where he remained until he retired in 1959.

Prior to his retirement Trujillo took courses for a doctorate at the University of California at Berkeley. Unfortunately, the responsibilities of his family, his job, and the fact that the university was so far away prevented him from obtaining his third degree.

After retiring from the BIA at age fifty-five, Trujillo returned with his family to Laguna Pueblo. There he continued to work for Indians through the National Indian Council on Aging. At this time he was a member of the American Legion Carlisle-Bennet Post 13, the Haskell Indian Club, the Laguna Colony Club of Albuquerque, and the Valencia County Selective Service board. He was employed by the New Mexico Department of Public Welfare, the Social Security Legal Administration, and the New Mexico Adult Education Association.

It was during these years that I first contacted him at his home in Albuquerque about his court case, not knowing that one day I would be seeking more information about this great man. Miguel Trujillo died on August 27, 1989. Since his death I have been in touch with his two children, Josephine and Michael, and am proud to have helped gain recognition for Trujillo's struggles in obtaining civil rights for Indians in New Mexico. I suggested to the city of Albuquerque that a tribute be made to him at the Martin Luther King, Jr., Memorial Park in Albuquerque, located downtown at King Boulevard. Subsequently, a picture of Trujillo with his wife was placed at the site.

On September 28, 1994, a Social Justice Convocation was held in memory of Trujillo at the University of New Mexico Continuing

Education Complex sponsored by the Albuquerque Human Rights Board. Two Indian attorneys gave a speech on American Indian civil rights in the twentieth century, "Surviving the System." The speakers were Christine Zuni, Isleta-San Juan, and Sam Deloria, Lakota. Another program was held in Trujillo's honor at the University of New Mexico Student Union on October 10, 1994.

For his noble action and public spirit, this humble Pueblo Indian man has earned a place among the great leaders of this country.

REFERENCES

Bronitsky, Gordon, "Isleta's Unsung Hero." *New Mexico Magazine,* August 1989.

Miguel H. Trujillo, Plaintiff vs. Eloy Garley, Defendant, U.S. District Court of New Mexico, No. 1353.

PART III

Consolidating Gains

CHAPTER 7

Joseph Filario Tafoya
Santa Clara Pueblo

A s the twentieth century unfolded, dramatic and sometimes traumatic changes swept through the world, leaving no society or culture untouched. New technologies in transportation and communication made the world a global village. Ancient cultures were subjected to the enormous pressures of modernity. The challenge facing the pueblo people was how to preserve their precious traditions in the face of rapid change—how to adapt to the modern world without losing their cultural anchors. This required foresight, courage, strength, patience, and wisdom—the characteristics exemplified in the life and work of Joseph Filario Tafoya, who helped lead his Santa Clara people through the stressful time of rapid change.

To appreciate Tafoya's contribution, it is necessary to understand the sometimes stormy politics of Santa Clara Pueblo. Disputes between various political factions have been noted frequently in the literature and other reports of pueblo societies by social scientists. However, despite the existence of conflicts and problems, the remarkable thing about pueblo history is the persistence of distinctive cultures among the pueblos, particularly in the face of the pressures of acculturation stemming in part from rapid changes occurring outside the pueblos.

Santa Clara Pueblo is a case in point, having been involved in a conflict between the Winter and Summer moieties (the two basic governing groups) since 1894. In the past it had been the custom in each Tewa Pueblo for the two moieties, Summer and Winter, to alternate seasonally in governing religious and secular affairs of the pueblo. Under the pueblo system, the Winter moiety directed governmental and ceremonial affairs from fall to the spring equinox, while the Summer moiety was in charge for the remainder of the year.

As the result of an incident which occurred in the late summer of 1894 at Santa Clara Pueblo, some of the members of the Winter moiety, who were in the minority, became a dissident group. Subsequently, the opposing Summer moiety, which was in charge of affairs when the controversy arose, refused to transfer authority to the Winter moiety when the time came that fall. Consequently, the Summer moiety remained in power year-round for forty years, having in its possession the governor's cane, while their opponents, the Winter moiety, had only the lieutenant governor's cane.[1] Ironically, as it turned out, Tafoya's grandfather, Felice Velarde, was the last Winter moiety governor of Santa Clara, beginning in 1893.

Three years before the rift in Santa Clara Pueblo politics, on October 6, 1891, Joseph Filario Tafoya was born to Thomas and Lucaria Velarde Tafoya, both members of the Santa Clara tribe. He was destined to become the leading figure in resolving the conflict.

As a young boy, Tafoya attended the local school. Later, he was educated at Santa Fe Indian School and Carlisle Indian School in Pennsylvania, made famous by James Thorpe, the athlete. As a result of attending the Carlisle Indian School, Tafoya's horizons were expanded and his interest in seeing the world was aroused. Consequently, he volunteered for the army and served during World War I.

After the war Tafoya returned to Santa Clara Pueblo, where he simultaneously became involved in politics and began courting a woman named Petra Swazo, also from Santa Clara. It was at this time, too, that he became employed by a firm in Manitou Springs, Colorado, for which he worked most of his life as an entertainer for tourists. Soon he took Petra Swazo to Colorado, where they were married in a little church in Manitou Springs.

In those days there was a narrow-gauge railroad, the Denver & Rio Grande, that passed near Santa Clara Pueblo. Called the "Chili Line," since it wound through a valley that was widely known in New Mexico for its chile crop, the railroad transported thousands of passengers between Denver and Santa Fe for many years.

The Chili Line was more than just a mode of travel for the people of Santa Clara; it was a tradition that played a role in the daily life of the community. The train would blow its whistle at high noon as it approached Santa Clara, and the people would know it was time for the noon break. Later, in the afternoon, the railroad workmen would toot the horn on their maintenance cart as they passed by the pueblo on their way to Española, signaling that it was quitting time. It was the Chili Line that Petra rode to her wedding; and the railroad was often used by the Tafoyas to travel to Santa Clara from Colorado.

The Tafoyas had three children: Joseph, who lives in Los Angeles; Paul, who has been governor of Santa Clara, last serving in 1974; and Mrs. Marie T. Gutierrez, who lives at Santa Clara.

Tafoya returned to Santa Clara from Colorado while still a young man and he began to participate in tribal government as a member of the Winter moiety, the moiety with the lesser role. Tafoya, however, had several advantages over others at the pueblo. He was the owner of the first automobile at Santa Clara, with which he chauffeured the Tribal Council. In addition, he was privileged because of his education at Carlisle Indian School and his experience in the army, which he put to use by offering his services to the council.

Soon Tafoya managed to become leader of his Winter moiety and, when the Indian Reorganization Act made it possible for the pueblo to establish an elective form of government, in 1935 Tafoya won the governorship of Santa Clara.

With his previous service as chauffeur and interpreter for his tribe, Tafoya had little trouble becoming a force in the All Pueblo Council meetings at Santo Domingo. It was no surprise, therefore, when Tafoya, known among all nineteen pueblos as a competent man, was elected second chairman of the council on May 31, 1940, at Santo Domingo. It was a position he held until October 12, 1946.

Tafoya's term as chairman coincided with World War II. This time of austerity, tension, and change had many effects on life in the pueblos, besides the absence of pueblo men serving in the military. Because of the priority of the war effort, Tafoya had to fight constantly for the Bureau of Indian Affairs to receive enough funding to carry out its commitment to the pueblo tribes. Not only were funds scarce, but employees were lost to the military and other federal programs. One prime example of this drain was the loss of United Pueblos Agency Superintendent Sophie D. Aberle, who had been in the post nine years when she was transferred to the National Medical Research Center in Washington, D.C., in April 1944. In addition to lack of funds and the loss of high-level employees in agencies affecting the pueblos, a shortage of teachers was a problem in many day schools in the pueblos as well as at boarding schools in Santa Fe and Albuquerque; such shortages often hampered the schools' operations.

Tafoya had a genuine concern for education throughout his life. For example, he was keenly interested in school attendance by the Pueblo Indian students. At a meeting in December 1943, Tafoya castigated the pueblo governors for allowing pueblo parents to withdraw their children from school so they could be sent to sheep camps (which occurred especially in springtime during the lambing season) or assigned to other tasks. At this meeting, the boarding schools were sent notice that they were not permitted to release children for work at home for more than one fiesta, and that this fiesta had to be the major one of the year and at the student's home village.

Tafoya also was concerned with establishing financial aid to pueblo officials, which remained a problem into the 1980s. Further, he began to support the idea that Indians should be permitted to vote for federal political offices; and this essential right was finally granted to New Mexico Indians on August 11, 1948, as a result of the court decision in *Trujillo v. Garley*.[1] (See pages 59–61.)

During Tafoya's tenure as council chairman, Felix S. Cohen was hired as an attorney to help interpret the complex legal and legislative problems of the times. In order to pay for the attorney's services, Tafoya asked the pueblo leaders to pay a yearly assessment of $50 from each of the nineteen pueblos. It is to the leaders' credit that the annual $50 levy continued to be collected even after Cohen's death until the entire amount owed him was paid.

Other tough issues that Tafoya faced as council chairman included providing road signs on pueblo lands (they are now available through poverty programs), determining a method of pueblo court appeals, finding appropriate procedures for itinerant trading in the pueblos (very rare now), and developing natural resources on pueblo land, depending on availability of financial backing.

Tafoya received no salary while he served as chairman. He had previously worked at St. Vincent Hospital in Santa Fe, and by the time he was elected to the chairmanship he was night watchman at the Santa Fe Indian School.

When he finished his six years as council chairman, he returned to Manitou Springs, where he worked as an entertainer for tourists. There he drummed and sang dressed in his Indian costume while his sons danced to the music. As his sons grew older, their sons took over the dancing, so it became a grandfather-grandson act. When his sons were performing pueblo dances, Tafoya would wear his Tewa costume; and when the dances were those of the Plains Indians, he would change into Plains Indian regalia. In this occupation Tafoya was very successful. Every summer thousands of tourists and Boy Scouts returned to Manitou Springs to watch him put on a show and to be photographed with him. In addition, many of his young friends sent him postcards and later brought their own children to see him perform.

In 1970, due to advancing age Tafoya retired and went home to Santa Clara. However, he could not forget his beloved Manitou Springs and after two years in retirement at Santa Clara, returned to Manitou Springs for the last time. He died there unexpectedly on July 8, 1972. His body was brought to Santa Clara Pueblo, where he was buried on July 11, 1972.

Tafoya typified the many dedicated men who struggled without pay for the benefit and progress of the pueblo people. His efforts on behalf of pueblo education came at a time when not all realized just how vitally important education would be to postwar generations. His foresight was a gift to his people.

NOTES

1. *Miguel H. Trujillo v. Eloy Garley,* County Clerk and Ex Officio Recorder of Valencia County, New Mexico, NM No. 1353, New Mexico Voting Decision.

CHAPTER 8

Abel Paisano
Laguna Pueblo

Laguna Pueblo is forty-six miles west of Albuquerque along Interstate 40. It has the largest number of Keresan-speaking Pueblo Indians (over 7,500) as well as the largest landholdings of the nineteen pueblos, just under 500,000 acres. The tribe was among the first in New Mexico to be affected by industrial development. The Santa Fe Railroad, which crosses the reservation, brought employment to tribal members, as well as marriages between Laguna women and white railroad workers. Although Laguna has profited from the railroad and more recently from other forms of economic development, the pueblo has been at odds with the federal and state governments on political and cultural issues.

Throughout New Mexico, Indians' and white men's ideas about formal education often have been in conflict, especially during the years soon after the American acquisition of New Mexico Territory. In the Indian view, education was only an attempt to incorporate Native American youth into the the so-called "melting pot" of American society, thus separating them from the traditional pueblo way of life. Indian leaders saw no other reasons for their youth to be subjected to the alien ways introduced to them at schools run by the United States government. Only recently has it been recognized how Native Americans have profited from the sacrifices of a few who attended either the Industrial and Normal Institute of Hampton, Virginia, or the Carlisle Indian School at Carlisle, Pennsylvania.

One such person who sacrificed her freedom and peaceful existence was a young girl of the Laguna Pueblo tribe named Mary Perry. A photograph now at the Smithsonian Institution in Washington, D.C., shows her wearing her Native manta dress as she arrived at the Carlisle Indian School in the company of two boys from Laguna Pueblo. Mary Perry's interest in education eventually was passed on to her son, Abel Paisano, who was to become secretary of the All Pueblo Council and later its

71

chairman. During his life he contributed much to the progress of the Pueblo Indian people.

Paisano was born at Casa Blanca, New Mexico, on the Laguna Indian Reservation on March 5, 1900. His grandfather had moved out of Old Laguna and settled at Casa Blanca after the Navajos were rounded up and marched to the Bosque Redondo near Fort Sumner, New Mexico, and the raiding Apaches had been fairly well pacified in the 1860s. Paisano's mother was of the Turkey Clan and thus so was her son. His father was William Holbrook Paisano of the Little Water Clan. Like Paisano's mother, his father also had attended Carlisle Indian School for a time. Given the fact that both his parents had had the rare experience of an American education in an era when, in frontier New Mexico, education meant learning to read and write in Spanish, it was almost inevitable that Paisano would become a leader and set an example for the majority of young pueblo people of his time.

For Paisano, formal education began in a little government day school at Paraje on the Laguna Reservation. Since the school only covered the first three grades, he transferred to the Albuquerque Indian School after completing the third grade. He attended AIS for the next eight years and then learned that Indians were being accepted into the United States Army as volunteers. In order to pursue adventure and fulfill a desire to see the world he had read about, Paisano and a friend from Isleta, Antonio Lucero, volunteered for the army. That was not an unusual action, for although Indian men were not subject to the draft during World War I, many volunteered. After the war, young men like Paisano and his friend heard about the opportunities in army life and enlisted. Not long before that time, the pueblo people believed that pueblo men should never fight a white man's war, even if a battle were taking place just outside the reservation. However, after some Indians volunteered for military duty, attitudes began to shift.

Paisano and his friend were assigned to Ft. Bliss, Texas, with the Seventh Cavalry, as members of the Cavalry Band. After their regular tour of duty, during which they took part in a few forays against the Mexican revolutionary Francisco "Pancho" Villa, the young soldiers were discharged and returned to their homes.

Since Paisano had learned the electrical trade as a high school student, after his return to civilian life he was able to find employment with Devoe Battery Company in Albuquerque. Now that he had a steady job, his next step was to marry Josephine Sarracino from Paguate, another of the Laguna villages. Subsequently, the couple had four children, Mrs. Daisy F. Abeita, William Holbrook Paisano III, Angus Paisano, and Mrs. Alice May Siow.

After a few years in Albuquerque, Paisano and his family moved back

Abel Paisano in his World War I uniform.

to the reservation, where he established an automotive service garage at New Laguna near old Highway 66. At this time his father was postmaster at Casa Blanca, and when the elder Paisano retired in 1930 Paisano assumed the position.

It was during this time that Paisano, through the influence of a local leader, Walter Sarracino, began to participate in tribal affairs. He subsequently served as secretary and interpreter for the Laguna Tribal Council.

In the mid-1930s, Paisano returned to Albuquerque to work as a mechanic in the garage of the United Pueblos Agency, which was under the authority of the Bureau of Land Management. By then the Laguna Tribal Council was well aware of Paisano's abilities so that when the council went to the monthly All Pueblo Council meetings, he was invited to join the delegation. This, in turn, led to recognition by the other pueblo leaders and on May 31, 1940, Paisano was elected secretary of the All Pueblo Council, the second man to fill that position since its establishment in 1922. In his role as secretary, Paisano was a presidential delegate to the Inter-American Conference on Indians at Patzcuaro, Mexico. He continued to serve as secretary under Chairman José Filario Tafoya of Santa Clara until October 12, 1946, when he succeeded Tafoya as the leader of the Nineteen Pueblos Council. Serving as Paisano's secretary was a young man named John Rainer of Taos Pueblo, the subject of Chapter 12.

Many of the elderly pueblo leaders had remained skeptical of the BIA since Indian Commissioner Charlie Burke read the riot act to the pueblos in 1926. At that time Burke had tried to dissolve the All Pueblo Council and substitute a federally controlled council, calling it the United States Indian Pueblo Council.[1] When pueblo leaders refused to accept Burke's proposal, he denounced pueblo culture. As a result, the pueblos refused to work with BIA employees; understandably, Chairman Paisano had a difficult time persuading the pueblos to consult with the BIA.

Because he was employed by the BIA while serving as chairman, Paisano often was criticized for conflict of interest—for either allegedly giving in to the federal agency or having BIA personnel dictate policy. When the All Pueblo Council adopted a constitution many years later, it was stipulated that no employee of federal or state government could be elected council chairman. Despite these criticisms and allegations, Paisano did a capable job of administering council affairs. Records of speeches by him during his tenure are indicative of what he achieved. In addition to many substantial accomplishments on behalf of the pueblo people, because he was a BIA employee, Paisano was able to secure the use of the Albuquerque Indian School auditorium for the council's use, which made meetings more convenient and efficient, although he was also criticized for this arrangement.

In an effort to improve communication and understanding between the Indians and BIA personnel, Paisano invited many government employees from various federal agencies and the Indian Health Service to the All Pueblo Council meetings, for which he was lauded by an old friend, Indian Commissioner William Brophy. It was the commissioner's belief that the pueblos should cooperate closely with all the federal agencies for the benefit of the pueblo people. This was not so easy as it might sound, for many of the older pueblo leaders had remained skeptical of the BIA since the early 1920s.

World War II was extremely hard on people in all walks of life. The war drew good employees away from their jobs and into the armed forces; others were lured away by high paying defense industry jobs. This created a dangerous shortage of personnel upon whom the Indian people relied. They already had lost their much-admired superintendent, Sophie Aberle to a research job in the war effort. Of special concern to Paisano and other pueblo leaders was the shortage of teachers in the day schools as well as the boarding schools in Albuquerque and Santa Fe. The threat to the schools was a part of the termination policy that was being promoted by the federal government to force assimilation and end tribal status and rights throughout the country.

In order to convey the seriousness of their problem to the powers in Washington, D.C., Paisano drafted a resolution which not only explained the problem of the loss of teachers but also urged restoration of funds cut from the BIA's education budget. This document was sent to congressional leaders, and many of its recommendations were later incorporated in House Bill 3123 as it moved through the appropriations process. Lacking needed funding, the Santa Fe and Albuquerque Indian Schools were ordered closed by the BIA as of May 29, 1947. In the face of this threat, the pueblos sent a special letter of appeal to President Harry Truman and, in order to court public support, to nationally prominent radio commentator Walter Winchell.

On May 10, 1947, Chairman Paisano called a special meeting to discuss the cuts in education funds under House Bill 3123. At this meeting, the pueblo leaders decided to contribute $60 from each of their tribal treasuries to finance a trip by a pueblo delegation to Washington. After the initial assessment, the All Pueblo Council continued to require $60 a year to be paid to the council as dues for official membership. In 1974, that was raised to $100 annually from each of the nineteen pueblos.

During Paisano's chairmanship other important issues were dealt with. For example, the federal Indian Land Claims Commission was established to resolve land claim conflicts between Indians and non-Indians. The All Pueblo Council selected James Stewart, at that time superintendent of the Navajo Nation, to head the body, sending telegrams to President Harry Truman recommending their choice. As chairman, Paisano was continually in touch with officials in the nation's capital, especially the New Mexico congressional delegation. He had corresponded regularly with Congresswoman Georgia L. Lusk, the only woman ever elected to the United States House of Representatives from New Mexico, and with Representative Antonio Fernandez and Senators Carl Hatch and Dennis Chavez, all of whom are now deceased.

When Paisano took the office of chairman, the position of interpreter was vacant, and the need for someone in that office became apparent at a meeting on June 18, 1948, when a resolution was passed and signed by seventeen pueblo governors expressing concern about the performance of the Extension Division of the United Pueblos Agency. As it turned out, some of the officials had misunderstood the resolution and, in reality, there were only a few complaints about the division's services. When the meaning of the resolution was fully explained to them, nine of the governors individually signed statements indicating that they had previously signed the complaint resolution without fully understanding its substance.

One of the milestones of Chairman Paisano's tenure occurred on November 22, 1949, when he attended the organizational meeting for the future Bernalillo County Indian Hospital, which later became the University of New Mexico Hospital, a center for teaching and treatment which continues to have a strong Indian component. Paisano contributed much in spearheading the drive for authorization of the proposed hospital, which was projected to provide much-needed health care for New Mexico's Indian population as well as other patients. Largely because of Paisano's efforts, the federal government eventually appropriated $40 million for the Indians' share of the development of the hospital. Because of his tireless effort to make the institution a reality, Paisano was selected to serve on the hospital's first board of trustees. He remained in that position until his death.

Throughout his career as a leader of his people, Paisano continued to work in the BIA garage. In time, with overwork and the stress of dealing with the many problems facing the Pueblo Indians, he developed high blood pressure. His physician recommended lighter duties. As a consequence, he was transferred to the administrative branch of the United Pueblos Agency, where he handled the mail and files.

One day at work, Paisano suffered a heart attack. He was rushed to the hospital he had helped found. Unfortunately, the overworked employees at the understaffed hospital treated him as "just another Indian" and did not attend to him until they were threatened with the statement that the sick man was a hospital board member and there might be serious repercussions if they did not treat him promptly. At this point, doctors were summoned, but it was too late. Paisano died November 1, 1958, at the Bernalillo County Indian Hospital.

All Pueblo Council Chairman Paisano was buried at the National Cemetery in Santa Fe. Although he died at a relatively young age in comparison with other Indian leaders he had been able to accomplish much for the pueblo people.

The passing of Chairman Paisano saddened many pueblo people and others who had known and worked with him. However, he bequeathed his ideas to the All Indian Pueblo Council, which changed its name from All Pueblo Council in 1965, when a constitution and by-laws were approved. He gave it a new direction, which it continues to follow. Another of his major contributions was his stress on cooperation with federal agencies to obtain tribal benefits—an effort which continues today.

NOTES

1. Joe S. Sando, *Pueblo Nations: Eight Centuries of Pueblo Indian History* (Santa Fe, N.M.: Clear Light Publishers, 1992), 97.

CHAPTER 9

Domingo Montoya
Sandia Pueblo

A teenager was topping beets in the hot August sun of western South Dakota near Belle Fourche. The work was difficult; the sun beat down unmercifully. But the heat did not particularly bother the youth nor did the backbreaking labor of bending over all day to top the sugar beets. The boy, Domingo Montoya, was used to the heat and hard work. He was a Pueblo Indian from New Mexico, where the August sun was at least as hot as in South Dakota, and he had worked in farm fields most of his eighteen years. The only thing that was different was the vastness of the field, something which at first had astonished him. Certainly his home village, Sandia Pueblo, had no farm fields on such a scale.

The job in the beet field was Montoya's first adventure so far from home. Like many other pueblo workers, he had been signed up for the job by a farm labor recruiter and had boarded a train near his home for the trip north. He had just completed the eleventh grade at the Santa Fe Indian School in June of that year, 1929. Because his father was in ill health, Montoya, as the oldest boy in the family, had to take responsibility for supporting the family of six in that first year of what would be called the Great Depression. Although he had been a promising student and one of his teachers had come to Sandia Pueblo to return him to the school in Santa Fe, Montoya felt strongly about his family responsibilities and was never able to continue his education.

It took the boy about two weeks to adjust to the new world of beet fields, but after his job became routine he was so busy he scarcely had time to be homesick. The weather was another matter. On September 10 of that year, the Belle Fourche area was blanketed by a ten-inch snowfall, and the cold wind stung like nothing Montoya had previously experienced. The snow continued to fall, and the temperature kept dropping so that by October the season ended and the workers returned to their homes. Montoya bought a bus ticket to return to New Mexico via

Denver, where he stopped long enough to buy a few gifts for his family with the money he had saved.

Back at Sandia, Montoya took over the management of the farm and crops that other members of his family had maintained during his absence. After that fall's harvest, he became a trapper, working his trap lines in the mountains east of the village and along the Rio Grande under the large, spreading cottonwood trees. He set his traps for coyotes, which were a menace to livestock, and for fox and skunk, whose pelts are valuable to Pueblo Indians, since they are worn by most ceremonial dancers. Customarily, a skunk pelt is split in half lengthwise and worn around a dancer's ankles after it is tanned. Also tanned first, a fox pelt is worn as a tail, hanging from the back of the waist of a male dancer.

For Montoya, the furs were commercial items to be traded with local residents or with other individuals from neighboring Indian pueblos. Thus, Montoya's family was able to obtain a few staples to augment its home-grown food supply during the Depression years. Later, as he grew older, Montoya was able to find other jobs to support his family. Struggling to meet daily demands, he did not even dream that he would one day be a leader of his people—chairman of the All Pueblo Council of New Mexico's nineteen pueblos.

Montoya was born on August 5, 1911, at Sandia Pueblo. His parents were Andrés Montoya and Isabel Pajarito. From his mother he inherited the blood of the Earth Clan. Montoya lives in the same family house today, although he remodeled the home. Over the years, he bought adjoining houses to add to the original, making it into a graceful eight-room home which stands on the northeastern corner of the Sandia Pueblo plaza.

Montoya's first encounter with the world outside Sandia Pueblo came in the fall of 1918 when he was seven and began his education at the Santa Fe Indian School, since there was no school in his home village. The trip to the railroad depot in nearby Bernalillo began in a horse-drawn wagon driven by his father. It was a radical adventure for a first grader who could not speak a word of English. But he soon met some other wide-eyed Indian youngsters from Santo Domingo and Cochiti Pueblos, who climbed aboard at Santo Domingo as the train chugged north.

Montoya did well in school. In addition to the usual subjects, he learned carpentry, blacksmithing, masonry, and farming. Unfortunately, because of his father's ill health he was forced to leave high school one year before graduation in the spring of 1929.

As it turned out, his father was not the only one with health problems that year. As the summer progressed, Montoya began having trouble with his right ear. His parents treated the pain with a variety of home remedies, but the situation grew worse, until one day in early July the teenager noticed blood trickling out of his ear. He knew he needed medical attention. On the Fourth of July, unaware of the Independence Day observance, he set out on foot in search of an Indian hospital that his family had heard was somewhere on Mountain Road in Albuquerque. (That Montoya would not know about the Fourth of July was not uncommon; many Indians at that time had little knowledge of American holidays.) He hiked the fourteen miles into Albuquerque in pain only to discover that the hospital was not where he thought it was. The infirmary had been moved to the Indian School campus. Montoya then retraced his steps to Highway 85, now 4th Street, to get directions to the hospital. By this time he was seriously weakened from hunger, as well as the illness. He had not eaten since leaving home in the morning, and it was well into the afternoon.

After walking another mile or more, the young man finally found the hospital. He knocked on the front door, but there was no answer. He leaned against the door for a few minutes, debating whether he should knock again. Always a shy boy, he did not want to create a disturbance. While he considered what to do, he watched as a German shepherd came close, wagging its tail in a friendly manner. Montoya decided against knocking and left, but as he walked eastward towards the mountains and the highway, the dog followed. Soon weakness overwhelmed him, and he had to sit under a tree to rest. The dog joined him, and he petted the animal, talking softly to it. After a while, the dog left, heading back toward the hospital. The Indian youth watched the dog until it disappeared and began to wonder whether he should follow the dog back to the hospital. Aching and weak, he retraced his footsteps and came again to the hospital, where he found the dog. He summoned his strength and pounded on the door. To his surprise, a nurse answered and invited him in to examine his ear.

"That looks bad," the nurse said, "I will have to find the doctor to see you. This is a national holiday, and I'm the only one here."

By about 4 P.M. a Dr. Hope arrived to take charge of the new patient. His examination quickly revealed the nature of the problem.

"It looks bad," Dr. Hope told the youth and the nurse. "I'll have to operate."

The following day Montoya underwent a mastoidectomy. He stayed in the hospital for a month before being released. On August 3, he again walked the distance between Albuquerque and Sandia Pueblo, but this time he was healthy. Two days later he celebrated his eighteenth birthday.

Sandia was a small village where everyone knew what was going on. The day after the youth's return, a man came to his family's house to ask Montoya to work for him cutting wheat. Montoya's mother told the man her son had just come home from the hospital, and she would not let him return to work so soon. The next month he was recruited to work in the South Dakota beet fields.

In 1931, Montoya was set to go to work as an oiler on a dragline for the Middle Rio Grande Conservancy District. However, the foreman who had offered the job to him broke his leg while cranking a Model-T Ford truck. The man who replaced the foreman hired someone else, and Montoya was given a job as a laborer. He worked periodically for the Conservancy District until 1935.

By this time, in an effort to counteract the effects of the Great Depression, the federal government had numerous programs in place. For the Indian people, the Emergency Conservation Work (ECW) program was a blessing since it rotated benefits among eligible workers. Under the program, a few men at a time took turns working one week out of each month. Montoya worked under the ECW Program for two years.

In 1934, Montoya married Eva Lucero, a resident of his home village. A son and daughter were born to the couple before Eva died and Montoya had to struggle on alone. Their son George gave him four grandchildren and three great-grandchildren. Their daughter, Mrs. Sophie Trujillo, is the mother of one son, from whom she also has a grandson.

After years of irregular employment, in 1937 Montoya obtained a steady job working as a member of a survey crew with the Bureau of Indian Affairs. However, again, events outside the pueblo world intervened. The project Montoya was working on ended abruptly with the beginning of the Finnish-Russian War just prior to World War II since funds used in the survey were diverted to the support of Finland's war effort.

However, this work hiatus did not last long. Montoya was soon hired as a laborer by the United States Soil Conservation Service (SCS), and worked his way up to farm equipment operator. In this capacity, he plowed, prepared seedbeds, and planted crops. The fine grass seeds had to be sowed by hand, one pound per acre, since there were no machines that could perform the task at the time.

As part of his work, Montoya planted wild plants such as New Mexico olive, chamisa, conifers, willows, and grasses from other arid regions of the world such as Africa and India. Montoya later said he potted conifers by the millions before they were used for conservation planting and reforestation. As he worked, he learned a great deal about good farming—what nutrients plants needed in the soil and what means could be employed to develop soils.

After several years as a single parent, Montoya married again in April 1945. His new bride was Mary Lauriano, also a Sandia resident. With his second wife, Montoya had two more sons, Sam, who now has two sons of his own, Dean and Keith; and Malcolm, who has a son Luke and a daughter Miranda. Sam also has a grandson from Dean. Montoya and

Mary had a daughter, Mrs. Fatima M. Tafoya, who has two children, Alan and Antonia. Sam Montoya served as superintendent of the Southern Pueblos Agency, where his father later asked for office space.

After nearly fifteen years with the SCS, Montoya resigned in 1950 to become a farmer himself. It was a big gamble. He withdrew all of his retirement funds from the SCS and, in addition, borrowed $6,000 from the Farmers Home Administration. He had wanted to begin farming much earlier, but when he tried to borrow money for the venture in 1929, no one would lend him any because he had no collateral.

"The first two years were a constant struggle," Montoya said of his venture in private farming. "But I never was delinquent in my payment which came due on December 1. Part of the hardship was due to my limited ownership of farming machinery," he added. "My only tractor was small, and I could not change the implements daily from plow to hay cutter. I either did without a tool, or I borrowed one someplace. Nevertheless, it was difficult to farm 125 acres with one small tractor.

"Bouncing around the sod on a hard seat and in various kinds of weather, like the hot sun with no umbrella and the cold wind with no cover, was hard, but I guess most farmers also put up with such situations or problems," he observed.

After the second year Montoya was able to buy another tractor and more implements to work with it. The third year he bought his own hay bailer. He was able then to level his farmland, fertilize it with commercial products, and plant thirteen acres of chile, melons, and sweet corn.

"I planted a few rows of sweet corn every two weeks so I was able to have corn all summer, and I sold most of it," he recalled. "I had 112 acres of alfalfa and with my two tractors and bailer I was able to grow all I could handle. I also kept some bales for my cows in the wintertime. People came from all over to buy green chile from me—from Albuquerque, Bernalillo, and the Indian pueblos."

Good luck seldom lasts forever; we live in a world of vicissitudes. Unfortunately, one day in 1963 a fire of undetermined origin broke out in a farm building that housed much of Montoya's equipment. Flames destroyed or badly damaged two tractors, a bailer, a swather, a combine, a welder, assorted other tools, approximately 8,500 bales of hay, and a huge woodpile. Montoya had no insurance to cover any of the loss.

"Naturally, I felt bad about the loss and especially because I worked hard for every piece of the property I lost," Montoya said. "However, I feel fortunate that I was healthy and was willing to work hard again to regain what I lost. The thing is, I had not owned those things very long, and I was not accustomed to the situation as much as I was accustomed to being poor and not owning very much. In a situation like I experienced, one really learns who the Great Spirit is. He can take it away as well as give it."

Montoya said he was still in shock from the fire when "one of our councilmen from Sandia came to my house after returning from the meeting at Santo Domingo to inform me that I had been nominated and elected as Chairman of the All Pueblo Council.

"I could not go to the meeting that day," Montoya recalled, "because I was trying to clean up my burned barn. I accepted because I had nothing else to do, and it was January and too early to plant and I was just finishing the job of clearing and cleaning the barnyard."

Among the first problems Montoya had to deal with when he took over administration of the All Pueblo Council on February 13, 1964, were lack of sufficient funds and adequate facilities. There was no funding for an office where he would be available to people who wanted to see him; and there was no money available to install a telephone for the council— he had to use his own.

Montoya found a solution to the office problem with the help of Southern Pueblos Agency Superintendent Kenneth Payton in Albuquerque, who located a room for him in the agency headquarters.

"My office was next door to the superintendent so some sobsisters began to question whether I was taking orders from the superintendent," Montoya said. "Actually, I was on my own and in time even employed my own secretary to handle incoming calls, make appointments, and, of course, handle the correspondence.

"Later, we found a vacant building on the Indian School grounds [old Albuquerque Indian School administration building] to which we moved," he continued. "We had partitions built to make the facility a three-room office building with a restroom. After the council contracted to administer the Neighborhood Youth Corps for the pueblos, we turned this building over to the administration of the NYC. Then I moved my office to another building, where we remained during my tenure."

The New Mexico State University Extension Division had employed this writer as a resources development officer, and in this position I began to work closely with the council chairman. Funding for the program by the Extension Division extended for a minimum of two years, long enough to help establish the chairman's office routine as well as seek out other programs. In this manner, two new federal programs were contracted by the council office. The first was known as Talent Search. The other, closely associated and initiated soon afterwards, was the pueblo Indian Scholarship Program. This writer took over as director of Talent Search, and Effie Marmon of Laguna Pueblo directed the scholarship effort. She was assisted by Tessa Archuleta of San Juan-Laguna heritage. I had as my secretary, Irene Gachupin Vigil of Zia Pueblo, whose services were shared with the chairman's office.

The Talent Search program was involved in visiting high schools in the state to identify outstanding students, and the scholarship program provided the money for these pueblo Indian students to attend colleges of their choice. The two programs triggered an explosion in the number of pueblo students attending institutions of higher education for the first time.

Although the Talent Search program no longer exists, the scholarship program continues, dispersed among several pueblos, which conduct their own programs.

Montoya began his council chairmanship of the All Pueblo Council when a very hot subject was under discussion statewide. For some time, pueblo leaders had been demanding that a vocational school be instituted with a program similar to that of the old Indian School. By mid-1963, most Pueblo Indian students were attending public schools near their reservations, but none of these schools had facilities to offer trade and vocational courses. Thus, the New Mexico congressional delegation was asked to present a bill in Congress to appropriate funds for establishing a vocational school.

As often happens in the political arena, the news media got wind of the proposal and reported that the pueblos were to receive several million dollars to start another boarding school where all the trades would be offered together with the regular curriculum. Unfortunately, before enough dialogue could be initiated to explain what the Indian leaders really wanted, misinformation clouded the issue. One New Mexico congressman voted against the bill. Vehemently and in unison, the public school superintendents opposed the proposed new vocational school. They each believed their schools should get part of the millions said to be earmarked for the institution.

In due time, however, following a few trips to Washington and a series of local meetings, civilized communications were established and there was general agreement that what the pueblos wanted was legitimate. Thereafter, another measure was introduced in Congress which resulted in the appropriation of $11 million to plan and construct a post-secondary vocational school in Albuquerque. Students would complete their high school instruction in their local public school systems or parochial schools; then, if they so chose they could attend the vocational school in Albuquerque instead of going to college.

Although some other problems between the pueblo leaders and the planners of the BIA school occurred, the school, now known as the Southwestern Indian Polytechnic Institute, was subsequently established to serve the purpose for which it was intended. The new school opened its doors in September 1971 with an Indian student body from around the nation.

Well known locally, the All Pueblo Council was not so readily recognized elsewhere. When Montoya began making trips to Washington, D.C., as chairman of the council, people in government occasionally would ask: "What proof do you have that you represent the nineteen pueblos of New Mexico? Do you have a constitution which I can examine?"

Despite being the eighth chairman since the modern council was formally organized in 1922, Montoya had no constitution to show skeptics. There had never been a need for such a document. The pueblo government had existed for centuries in a common union, or council, for mutual protection. However, seeing that such a document might now be advantageous, Montoya began to discuss the merits of a constitution with his colleagues on the council. Subsequently, after many meetings and debates, a constitution was drafted and approved.

Among the other major issues confronting Montoya and his colleagues on the council were the ever-present and always convoluted problems concerning water rights. Despite the council's best efforts, more than two decades later, while some attorneys undoubtedly have become rich, water problems still plague the pueblos. Some situations remain unsolved while others are on appeal.

Other issues the members of the All Indian Pueblo Council* had to deal with during Montoya's tenure included Public Law 90-284, also known as the Indian Civil Rights Act or the Ervin Bill. A great threat to the pueblos, it imposed non-Indian standards of government on tribal structures. It also proposed the updating of the handbook of federal Indian law, among other things. To counter the possible negative impact of the bill, the council urged New Mexico senators Clinton P. Anderson and Joseph M. Montoya (no relation to Domingo Montoya) to draft an amendment to the Ervin Bill. This they did in the form of Senate Bill 211.

As threatening as the Ervin Bill was during this era, time has rendered it obsolete as a result of changes within the pueblos. Now, more than twenty-five years later, few people remember it. The swirl of controversy around the flawed legislation was one of those human dramas that arouses the collective Indian mind for a period of time and then vanishes along with its supporters. The Indians live on, awaiting the next crisis resulting from actions outside their pueblos, hopefully to be resolved by other leaders as outstanding as Domingo Montoya.

During Montoya's tenure, the All Indian Pueblo Council was able to obtain 11.6 acres of government land between Indian School Road and Menaul Boulevard on 12th Street in Albuquerque. This plot was on the west side of the Albuquerque Indian School grounds, cut off from the main site by 12th Street. It became the focus of many dreams and plans which finally, after much government "red tape," became reality in the form of the handsome and much-visited Indian Pueblo Cultural Center.

*The All Pueblo Council changed its name to All Indian Pueblo Council in 1965.

The Chairman of the All Indian Pueblo Council has many demands on his time and services, among them a variety of committee memberships with their attendant plethora of meetings. One of the committees that made its share of calls on Montoya was the National Indian Education Advisory Committee, which met quarterly in different parts of the country from Alaska to Florida. Another was the New Mexico Commission on Indian Affairs with its office in Santa Fe. Montoya was chairman of this group in 1971. Still another important assignment was membership on the Advisory Committee of the Small Business Administration. This panel was an advocate of minority enterprise in deprived areas, usually rural regions.

In the late sixties, Texas Senator Ralph Yarborough introduced a bill in the U.S. Senate calling for the Tiguas from Ysleta del Sur (Isleta of the South), southeast of El Paso, to be recognized as descendants of an American Indian Tribe —Tiwas who fled south in the 1680 Revolt, leaving the territory with the Spanish colonists. Chairman Montoya was appointed to verify whether there was any segment of the pueblo heritage and culture still maintained by the Texas Tiguas. This writer, as Secretary of the All Indian Pueblo Council, accompanied Montoya to Ysleta del Sur to observe the people firsthand.

We found a Spanish-speaking people when we arrived at the village. Since Montoya spoke fluent Spanish, he had no trouble communicating with our hosts. After we had become acquainted—the Tiguas knew why we were there—Montoya asked the people to demonstrate to us their Indian culture. The men who had gathered with us were ready. They had their drum and their dance regalia. The drum, their bows and arrows, and their rattles all were painted red. One or two men stuck turkey feathers in their headbands as they lined up to perform. When they were all ready, their leader announced, *"Numero uno,"* and they started dancing.

"Numero dos," the leader called out when they completed their first dance. The men performed a second time. We recognized the dance as a Tiwa dance called *Ya-hayna.*

Satisfied with our findings, we sent a report to Congress indicating that the Tiguas still maintained a pueblo tradition, customs, and dances. The only drawback was that they had lost their Tiwa language and spoke only Spanish. Since that time the tribe has been recognized by the federal government as an organized Pueblo Indian tribe. A book titled *The Tiguas: Pueblo Indians of Texas,* by Bill Wright, was published in 1993, confirming recognition on a less official level.

In his role as chairman, Montoya was called to testify before U.S. Senate hearings on many occasions. Later he would say of this, "One lesson I have learned is that, despite the fine language, enthusiasm, and good intentions contained in the policy statement, how well policies are carried out and whether they are acted on at all depends to a large extent on the Indians' ability to have adequate legal advice from trusted counsel."

Time has proven Montoya right. During the past thirty years, as Indian tribes have retained their own legal advisors or attorneys, they have begun to win court cases. Previously, the lawyers for the Indians were employed by the Interior Department. Usually they were younger professionals going up against senior attorneys in other branches of the Interior Department such as Agriculture, Forestry, and the Bureau of Land Management.

During the years after he was named chairman, Montoya and his wife Mary were host to thousands of people at their spacious home, especially on feast days. Among them were both old and new friends from all ethnic groups, governors, bank presidents, United States senators, foreign visitors, and tourists. In spite of his broad contacts and the fact that he was known by people in all walks of life, Montoya accepted his calling to serve his people as a typical pueblo leader. That is, he served in humble dignity, knowing that dignity demands respect. Long after his term as chairman ended, he remained available to his people and the council. Later chairmen occasionally called on him for advice. In the pueblo world, a man of his advancing years was justly valued for his experience.

His colleagues on the council, government officials, and staff members who have worked with him agree that it was Montoya's nature to be sensitive, cooperative, and helpful to others. He had many friends, but he would have had them even had he not been council chairman, for it was Montoya's way to be very friendly and meet people easily. As a coworker of Montoya during his days as chairman, this writer feels as though he knew the man well. The two of us spent many hours together finalizing speeches and presentations and traveling together to meetings and conventions.

After stepping down as council chairman on January 30, 1971, Montoya returned to the life he enjoyed the most—farming and cattle raising. He continued to farm until 1983, when he leased his beloved land to a non-Indian. Under the lease agreement, Montoya was paid mostly in alfalfa that he fed to his cattle, which ranged east of the pueblo at the foothills of Ki Pien, the Sandia Mountains.

The years had taken a toll but Montoya continued to deliver bales of alfalfa to his herd and check the water tanks regardless of the weather. On weekends he got help from his grandsons and sons, who worked at other jobs during the week. Although he was still physically able, he had to be more careful how he slung the bales and jumped off the truck.

The young beet field worker who could not finish high school was able to accomplish much for his people as governor and village councilman and chairman of the All Indian Pueblo Council representing the nineteen Pueblos of New Mexico. His name and accomplishments will continue to be remembered.

On May 30, 1993, Montoya went on his daily chore of inspecting and feeding his cattle. He arrived there, he probably left his new truck parked uphill with the automatic gear shift in drive, but he had put his brakes on, thinking that would hold the truck.

After he opened the tailgate, he started to pull a bail of alfalfa so he could spread it for the cattle standing around him. But the truck apparently rolled backwards, knocking Montoya down and a wheel rolled over him.

Being Sunday, and Memorial Day as well, his boys were home and since their father was unusually late returning, Sam went to look for his dad and found him already expired.

Thus ended the life of a great pueblo man. He would have been eighty-two years old in ten more weeks.

At a gathering of family and friends, Sam said about his father, "He was very healthy and was working on his land right up to the end. He died doing what he loved to do. He was a great husband, father, and tribal leader."

PART IV

Sovereignty and Development

"I consider the signing of Public Law 91-550 one of the most significant achievements of my Administration. It is more than just a land settlement: it is a symbolic turning point in the history of those who were the first Americans. It is the beginning of a new era which will finally achieve for you the fullness of the prosperity and progress you deserve as citizens of this richly endowed land." —Richard M. Nixon

Left to right: Paul Bernal, Taos Cacique Deer Bird, and President Richard M. Nixon (seated). Courtesy of Bethel Agency, New York.

CHAPTER 10

The Blue Lake Story
Taos Pueblo

Imagine somewhere in America a beautiful church in a serene pastoral setting serving the religious needs of a devout community for centuries. Now, imagine the United States government declaring this church public property and opening it to people from anywhere and everywhere for meetings, luncheons, or dances. Such a sacrilege could never happen, you say? But it did. Only in this case the "church" was not a building but a beautiful small lake and the land around it in the Sangre de Cristo Mountains of northern New Mexico.

Blue Lake is its name. It is the most important place for the spiritual life of the Taos Pueblo people. According to pueblo oral history, Blue Lake is the mystic primordial home of Taos Pueblo, the place where the Taos people came into this world. It also is the place where the people return after death, to enter into the spirit world and eternal life—a place called heaven in the white man's religion.

It is difficult to describe and discuss the sacredness of Blue Lake. Indeed, the people of Taos do not speak of its true spiritual meaning outside the circles of the initiated ones of the various kivas. However, Severino Martinez, a former governor of Taos Pueblo, once said:

> Blue Lake is the most important of all shrines because it is a part of our life, it is our Indian church. We go there for good reason, like any other people would go to their denomination. Different people would go visit and give their humble word to God in any language that they speak. It is the same principle at Blue Lake. We go there and talk to our Great Spirit in our own language and talk to nature and what is going to grow and ask God Almighty like anyone else would do.[1]

Despite the fact that Blue Lake was a church to the Taos people, in 1906 the president of the United States, ignoring the Constitution, declared the area—including the sacred lake and surrounding land—to be

93

part of a national forest. This action was taken in the name of conservation, but it overrode Article 1, Section 8 of the United States Constitution. That section states: "Indian tribes, like foreign countries and states, will be consulted on important transactions." Even though nothing could be more important than the desecration of a people's religious shrine, and the confiscation of their land, there are no records which show that Taos Pueblo or even the United States Indian Service was ever consulted on this most serious matter.

In the mid-nineteenth century, when the United States acquired sovereignty over New Mexico by virtue of the Treaty of Guadalupe Hidalgo, the Pueblo of Taos, under Mexican law and previously under Spanish law, was owner of all lands that it had historically exclusively used and occupied. Those lands included the Blue Lake region. In line with Articles VIII and IX of the treaty ending the Mexican War in 1848, the United States agreed to respect and protect all property rights within the vast area ceded to it. With the inclusion of Blue Lake and its environs in the Carson National Forest, that provision was ignored.

The Taos people were deeply hurt by the loss of their land and lake; a major taproot of their culture had been cut. They spent many years learning how to battle politicians and bureaucrats on their own terms in order to redress the wrong done them. For sixty-four years, the Taos people would fight against impossible odds to regain their hallowed site. Taos Pueblo's struggle to regain its holy place is one of America's epic stories. The sixty-four-year effort became a symbol of the plight of the American Indian. Before it ended, it expanded to become the focus of all Taos Pueblo efforts and gained the support of most American Indian tribes as well as of people all over the world who recognized in this confrontation an example for aboriginal people wherever their claims. Through all those frustrating years, the Taos people rallied united to defend their most sacred ground.

Many people played important roles in the long struggle to have Blue Lake returned to the Taos people, but none more than Juan de Jesus Romero, the Christian name of Deer Bird, the longtime Taos cacique who never wavered in the cause. In a sense, the story of the long, difficult legal and political fight to regain Blue Lake is the story of Deer Bird's life.

Deer Bird lived to be more than a century old and devoted much of his life to the effort to regain Blue Lake, but he was not alone. Often at his side during this critical struggle was Pablo José (Paul J.) Bernal, interpreter and secretary of the Taos Pueblo Tribal Council. Many others also contributed significantly to the effort, including successive governors of the pueblo, who tried to bring about an equitable solution. Even after their terms ended, these governors continued as councilmen to accept responsibility and concern for the return of their lost shrine.

According to the Taos Pueblo census, Deer Bird was born at Taos Pueblo sometime in 1886. *The New York Times* gave his age as 103 when he died, but a publication of the Chicago Indian Council Fire listed him as 104 at death. In 1974, the Chicago Indian Council Fire had honored the Taos patriarch with its forty-second annual award demonstrating continuity in achievement among American Indians.[2] (Five other Pueblo Indians have been honored by the Chicago-based organization: Maria Montoya of San Ildefonso Pueblo; Hopi leader Fred Kabotie; George Blue Spruce, Jr., of San Juan-Laguna Pueblo; Robert E. Lewis of Cherokee-Zuni Pueblo; and Alfonso Ortiz of San Juan Pueblo.)

First as governor, later as a councilman, and finally as cacique, Deer Bird joined in the campaign to regain the land for his people. Throughout those difficult years, Deer Bird was a symbol of strength, determination, and optimism. At one point, he was quoted as saying: "If our Mawhalo [mountain peak near Blue Lake] is not returned to us, then it is the end of our Indian life. Our people will scatter as the people of other Indian nations have scattered. It is our religion that holds us together."[3]

Because Deer Bird was assigned to the Old Axe kiva fraternity by virtue of his birth (membership is passed on through paternal bloodlines) he was eligible to become cacique of Taos Pueblo when the incumbent died. The cacique is the titular head of most pueblo Indian villages, and the majority of the nineteen pueblos in New Mexico still maintain the office. The word cacique is of Caribbean area Indian origin. It was learned by the Spanish from the Arawaks on the islands of the Caribbean early in the era of conquest and brought to the Americas by the invaders. When the Spanish encountered a pueblo tribe, they immediately asked for the cacique, applying the term to any leader with whom they negotiated.

As a young man, Deer Bird was initiated into the practices of the Taos religious society of the Old Axe kiva, one of six kivas at the pueblo. There are three each on the north and south sides of the pueblo. With Old Axe on the south side are Water and Feather kivas, on the north, Knife, Day, and Big Earring.

Deer Bird was cacique of Taos during the last twenty years of the struggle to regain Blue Lake, from 1958 to 1978. In that post he was a symbol of the religion of his people and kept them rallied in spirit to obtain the return of their sacred site. While other tribal officials were selected by religious leaders for yearly appointments, the cacique held his place for life. Thus, Deer Bird provided the continuity needed to sustain the tribe in its battle with the United States government for Blue Lake, and in this capacity he never faltered. As tribal secretary and interpreter, Bernal also was a long-term appointee, especially well equipped for the role he played.

Bernal was born at Taos Pueblo February 22, 1913, the son of José

Ignacio Bernal and Maria Romero. Volunteering in 1942, Bernal served six years in the United States Navy before being honorably discharged in 1948. On his return from the service to Taos, he began to work for the Indian Health Service, which was then administered by the Bureau of Indian Affairs. Two years later the tribe appointed him secretary and interpreter. Bernal joined the effort to regain Blue Lake with his tribal appointment in 1950. For two decades he stood at Deer Bird's side with the other officials who were appointed annually and experienced many bitter disappointments before the joyful moment of victory. He was the constant companion of Deer Bird at meetings at the pueblo and in Santa Fe, Albuquerque, and later Washington, D.C., where they went to lobby and learn the ways of the white man's politics and bureaucracy. Together with Deer Bird he became a symbol of Taos Pueblo's fight against overwhelming odds for the return of Blue Lake.

Bernal's language skills as an interpreter helped bring a clear message to United States officials concernig the Taos people's claim. There was the time, for example, when Seferino Martinez, a tribal councilman who spoke a mixture of Spanish and Tiwa but very little English, was designated as tribal spokesman. With Bernal at his side, this deficiency did not keep Martinez from being heard nationally in high places. On April l8, 1961, when he was serving as governor of the pueblo, Martinez spoke to the Association on American Indian Affairs in New York City. In part, he said:

> You have beautiful statues, beautiful figures of representative scenes which we now worship, you and I together. We don't have the beautiful structures, and we don't have gold temples in this [Blue] lake, but we have a sign of the living God to whom we pray—the living trees, the evergreen and spruce, and the beautiful flowers, and the lake itself.
>
> We have to pray for what we receive from the sun that gives the light and the water we drink. They are provided by God. We are taking that water to give us strength so we can gain in knowledge and wisdom about the work that we are engaged in. Without energy provided by God, we are helpless. Religion is the most important thing in our life. That is the reason why this Blue Lake is so important to us.[4]

One gauge of the importance of Blue Lake and surrounding land to the Taos people is economic. Taos Pueblo is not rich. During the two-thirds of a century that the pueblo fought for the return of its sacred lake, the people were living on scarce resources, almost below the subsistence level. Given this, the added hardship of providing the fares for trips to Washington, D.C., or managing the cost of all the legal actions is evident.

Despite unified defense of the Taos people, at times they became discouraged or even disillusioned. Sometimes there was dissension as, for example, when the tribe was offered monetary compensation for the lost site. Some wanted to take the money, but the majority only wanted the land and lake. Consequently, the struggle continued, as the tribe took on the highest-ranking politicians on the politicians' terms—and won. The Taos people emerged victorious mainly through this courage and tenacity.

The story of Blue Lake began on November 23, 1903, when the area was withdrawn from public entry as a first step towards inclusion in the newly formed Forest Service venue. This action was not opposed by the pueblo, for the land was thus protected from mining and other non-Indian speculators. The Taos people had maintained the land and the lake for their religious purposes for centuries, and they feared the intrusion of outsiders on their privacy and the destruction of the land non-Indians caused for the sake of material gain.

When the land was first withdrawn, the pueblo had an ally in a trusted white friend, Bert Phillips, who became the first forest ranger for the area. He was aware of the pueblo's concern about encroachment, and when government surveyors came to Taos, Phillips asked the two men if they would recommend to the president of the United States that the area be set aside for exclusive use by Taos Pueblo.

Instead, on November 7, 1906, President Theodore Roosevelt proclaimed Blue Lake part of the Taos Forest Reserve, making it public domain. Under an executive order dated June 26, 1908, the Taos shrine became part of the Carson National Forest. One consequence was that the region was now open to miners, fur trappers, and traders. The people of Taos soon saw their shrine become profaned and polluted by outsiders. The executive order also increased the possibility of encroachment by Spanish-heritage neighbors.

There always had been an uneasy relationship between the Indians and Spanish in the area, marked by strife and many court cases. The Supreme Court's ruling on the *Joseph* case of 1876 (94 U.S. 614, 1876) was an unfortunate example of the Court's failure to stop non-Indian intrusion on Taos Indian land, resulting in a loss for Taos and many other pueblos.[5] An earlier loss of land to the Spanish resulted from an insurrection planned by the Taos Indians and their Spanish neighbors in January 1847 to show their discontent with the invasion of northern New Mexico by American miners and trappers after the acquisition of the territory by the United States. The Taos Council agreed to provide some men to assist the Spanish in the plot to kill American governor Charles Bent. When the time came, the Indians were in place to carry out the plan, but instead Colonel Sterling Price and his soldiers cornered the rebels in the Taos Pueblo church. In an effort to save the insurgents, who were sentenced to death, the Taos Council went to Antonio José Martinez, better known to history as the controversial Padre Martinez, for legal help.

Martinez insisted on being paid in land for his assistance, and thus the council gave him the El Prado section of their reservation. Nevertheless, the rebellious Indians were executed, while today El Prado is part of the town of Taos.

During the early years of the struggle to regain Blue Lake for Taos Pueblo, the only consolation was that the Indians' forest ranger friend Bert Phillips, who had homesteaded north of Taos, did not grant permits for entry to the Blue Lake area to non-Indians for any reason, including mining or grazing. Unfortunately, Phillips left in 1912 after six years on the job, and, by contrast, his successor, Elliot Barker, who later became director of the New Mexico State Game and Fish Department, stocked Blue Lake with fish and built a trail to the area. This demonstrated the white man's drive to control or change nature when the department dynamited Star Lake, a small lake near Blue Lake, because it was overstocked with fish. Star Lake also is a shrine used by the Taos Indians in their religious ceremonies; thus, one of their shrines was desecrated by dynamite in order to manage nature.

As the years passed the people of Taos felt the invasion of their privacy and religion more and more. Grazing permits for sheep and cattle were issued to non-Indians for the Blue Lake area, further despoiling the shrine. In 1912 the Taos Indians began trying to have the Blue Lake area declared an "executive order reservation by the secretary of the interior." Although the interior secretary sought the cooperation of the secretary of agriculture, whose office had jurisdiction over the Forest Service, the latter declined. In 1916, the pueblo again fought the change, but to no avail.

Encroachment on Pueblo Indian land became so bad in Taos and elsewhere that the Taos Indians began, literally, to throw trespassers off their property, but the government held the upper hand. Then, in 1924 the pueblo thought it had regained its land when on June 7 Congress passed the Pueblo Lands Board Act (43 Stat. 636), designed to determine prior Indian land claims, and the Pueblo Lands Board began to make favorable decisions. Taos, like the other pueblos, believed, innocently, that their government representatives would be advocates for them but discovered this had not been the case with then Indian Commissioner Herbert Hagerman when they read the newspaper headline "Senate Group Votes Ouster of Hagerman" and learned about the charges against the man who had been appointed to help their cause.

Herbert J. Hagerman, who had been appointed special Indian commissioner by the president of the United States, had been under investigation by a Senate committee for neglect of duty and misconception of his position. He also had been questioned about his conduct as a former member of the Pueblo Lands Board with accusations that he had not complied with the mandate of Congress in that he "failed, neglected to find fair market value and to award fair compensation to pueblos when ownership of land and water rights were extinguished."

Hagerman had served as twenty-first territorial governor of New Mexico from 1906 to 1907, having been appointed by President Roosevelt on January 22, 1906, but then asked to resign fourteen months later for reasons similar to those later investigated. In spite of his previous inadequacies, Hagerman was later appointed to serve on the Pueblo Lands Board in the 1920s and later as special Indian commissioner to negotiate with Indian tribes in New Mexico, Arizona, Utah, and Colorado concerning lands they had lost.

Although Hagerman clearly did not provide the representation the Indians had hoped for, Taos Pueblo did not give up hope and again experienced the illusion of victory in December 1927 when the Cooperative Agreement was signed, defining the responsibilities and privileges of the Indians and the Forest Service in the Blue Lake area. Following this, several attempts were made in Congress to enact legislation that would settle the problem. In January 1932, New Mexico Senator Bronson Cutting introduced a bill (S. 2914), which would have authorized a patent to Taos Pueblo for 30,000 acres of the land covered by the Act of 1928, which stipulated that the Forest Service should continue to manage and administer the acreage. The Senate favored the bill, but the House of Representatives rejected it. A substitute to Cutting's proposal (H.R. 4014) was considered in the House. However, it would have authorized only the segregation of the same 30,000 acres with a fifty-year special use permit to the Pueblo of Taos.

In the climate of this attempt at illegal land appropriation by the federal government, Special Commissioner Hagerman appeared not to help the Indians he was sworn to assist, but to testify against them. Hagerman, on February 11, 1932, testified at a congressional hearing that he saw no reason why the Blue Lake area should be patented to Taos Pueblo. His motive for such testimony is uncertain, but it might have been related to action a month earlier by a congressional subcommittee recommending that Hagerman's position be abolished and that there be no further appropriation for his salary and expenses. The result of these hearings was that the 1927 Cooperative Agreement was followed by the Act of 1933, which withdrew the area from entry for mineral extraction.

After the Cooperative Agreement and the Act of 1933, the people of Taos Pueblo felt some relief, since they thought their problems with the federal government had been reduced to manageable proportions, if not settled according to their desires. The 1933 legislation would serve to keep miners from trespassing and staking claims in the Rio Pueblo watershed, protecting the land from degeneration and the waters from pollution. However, as it turned out there were loopholes in the legislation.

Careful scrutiny of the two acts revealed that they did not cover the entire watershed of 48,000 acres but only 32,000 acres and the Indians were not even granted exclusive occupancy and use of that tract. Instead, non-Indians were eligible for permits to sightsee, camp, and fish and ranchers could be given ten-year grazing permits. Insult was added to injury when Taos Pueblo learned that the Forest Service had allocated only three days in August for their centuries-old religious ceremonies—provided the pueblo informed the Forest Service ten days in advance.

This latter provision was especially distasteful to Deer Bird and other Taos religious leaders, whose duty it was to see that the ancient religious ceremony was observed in its entirety uninterrupted rather than rushed through in three days. Further aggravating the situation was the dictate that the Forest Service was to be the sole authority for issuing permits to enter the area for any purpose.

Taos tribal officials then protested the new and unilateral decisions of the Forest Service to the Indian Agency. The resulting controversy spawned a great deal of misinformation and misunderstanding between Taos Pueblo and government authorities. The Taos Indians thought no one was to be admitted to the Blue Lake site without written permission from both tribal authorities and the Forest Service. They contended that members of the public wishing to enter the area should go to the tribal officer first and then have their permits countersigned by the Forest Service; the governmental agency claimed the procedure should be the opposite. The Forest Service's interpretation of the law was that Congress had not intended to give exclusive use of the land to Taos Pueblo, merely exclusive use of wood, water, and forage; it further insisted that the Taos Indians should abide by state game laws.

In spite of formidable opposition, some of the pueblo's non-Indian friends, notable among them John Collier, supported the final form of the bill providing for special use and a provision for the Taos Indians to cosign all permits for tourists entering the Blue Lake area. The Forest Service agreed to this provision and on May 31, 1933, Congress enacted the legislation (48 Stat. 108).

The following year, on April 30, H.R. 9407 was introduced to expand the special use area to 39,000 acres. However, this House bill died because of pressure from ranchers who wanted permits. (It is ironic that Indians at this time were not allowed to vote in federal or state elections. Later, when they won the right to vote, many older Taos Indians refused to register because they did not want to be a part of the white people's system of government, which they felt could not be trusted.)

In March 1935, there were new attempts in both House and Senate to expand the special use acreage by 9,000 acres. Both failed. Four years later, in March 1939, another House bill identical to the 1935 proposal was introduced but met the same dismal fate. There was a recurring pattern to the unequal struggle. Each time the Taos Indians won a minor legislative victory, the advantages that seemed to accrue to them under the law would first be eroded by interpretation and then further diminished by the actions of entrenched bureaucrats and non-Indian interest groups.

The flame of hope shot up again for Taos when the Indian Land Claims Commission was established in 1946. In 1951, the pueblo filed a claim to their aboriginal land, alleging it had not been alienated but taken by the government and demanding trespass damages. The Indian Claims Commission, however, could award only monetary reparations for lands taken by the government. The Indians' attorney then advised the pueblo to delay its legislative efforts for land return until the Indian Claims Commission could establish aboriginal title, thus building a stronger base for their claim. Once again the Taos Indians waited patiently for justice. Finally, in 1965 after fourteen years, word came from the Indian Claims Commission that Taos Pueblo did, indeed, have valid title to the land and that the federal government was liable for taking the property from the Taos Indians. Their repayment was to be monetary, but this was not acceptable to the Taos Indians, who only wanted the return of their sacred Blue Lake area as compensation.

As they studied the decision further, the people of Taos found the action of the Indian Claims Commission to be as confusing as many past governmental decisions. The amount of compensation awarded the pueblo was $297,684.67 (how they had arrived at the uneven figures was a mystery) and was for land lost through encroachment by the town of Taos. It was the Taos Tribal Council's intention to file for title to Blue Lake only. The tribe was ready to forego the compensation awarded for the land in the town of Taos if they could just recover their shrine. However, to have it returned they had to endure still more legislation.

In 1966, New Mexico Senator Clinton P. Anderson introduced a bill (S. 3085) at the "request" of the Taos Tribal Council, which would have added 50,000 acres to their reservation. To their disappointment, the Taos Indians learned that introduction of a bill "by request" meant that the sponsor had no real interest in its outcome. Consequently, the Anderson Bill got nowhere. The Forest Service objected to the proposal because it could not take care of land outside national forest boundaries, it argued. And no one outside the tribe came forward to support the bill.

Disheartened but not defeated, the Taos Indians did not give up. They had learned the hard way that public opinion was one effective way to lobby Congress, and by that time the pueblo had gained support from friends outside the tribe. Among them was a local champion of Indian rights, New Mexico Governor David Cargo. Through his ties to the federal administration and, especially, Vice President Spiro Agnew, the tribe was able to make broader contacts with politicians and the media. For example, through the efforts of Vice President Agnew, Taos Governor Quirino Romero and John C. Rainer, Sr. (whose life is discussed in Chapter 12) appeared on the Dinah Shore television show to champion their cause.

Cargo, dubbed "Lonesome Dave" by the media, had for the first time in state government appointed a number of Indians to state commissions and boards, giving them broader public exposure. John Rainer of Taos Pueblo was appointed director of the State Commission on Indian Affairs, making that office a valuable avenue of communications.

With wider exposure came more support for the Taos Indians' cause; they gained an ally in Congress, Representative James A. Haley of Florida, chairman of the House Subcommittee on Indian Affairs. In 1968, Haley introduced H.R. 3306, which was designed to give trust status to 48,000 acres of Taos land in the Blue Lake area. Predictably, there was loud opposition. Many legislators argued that in the past American Indians had lost so much land through legislation and action in the white man's courts that restoration of the Taos land might set a dangerous precedent. Historically, politicians had relied on the old military axiom "sacrifice the few to save the many." Recreation interests and the Forest Service also mobilized their forces against the Haley Bill, and it died in the Senate as the result of New Mexico Senator Anderson.

In spite of his initial failure, Haley was convinced the Taos Indians had been wronged by the government in having their aboriginal lands taken from them. Early in 1969, at a time when the plight of American Indians was coming to light across the country, Haley introduced another bill (H.R. 471) on behalf of Taos Pueblo. The House held hearings on May 15 and 16, and the Senate reviewed the bill on July 9 and 10. This time the proposed legislation got nationwide media coverage and, more importantly, editorial support from influential newspapers.

Editorials supporting the Taos Indians' claim appeared in scores of newspapers around the country and major magazines featured articles about the problems of Indians, many focusing on Taos Pueblo's quest for the return of Blue Lake. As a result of this media coverage, people all over America came to know about Blue Lake and most sympathized with the concerns of the Taos Indians. A few of the major newspapers that provided editorial support to the Taos Indians were the *New York Times, the New York Journal American, the Washington Post, the St. Louis Post-Dispatch, the Minneapolis Star-Tribune,* and the *Denver Post.* The common themes in their editorials were the constitutional guarantee of freedom of religion and the return of the land to its rightful owners.

Finally, the Taos Indians were gaining publicity and widespread support for their cause. Many religious organizations also endorsed the claim of Taos Pueblo. Some of the organizations that spoke out for the Taos Indians were the New Mexico Council of Churches, the National Council of Churches of Christ, and the American Jewish Congress.

Meanwhile, the grand Indian lady of Washington entered the controversy and began doing her part to educate and persuade the stern and staunch opponents in Congress with her charm and knowledge. This lady was LaDonna Harris, a Comanche and president of Americans for Indian Opportunity, an Indian advocacy organization based in the nation's capital. She also was the wife of former Oklahoma Senator Fred Harris, now a professor at the University of New Mexico.

To old-timers on the Indian scene, the situation was much like the days of the fight against the Bursum Bill by Pueblo Indians in 1922, when they marshaled forces to defeat that destructive and unfair legislation. This time, however, a more experienced lobbying force of Indians and friends was working unceasingly and visiting influential persons in key states around the nation. In addition, influential persons, such as Kimberly Agnew, the daughter of Vice President Spiro Agnew, also visited Taos Pueblo to show their support. She would return later for a victory celebration.

Early in 1970, a Taos Pueblo delegation attended the executive council meeting of the National Congress of American Indians (NCAI) in Washington, D.C. John C. Rainer was vice president of this association as well as chief Indian member of the National Council of Indian Opportunity under Vice President Agnew. The Taos delegation traveled to Washington hopeful that the NCAI would use its influence to convince the president of the United States to publicly support the return of Blue Lake and the pending legislation.

Support for the Taos Indians also came from another source close to President Richard Nixon, although he has not publicly been given credit. Top presidential aide John D. Ehrlichman, like Congressman Haley, was convinced the people of Taos Pueblo had been wronged and reportedly urged Nixon to support the return of Blue Lake.

As a result of all these efforts, and ultimately because truth triumphs, on July 8, 1970, President Nixon announced his support of the Taos Pueblo claim. This pronouncement gave the Taos cause a great boost at a critical time.

At this point Senator Anderson introduced another bill that appeared to give Taos Pueblo use of some of the land. Closer investigation of its terms, however, revealed that the legislation would have separated the land into parcels for different purposes, including logging. It was quickly denounced by Taos. Nevertheless, the bill came out of committee November 16, 1970. It was challenged immediately by Democratic Senator Fred Harris, a strong advocate of justice for Indians, and Republican

Senator Robert Griffin of Michigan. Together, they moved to substitute Haley's H.R. 471 for the Anderson Bill.

The Senate was scheduled to vote December 2 on which bill would be adopted. To aid the Taos cause, Domingo Montoya, chairman of the All Indian Pueblo Council, sent a telegram to New Mexico's junior senator, Joseph M. Montoya, asking him to vote for the House bill. He replied that he could not go against the state's powerful senior senator. As it turned out, Senator Montoya was conveniently out of the country on a trip to Mexico when the vote was called.

Taos Pueblo officials and their friends were tense as the vote was taken. They thought the numbers were on their side, but they could not be sure until the votes were counted. Anderson's bill was defeated 56 to 21. Then came the vote on the legislation that would give the shrine back to the pueblo. It passed overwhelmingly, 70 to 12.

During the tabulation, John C. Rainer was sitting with network broadcaster Roger Mudd at Vice President Agnew's seat in the Senate. That evening Mudd broadcast information about the Taos situation given him by Rainer.

With victory, the Taos Pueblo Council and their friends wept with joy. The jubilant news spread from Washington across the continent to all American Indians on this most momentous day when the David that was Taos Pueblo defeated the Goliath government.

At 11 A.M. on December 15, 1970, in the state dining room of the White House, President Nixon signed into law H.R. 471 giving Blue Lake and its environs back to its rightful owners. Of the many pens on the table, the one Nixon used to sign the document was given to Deer Bird, a man who had devoted much of his life to the quest for the return of Blue Lake. With great dignity, Deer Bird accepted the pen and said: "Now when I die, I will die at peace." When Deer Bird died eight years later, the *New York Times* printed an obituary of this dedicated man with the head-line: "Taos Tribe Leader, In West, At Age 103, Juan de Jesus Romero, a Spiritual Head of New Mexico Indians."

With Deer Bird at the bill signing ceremony in the White House were Quirino Romero, governor of Taos Pueblo; James Mirabel, tribal senior councilman; Deer Bird's constant companion, Paul J. Bernal; and John C. Rainer. At the ceremony Rainer was the only Indian wearing a war bonnet, which was worn to represent all American Indians. The war bonnet had belonged to Leo Vocu, a Sioux from Pine Ridge, South Dakota. Vocu had given it to Robert Jim, Chairman of the Yakima Nation, when Jim was going to South America as a representative of the American Indians. When Jim learned of the date of the signing ceremony, he flew from Yakima, Washington to the capital the day before to give the headdress to Rainer.

NOTES

1. "Handbook of North American Indians," Vol. 9, *Southwest* (Washington, D.C.: Smithsonian Institution Press, 1979), 257.

2. Lola L. Hill, "A 50th Annual Report of the Chicago Indian Council Fire," Chicago, 1982, 27.

3. Speech, April 18, 1961, Assocation of Indian Affairs, New York City. Cited in Marta Weigle and Peter White, *The Lore of New Mexico,* (Albuquerque: University of New Mexico Press, 1988), 250.

4. Ibid.

5. In the *Joseph* decision the court ruled that federal statutes authorizing the Indian commissioner to regulate Indian treaties had no application to the Pueblos.

REFERENCES

Archibeck, Ronald P. "Taos Indians and the Blue Lake Controversy." Masters thesis, University of New Mexico, Albuquerque, 1972.

Bernal, Paul J., private papers, New Mexico State Records and Archives, Santa Fe, New Mexico.

Porfirio Montoya

Roy Montoya

CHAPTER 11

Story of the Tamayame
Santa Ana Pueblo

The story of the Tamayame is somewhat like the story of Taos Pueblo's struggle for Blue Lake. Both were community struggles. Tamaya is the Keresan name for the old village of Santa Ana Pueblo, so the people refer to themselves as Tamayame. Tamaya became known to non-Indians as Santa Ana after the village received its patron saint of that name from the Spaniards in the sixteenth century. Instead of Santa Ana they say "Santana."

Santa Ana is a small Keresan-speaking tribe numbering approximately 650, counting the Indians who live off the reservation. Like the Indians of Acoma Pueblo, the Tamayame live at two places. They spend most of their time along the banks of the Rio Grande at El Ranchito, where they have their farmlands and modern homes. But they return to old Tamaya, on the banks of the Rio Jemez a few miles west of El Ranchito, for their annual feast on July 26 and other celebrations and ceremonies. Today, one can describe the Tamayame as successful business people considering that the tribe has minimal unemployment due to an assortment of businesses located on their 61,931 acres of land (as of 1990). A few non-Indians and non-tribal member Indians are also employed.

Tamaya is located away from the main routes followed by later travelers through the Southwest. Because of its small size and relative isolation, in the past Tamaya was often disregarded by social scientists and other writers. However, in 1994 a book co-authored by Laura Bayer and Floyd Montoya of Tamaya and titled *Santa Ana: The People of the Pueblo and the History of Tamaya* was written about Tamaya. In this book the authors combined written history with the rich oral tradition that has preserved Tamaya's own account of the past.

It was only natural for Floyd Montoya to be the co-author since he is the son of Porfirio Montoya, once interpreter and spokesman for Tamaya. His family related to me that Porfirio was a teenager attending the Albuquerque Indian School when his pueblo leaders appointed him to the position, in which he served for many years, until he died at a ripe old age. Many of the developments that took place in Santa Ana during his lifetime and since were the result of Porfirio's work and dedication. He was known as "Mr. Tamaya." I can recall listening to Porfirio as he detailed accounts of his people's origin, land use, migrations, traditions, and twentieth-century history in preparation for hearings before the Land Claims Commission, which was established by an act of Congress on August 13, 1946. At that time, Jemez, Santa Ana, and Zia Pueblos were united in their struggle to retain part of their aboriginal lands.

As I remember Porfirio relating, after the Tamayame emerged at Shipapu they traveled for a long time, searching for the center of the earth, where they would make their homes. Although they passed through many fine lands, they did not settle in any of them. When they grew tired and hungry, they stopped to gather the nourishment Mother Earth provided for them. At last they reached Kashe K'atreti (White House). There, after many years of traveling they settled for the first time. As a historian, I am aware of two places that could be Kashe K'atreti. First, it could be Chaco Canyon since pueblo oral history often talks of the Keresans at Chaco Canyon. It is repeated that the Acume (Acoma), Tsiyame (Zia), and Tamayame came directly south from Chaco Canyon while the other Keresans went east from the Four Corners area and eventually came south to the middle Rio Grande area, where most live today.

Second, another pueblo legend suggests that Kashe K'atreti was in Florida. This pueblo legend was turned into a book by John M. Gunn,[1] part of which was published in 1904 in *Records of the Past* in Washington, D.C. This book suggests that Kashe K'atreti was in Florida since the White House, supposedly the home of the cacique, was finished with white sea shells on the outside. The Keresans, like most Pueblo Indians, do talk about migrating in their oral history, and the Caribbean area contains many place names that also have meaning in the Keresan language. For example, the land Columbus discovered in 1492 was called Guanahane by the Natives, a name that means "It comes from the east" to some Keresans. *Ha* or *hane* means east. The word *cacique* also originated in the Caribbean and was brought to the Southwest by the Spaniards. There the cacique was called *Hatuey* or *Hataway*, expressions commonly used by the Keresans when speaking about the pollen of corn tassel.

In their oral history, the Tamayame speak of temporary settlements. One of the first settlements in the currently occupied area was Paaku, on the northeast side of the Sandia Mountains. While they were residing at Paaku, a group split from the main group and began using the valley near the Rio Grande for farming. According to their oral history they were also on the San Felipe mesa at one time. Some of their migrations may have resulted from attacks by the Athabaskans, either Apaches or Navajos, who reportedly had arrived in the area by A.D. 1400.

The faction of the Tamayame that split off from the main group went west and settled by the Rio Jemez, south of San Ysidro. Later the group went south to the Rio Puerco and settled there. Later they moved west to a place near the current village of Paquate, north of Old Laguna. This seems to be where Coronado's men saw ruins while traveling to the Rio Grande from the Zuni area in 1540. After this, the Tamayame again moved south, passing by Acoma and settling in the present-day Socorro area. A few years later they traveled north, returning to their kin at Paaku.

The Tamayame developed small farming plots at the foot of San Felipe mesa, where they were able to irrigate with runoff. They could not use water from the Rio Jemez since it was too saline for irrigation. They occupied many farming villages along the Rio Grande until their farm lands were confiscated and granted to the early Spanish settlers by the Spanish governor. They also utilized the farm lands of modern Corrales and developed two communities north of Corrales. One was called Buraikana and the second one Kwiiste Haa Tamaya. Coronado wintered near one of these settlements.

In a series of land transactions with the Spaniards, Santa Ana eventually began to recover its farm lands. These transactions were documented by the Spaniards in detail, and Santa Ana carefully preserved its copies, keeping many of them in frames. Some of these documents are nearly 300 years old. These are the only papers that I have ever seen kept by a pueblo tribe. They tell a story of an Indian tribe for which no sacrifice was too great for the recovery of its sacred lands. The earliest transaction for which they have records occurred on June 27, 1709. Captain Manuel Baca sold the pueblo a portion of land that he had received by grant in 1695, and other lands that he had acquired in 1706. Three other land purchases were made in the next few decades.

In 1763, a huge tract of prime farm land on the east side of the river between Bernalillo and San Felipe Pueblo was made available by the Contreras family. The price agreed upon was 3,000 pesos. The appraisers, who were appointed by the governor, set up a station beneath a cottonwood tree. All the members of the pueblo lined up with their animals and possessions. Each brought such possessions as he or she could afford to give toward the purchase price. The appraisers determined the value of each item brought, until the sum of 3,000 pesos had been reached. In all, the Tamayame paid 67 cows, many with new calves, 29 oxen, 8 bulls, 74 goats, 50 sheep, 3 mules, 4 blankets, a bowl, 8 horses, a mare, a colt, and 2 bridles.

Today, the land acquired in this purchase makes up the bulk of what is known as Santa Ana's El Ranchito Tract. It is the pueblo's principal residential area, while old Tamaya remains the site for feasts and ceremonial occasions.

In recent years the Tamayame have developed a number of profitable businesses. Their current financial success is a tribute to their business acumen and their tenacity. In 1980 they were operating a sand and gravel enterprise that nearly failed financially. Consequently, they decided to lease the operation. With the prospect of some monetary gain through leasing, the Tribal Council decided to lease additional land. First they leased fifty-two acres for a mobile home park. It included the renovated Harold Brooks building, which later was leased to Americans for Indian Opportunity, an American Indian advocacy organization headed by LaDonna Harris, a Comanche. Then in 1985 the Tribal Council, consisting of the secular officials for the year and young men eighteen and older, decided to collect the Possessory Tax from any corporate business that used their land, such as the Santa Fe Railroad and companies that owned pipelines, telephone lines, and relay stations. With the money accumulated from this taxation, they opened a smoke shop. In 1986 they leased a building to another company, which established a high-class restaurant called the Prairie Star. With the relative success of these business endeavors, the tribe could consider further development.

The Tribal Council proposed establishing a golf course, which today is located next to the Prairie Star restaurant. The twenty-seven-hole course opened in July 1991 and is called the Valle Grande. The Rio Grande flows on the east side nearby, and the majestic Sandia mountains form a backdrop only a chip shot across the river to the southeast. Located eighteen miles from Albuquerque, it is a pleasant relief from the overcrowded golf courses in the city.

With all this business experience, the tribe then opened a casino alongside State Road 44, which is located near the entrance to the golf course and the Prairie Star restaurant. Customers include people from the pueblos, Bernalillo, Albuquerque and its suburban communities, as well as tourists.

How did a tiny community accomplish all this growth in business? A key to Santa Ana's success was undoubtedly the united effort of the council and officials. Of course, there were several individuals who were instrumental in fostering business development. Clyde Leon, a former governor, may have been the first to fill the position that came to be called tribal administrator. The position was originally established to put the tribal office on a business footing by keeping the office open during working hours. The administrator also maintains continuity by informing incoming governors about problems and procedures connected with tribal affairs. Eventually, as Santa Ana and other tribes built sufficient operating budgets, the position of tribal administrator became funded. After

Leon resigned in 1983, the Tribal Council discussed the importance of the position. They asked a nephew of Porfirio Montoya, Roy Montoya—who had established the accounting and personnel systems while he served as an aide—to take over the position. Roy has been reappointed to the position several times.

I interviewed Roy for most of the Tamaya story though I had worked with Floyd Montoya before his early death on February 24, 1995, and had learned much from Porfirio many years ago.

Roy was born at El Ranchito on December 5, 1940. After attending the local BIA Day School, the Albuquerque Indian School, and Bernalillo High School, he enlisted in the Navy, serving for three years and ten months. After a year at Ft. Lewis College in Durango, Colorado, he completed an eighteen-month business and accounting program at Draughon's Business School in Albuquerque. During this training, which he completed in a year's time, Roy developed the expertise that would prepare him to serve his community.

He worked for the BIA for nearly twenty years, first as an accountant, later as a computer operator and by the time he resigned, as a fiscal computer systems analyst. Roy was first appointed as an aide and on the tribal governor's staff in 1965, when he began to help with tribal administration by installing the personnel and accounting system for the tribe. In 1979 he was appointed lieutenant governor under Governor Sam Armijo. During this time he was still working for BIA and worked for the tribe after returning from his regular job. When the council asked him to consider the position of tribal administrator, he had to search his mind. He had a guaranteed well-paid job with good benefits and a retirement pension. Would the new job equate with his present one? Like many other pueblo leaders, he realized that it was more important and rewarding to his life to work for his people, to make use of his training, skills, and experience for the benefit of the community.

In February of 1996 Roy was one of a half dozen Native Americans selected to meet with President Clinton to discuss any subject they wished to bring before the president of the United States. While Roy has played an important role in Santa Ana's economic success, he is widely recognized outside the pueblo. He is considered a bright star on the horizon, a leader with great potential for Pueblo Indian affairs and statewide political action.

NOTES

1. *Schat-Chen,* John M. Gunn, (Albuquerque, N.M.: Albright and Anderson, 1917).

CHAPTER 12

John C. Rainer, Sr.
Taos Pueblo

As director of American Indian Scholarship John Rainer received a great many letters such as the following:

Dear Sir:
I was able to get my bachelor's degree, as a veteran, several years ago. Currently, I am teaching at a high school near my reservation. I realize that without a master's degree I cannot advance very far. . . . I have a small family of two children and a wife. I have a small amount saved, but with the family I need help to return to graduate school. I understand you have a program to help Indian graduate students.
Sincerely,

Dear Mr. Rainer:
Through the resources of my tribe I was able to get my nursing degree. I would like to get a master's degree in nursing so I can teach other Indian girls. However, the tribal scholarship committee is not willing to approve an additional grant for me to return to graduate school. Can you help me?
Yours truly,

Dear Mr. Rainer:
The Bureau of Indian Affairs from my agency has helped me the past four years. I will be graduating in June. However, I am planning to stay on campus and begin graduate work. I may obtain a graduate fellowship during my second year of graduate study. I only need help the first year. Please write me at the following address.
Sincerely,

In a great many instances, the writers of such letters were helped largely thanks to John C. Rainer, Sr., of Taos Pueblo. Rainer and Robert L. Bennett, who earlier was commissioner of Indian affairs, designed the American Indian Graduate Scholarship (AIGS) program early in their careers to aid Indian students with graduate work. Rainer served as director of AIGS for fourteen years, retiring on December 31, 1983. He was succeeded by Lorraine P. Edmo, a Shoshone-Bannock from Idaho. During this time the AIGS headquarters, which had been in Taos Pueblo for nine years, was returned to Albuquerque, and the school was renamed the American Indian Graduate Center. Subsequent directors were Oren LaPointe, a Lakota from South Dakota, Reginald Rodriguez of Laguna Pueblo, and Hilton Quetone, a Kiowá-Seminole, the current director.

The graduate scholarship program was an outgrowth of Rainer's lifelong dedication to the needs of the Indian people and his belief in the preparation of young people for responsible, rewarding careers. Like most innovative approaches to a problem, the program had a slow start, but once the "moccasin telegraph" started operating in high gear, the office was flooded with requests for scholarship aid. By the end of the school year 1987, AIS had awarded 280 fellowships for the year to graduate students representing 81 tribes from 22 states.

Of the recipients, 163 were studying for graduate degrees in the AIS priority areas of health, education, law, business, engineering, and natural resources. The other 69 were studying in fields such as anthropology, music, and ministry. Unfortunately, owing to a limit on available funding, AIS was able to finance somewhat less than half the fellowship applicants.

The granting process works like this: once a letter is received, the director reviews its content. If all requirements are met, the student-applicant is sent an application. Completed applications are evaluated by the members of the AIS board of directors, who must examine financial need, degree of Indian blood, and urgency of need, as well as establish the authenticity of the graduate study. Once all criteria are satisfied, the grant is made, if money is available.

The seed for AIS was planted when Rainer and Bennett met as co-workers in the Arrow, Inc. project sponsored by Will Rogers, Jr., to help Navajos struggling to survive severe winters. Later, Rainer and Bennett also established the first office of the National Congress of American Indians in Washington, D.C., of which Rainer became executive director. As the two men worked together, they lamented the lack of Indian professionals in all fields due to insufficient tribal funds and the unavailability of money from the Bureau of Indian Affairs for Indian graduate study. Up to this point, the BIA had mainly funded Indian education only through high school, with a little also being spent for a few undergraduate college students. Rainer and Bennett set out to remedy the situation. Their dream became a well-documented success story for thousands of recipients and the Indian communities that the new professionals now serve directly.

Rainer joined the graduate scholarship program in August 1969. Just prior to this appointment, he was executive director of the New Mexico

Commission on Indian Affairs with an office in Santa Fe. He was appointed on January 4, 1969, the unanimous choice of a board of commissioners, and confirmed by governor of New Mexico David Cargo. Before the appointment, he had been a member of the commission's board and had served as its vice-chairman from 1956 to 1969. Rainer resigned his board membership before assuming the duties of executive director of the New Mexico Commission on Indian Affairs.

In his position as executive director with the state commission, Rainer often was the personal representative of the New Mexico governor at various state functions, where he spoke expressing the governor's views. He also was the governor's representative on the Governors' Interstate Indian Council, and at a meeting in Rapid City, South Dakota, in September 1969, Rainer was elected chairman of that interstate organization. The council represented Indian populations in thirty states.

Born at Taos Pueblo on June 12, 1913, Rainer was the son of Hilario Reyna and Crucita Mondragon, the second oldest of eight children. Originally, the family surname had been Reina, which in Spanish means "queen"; over the years, it evolved into Reyna.

Later, when he started working at Dulce, New Mexico, with prospects for a regular paycheck, he became concerned about the fact that there were four John Reynas in his extended family and chances for confusion or misidentification were numerous. Consequently, he changed his surname to Rainer.

Like many reservation Indian youngsters, Rainer spent much of his preteen life on horseback, usually without a saddle. Education for Indian youth in the American system was considered unimportant in those days; Thus, he did not start school until he was thirteen years old.

Reminiscing about his early days in school, Rainer once said:

> *I remember when I started school, I sat at a double desk with another young boy. The teacher put our names on the blackboard, and for some reason I learned my deskmate's name first, and I thought my name was Ben. Ben learned my name also and he thought his name was John. We could hardly talk to our teachers as we didn't know how to speak English. We spoke our dialect to communicate in the classroom, and I spoke that language strictly until I was able to speak a little English.*
>
> *One day, when I was in about the fourth grade a Mr. Marks, who was the principal teacher and teaching fifth and sixth graders, came into our room and asked our class if there was anyone in the room who could draw a rectangle three inches by six inches. I raised my hand and was taken into the next classroom to draw the rectangle before the upper grades. From then on I became a favorite of Mr. Marks.*

Unfortunately, a crisis arose soon after. Taos had a custom or practice of initiating young boys and training them for manhood for eighteen months. This particular year a boy named Henry Lujan and I were selected by our kiva to take the training. Mr. Marks refused to let us be taken out of school for the eighteen-month training period. He tried to negotiate with the Taos Council, but the council failed to agree that we should remain in school. The religious leaders and kiva members had already, many months earlier, prepared for the training, and not going on with it was unthinkable. Arrangements for lodging, clothing, and personal counselors all were in readiness long before the Taos Pueblo Council formally asked for us boys to be released from school for the eighteen months.

The superintendent of the Pueblo Agency in Santa Fe was informed of our plight by Mr. Marks, and I guess the agency people were ready to send up the militia to enforce school attendance and make a stand before the council.

In order to understand this conflict between the Taos Council and the Indian Agency regarding school attendance versus pueblo religious training, it is necessary to put this incident in historical perspective. This was a bad era for Pueblo-Bureau of Indian Affairs relations. The pueblos were being subjected to strict, quasi-"God-fearing" and proselytizing Christians bent on imposing their own religion upon the Indians. Strict regulations were enforced through both the BIA and the Religious Crimes Act, and offenses against both were assiduously punished. Government agents, superintendents, and federal commissioners made it punishable to practice Indian religious ceremonies. In 1924, Indian Commissioner Charles H. Burke directed that propaganda be conducted against Indian religions. He circulated documents to churchmen, members of Congress, and newspaper editors asserting that Indian religious observances were sadistic and obscene. He further expressed the belief that Native religion was a crutch preventing the useful assimilation of Indians into white society. Ultimately, Burke issued orders to BIA personnel to tell the pueblo people to rid themselves of their Native religion "within a year."

During a meeting in 1926 in which Burke addressed the Taos Council on the issue of Blue Lake, he rebuked the council for their stand in favor of initiation rites for young boys and told the council they were "half animal" because of their pagan religion. In the incident regarding Rainer's and Lujan's initiation training, a man named John Collier volunteered to help the Taos Council and proved to be successful in his effort to keep John C. Rainer and Henry Lujan out of school for their training.

Non-Indians doubted the value of the Indian religion, especially such practices as keeping young boys out of the white men's classrooms. Ugly rumors of immoral activities during the annual religious trips to the sacred Blue Lake turned into serious charges by officials of the BIA, as cited by the Indian commissioner. Collier decided that the only way the Taos Indians could clear themselves of the charges was to have an un-biased, non-Indian accompany the Indians to Blue Lake. The Taos Council agreed. Collier himself made the journey in order to be able to file a report with the government to prove the authenticity of the religious practices and to show that, in fact, the experience was an educational ex-ercise for the boys.

Under ordinary circumstances, the trek from the pueblo to Blue Lake would have begun as the sun was setting in the western horizon. But since a white man was going along, the kiva leader responsible for the boys' training allowed the trip to start at high noon. As it turned out, Collier accompanied the band only halfway to Blue Lake. It was from that point onward that the trainees entered into a religious ritual that would con-tinue until they reached the shrine. The idea of having a white man witness the most sacred portion of the Blue Lake annual homage proved to be too unsettling for some tribal leaders. Consequently, Collier was put on a horse and escorted back to the village. It is to Collier's credit that he wrote an excellent report of what he had witnessed and was able to soften criticism of the Taos rituals.

After young Rainer's eighteen months of training was completed, he returned to the Pueblo Day School and finished six grades in less than six years as the result of good school work. Next, he attended Santa Fe Indian School, since at that time, pueblo students were required to go to either the Santa Fe Indian School or the one in Albuquerque. Neither school had what is now called aptitude testing. At these schools students were exposed to an academic curriculum half the time and vocational training the other half. The vocational skills taught included carpentry, blacksmithing, cabinet making, masonry, leather work and shoe repair, and plumbing; work assignments were changed every six weeks.

Rainer remembers the Santa Fe Indian School as being "very strict" and military in operation. The classroom teachers were all white; one of Rainer's distinct memories was of a history teacher "who openly told us that Indians were cowards and that was why they camouflaged themselves into trees and rocks so they couldn't be seen." Of course, World War II, when the practice of camouflage became important, was years away.

Not knowing the English language often made learning difficult at the school, but Rainer managed to stay at the head of his class and was made Captain of Company "C."

"We dressed in castaway bits and pieces of World War I uniforms," Rainer recalled. "We had rifles and drilled. We marched to the dining room and raised and took the flag down military style."

During his senior year, Rainer began to take a special interest in cabinet making, partly because the instructor was a pueblo Indian who was very well informed about the non-Indian world. He was George Blue Spruce, Sr., a Laguna from Paguate. Blue Spruce had attended Haskell Institute and had done some college work in northern Colorado.

Also during Rainer's senior year, a bright, college-educated Indian—Alvin Warren, a Chippewa from Wisconsin—began his teaching career at the Santa Fe Indian School. Warren, who had attended Bacone Junior College in Oklahoma, identified Rainer as a promising student, urged him to pursue higher education, and recommended that Rainer apply to Bacone. At first Rainer was skeptical about college study, but after winning an academic prize he began to gain confidence that he could handle a college curriculum.

During Rainer's last year at the Indian School some Santa Fe businessmen began to take an interest in the Indian students. As a result, one of them, Henry Dendahl, offered a gold medal for the best academic performance. Rainer won the medal, becoming the outstanding graduate of his class.

The class of 1934—Rainer's graduating class—was the first to graduate from the Santa Fe Indian School. With the nation then engulfed in the Great Depression and with the disadvantage of being an Indian youth with a limited educational background, Rainer found it difficult to contemplate a bright future. In retrospect, recalling his high school graduation, Rainer said, "To my credit, I knew I did not know anything."

Rainer spent that summer in the Santa Fe Indian School cabinet shop, earning $1 a day. But fortunately, in midsummer he received word that he had been accepted for fall enrollment at Bacone College.

In September, carrying a small box (since he did not own a suitcase) packed with an extra pair of pants, a shirt, and a rock—for good luck—Rainer boarded the Greyhound bus that would take him to Muskogee, Oklahoma, where Bacone College was located. When he arrived on campus, Rainer had $25 in his pocket—all the money he had in the world. During registration, when the college president asked if he had all the money he needed for tuition, books, and supplies, Rainer answered that he had only $25. The following exchange took place:

"Are your parents going to send you more later?" asked the president.

"No, sir, they don't have any money either," Rainer replied.

"If you have no money, why did you come?" the president wanted to know.

"Well, sir, I asked for an application. I filled it out and you accepted me, that's why I'm here," Rainer responded with a gently ironic look.

"Well, what kind of skill do you have for work?" the president asked.

"I took cabinet making in high school," Rainer told him. The president took him into a room more than fifty feet long full of broken tables and chairs and asked Rainer what he could do with them.

"I could fix them," Rainer said. So Rainer stayed. By Christmas he had repaired all the chairs and tables and had gone on to fix broken doors and windows on campus.

Eventually the question of religion was raised for Rainer at the college. Bacone Junior College was a Baptist school, and Rainer had been born a Catholic. After he had been at the college awhile, the president called him in and said, "Well, John, you've been here this long, I would like to baptize you."

"I was yet so adamant a Catholic I told him, 'No,' outright," Rainer said. "He didn't press me. Then I went to my room, pulled the cot down from the closet wall, and lay on it with my head in my hands thinking, 'Here's this man who gave me a chance. The least I can do in appreciation is to have him baptize me,' and I did. I know there is a God, but he is not Baptist or Catholic," Rainer said.

"The first semester was really hard on me, I was so homesick I would have been glad to fail a course so I could come home," Rainer confessed. "But I was over it by Christmas."

During the Christmas vacation, Rainer did not have enough money to go home, although he wanted to—especially to go to Santa Fe, where a lovely young girl he had met in high school lived. Since the dormitories were closed over the holiday, the few students who remained on campus were transferred to an orphanage, where they stayed until classes resumed.

Rainer graduated from the junior college in June 1936. In addition to his work in academics, carpentry, and furniture repair, he had also left his mark on the college as an outstanding football player and vocalist in the Bacone choir. He returned to his family at Taos Pueblo thinking his opportunity for higher education had come to an end.

When Rainer arrived home, a hospital was being built at the pueblo. He was hired as a carpenter at $4 a day. While he was working all summer he kept wishing he could return to college with the money he was earning. He thought of the good times and the good friends he had made. Now and then, he prayed for another chance.

Suddenly, on September 6, he received a telegram from the University of Redlands in California. On the recommendation of a Professor Weeks at Bacone College, Rainer had been accepted and granted a scholarship at Redlands. Rainer had no time for preparation and immediately boarded a bus for Albuquerque, where he then took a train to California.

When he arrived at the University of Redlands, he discovered that no living arrangements had been made for him. Finally, the president asked the college treasurer to find him a place, and the new student was taken to a rooming house for the night.

When Rainer went to register, he was asked, "What does your scholarship cover?"

"I don't know. The telegram I received said only that I was being granted a scholarship," Rainer answered.

"If it covers tuition, which it must, where will you get the money to pay for your room and board?" the man at the desk asked.

"I will work for it," Rainer told him.

Subsequently, the university found Rainer a job cleaning classrooms. He also managed to find work at the rooming house washing dishes, mowing the lawn, cutting weeds, and cleaning the house. Sometimes he even drove the landlady to town to do her grocery shopping.

Rainer graduated from the University of Redlands with a Bachelor of Arts degree in Education in May 1938. In order to clear all his debts at the university, he had to borrow $1,000 from the Bureau of Indian Affairs—a loan that was contingent on his participating in a BIA apprenticeship program. In the program, a first-year teacher was to work under an experienced teacher. Salary for the regular teacher was $1,620 a year and for the apprentice half that amount—$810. This arrangement was unacceptable to Rainer, who argued that he was as well prepared to teach as anyone with a bachelor's degree. He refused to work for $810 a year. In the end, his salary was set at $950, and he was assigned to teach Apache youngsters in Dulce, New Mexico, on the Jicarilla Reservation.

The fallacy of the apprentice program, as Rainer had argued from the beginning, quickly became apparent. The Dulce school principal had combined the seventh, eighth, and ninth grades and asked Rainer to teach the combined class while he observed. Rainer taught one whole day—and one day only—under observation. Apparently, the principal liked what he saw, because he never again supervised or observed Rainer's teaching.

Rainer stretched the $75 a month that he earned to pay off his loan as well as provide for his room and board and personal necessities. There was nothing left for savings, but with the raise he had been promised at the end of the fiscal year, he hoped to help ease the strain. Unfortunately, he never got the raise. Always self-assertive, Rainer wrote in protest to Dr. Willard Beaty, director of Indian education in the BIA central office in Washington, D.C. At about this time, John Collier, Rainer's old benefactor, came to visit the Apache school. By this time, Collier was very active in assisting with Indian causes. Rainer told Collier about his promised promotion and threatened to resign. Soon after Collier's visit and after Rainer had been at Dulce for two years, Rainer received a telegram from Washington directing him to transfer to Zuni Pueblo with a raise in salary to $1,200 a year.

His future now brighter, in 1939 before moving to Zuni Rainer married his high school girlfriend, Wynema Freeman, a beautiful Creek

Indian girl from Henryetta, Oklahoma. The couple remained at Zuni for a year before Rainer was transferred again, this time to Santa Ana Pueblo Day School as teacher-in-charge. He reported to his new assignment in August 1941, at a full teacher's salary of $1,620 annually.

While at Santa Ana, Rainer learned of an opening for principal at the Santo Domingo Pueblo Day School, a position that paid $2,240 a year. He applied, was hired, and the Rainers moved to Santo Domingo, where they stayed five years.

During this time the nation was preparing for war, and the young teacher had registered for the draft. Rainer was called to serve while he was at Santo Domingo. However, the pueblo officials lobbied successfully to obtain a deferment for him.

In August 1947, Rainer transferred to his home, Taos Pueblo, as principal of the junior high school. As principal, Rainer was not satisfied with the ordinary classroom curriculum and urged the teachers to organize Boy Scout and Girl Scout troops as well as a 4-H Club. Through this latter organization, a Duroc Jersey hog program was introduced at the pueblo. Club members bred the hog to family-owned sows. When a sow had a litter, the club member returned one piglet to the school program and kept the rest. Then the returned piglet was given to a club member who did not have an animal. Later, Rainer was able to get a purebred stallion categorized as surplus from the cavalry base at Fort Sill, Oklahoma, to improve the riding horses on the reservation. Rabbits and chickens also were ordered for club members and other interested families in the pueblo.

Garden seeds were furnished by the Extension Division of the BIA, but otherwise the Education Division had no funds to assist the 4-H Club; Rainer said he had to "bend" a few regulations to provide operating money. The community also helped the school. For moving their livestock, 4-H Club members borrowed trucks from local non-Indian citizens and businessmen in Taos. The businessmen also donated food for refreshments and prizes for bingo games at club events. The profits from such fundraisers were used to buy educational and recreational films for the youngsters and their parents. Rainer laughs when he recalls the "little big men in the BIA" who did not appreciate his unorthodox methods as principal.

In 1949, Rainer's life changed significantly once again. On a hot day in August there was a knock on Rainer's office door. The man who stepped in introduced himself as Will Rogers, Jr., from Culver City, California. Rogers told Rainer that on the recommendation of many people he had come to Taos to discuss the possibility of Rainer going to California to help administer a program called Arrow, Inc. This was a new endeavor which was a consequence of Operation Navajo, a livestock rescue program created in response to the extreme hardship caused to the

Navajos by unusually heavy snowfall in the Southwest. The salary Rogers offered was three times what Rainer had been making as principal of the school in Taos, and Rainer wasted no time in asking for and receiving a leave of absence to take the job in California.

It was while he was working with Arrow, Inc., that Rainer attended his second conference of the National Congress of American Indians at Rapid City, South Dakota. The NCAI was a fledgling organization at that time with no official office except for a basement room in the home of Ruth Muskrat Bronson, a Cherokee. Rainer was approached by officials of the congress to become part of the effort to develop the group into a national Indian organization. Subsequently, he became the first executive secretary of the National Congress of American Indians and moved his family to the nation's capital.

While he was working in Washington, Rainer received a John Hay Whitney Fellowship to do graduate work at the University of Southern California, which he accepted. Following a year of intense study, Rainer earned a master of science degree in education in August 1951.

After achieving this milestone in his education, Rainer and his family once again moved back to Taos Pueblo, where he established the Taos Pueblo General Store and entered the cattle business with his father. To establish a herd of cattle, Rainer borrowed $1,500 from a bank in Santa Fe and found the type of cattle he wanted at a Hereford ranch near Tierra Amarilla, New Mexico. At that time, except for a strain of "I.D." branded cattle brought to the reservation from western Kansas and Oklahoma during the Great Depression, most of the pueblo cattle were lean frontier or Mexican cows. At the time there was not much opportunity to improve a herd because most cattle grazed in communal pastures, and the bulls were generally of the same poor quality.

With his objective of upgrading agricultural practices on the reservation to bring good prices and produce a decent income for pueblo cattlemen, Rainer began a program of herd improvement. In order to set an example for other cattlemen at Taos Pueblo, he and his father went to a registered bull sale in Clayton, New Mexico, where they purchased two registered bulls. Soon the other Taos cattlemen noticed the difference between the registered animals and poor quality bulls, and they, too, began to buy registered bulls.

Rainer's next step was to organize a cattle sale. Traditionally, individual cattle buyers would purchase cattle from the Indian ranchers on the buyers' own terms. Rainer reasoned that if the pueblo cattlemen sold their stock as a group they could command better prices. After many organizational meetings, a sale was held at a borrowed corral using slaughterhouse scales. While only thirty-two head were sold, the cattlemen received good prices for their cattle.

The following year, the Taos cattlemen officially organized, borrowing $1,500 from the Santa Fe National Bank in Rainer's name. They installed scales of their own in a newly completed sales corral and that fall held their second sale. Buyers were invited from New Mexico, Colorado, and Kansas. To nobody's surprise the prices of the Indian cattle were equal to those commanded in Denver; the Taos cattlemen had become viable competitors in the national cattle market.

Today, Rainer says, "No Taos cattleman is without a registered bull." Of all the things Rainer has accomplished, he is most proud of the role he played in bringing registered bulls, improved cattle herds, and organization to the Taos cattlemen.

Rainer had begun to assist the All Pueblo Council as early as his tenure at the Santo Domingo Day School. And in the election of October 12, 1946, Rainer was elected secretary of the council, serving under Chairman Abel Paisano until November 2, 1950, when he began graduate work at the University of Southern California.

While in business at Taos Pueblo, Rainer was called on again for another special assignment. He was asked to establish the Ute Mountain Ute Tribal Rehabilitation Program at Towaoc, Colorado, near the heart of the Four Corners area, where New Mexico, Colorado, Utah, and Arizona meet. He directed this program until 1953 and saw it become firmly established before returning to his business interests in Taos.

After returning to Taos, Rainer resumed his activities with the All Pueblo Council and on February 12, 1955, was elected chairman, a position which he held for the next two years. During his administration, some of the most difficult issues facing the pueblos were indifference to the tribes and *de jure* discrimination by the state of New Mexico. At that time Indian people of the state were not eligible to receive welfare aid or Social Security, nor were they permitted to vote in state or national elections. This has all changed as a result of many conferences and legal battles; today, the Indian people of New Mexico are considered the equals of all other citizens and entitled to all their privileges as Americans.

Rainer served as chairman of the All Pueblo Council until March 1957, when he was succeeded by Martin Vigil. However, Rainer continued to serve the council as vice-chairman for another two years. On February 7, 1959, Rainer stepped down as an All Pueblo Council official to devote his undivided attention to personal business and to provide for the education of his three children.

At the forefront of Indian leadership in those eventful times, assisting in the fight for Indian rights, were David Dozier of Santa Clara, an extension agent with the United Pueblos Agency; Alvin Warren, a Chippewa and education administrator with the United Pueblos Agency; Martin

Vigil of Tesuque Pueblo; and the best legal representative in the Department of the Interior, solicitor Felix S. Cohen.

In addition to his work with the All Indian Pueblo Council, Rainer was involved in other civic activities. On the national level, besides being executive secretary of the National Congress of American Indians at one time, he also served as treasurer of that organization from 1953 to 1963. At the October 1969 NCAI meeting, Rainer was elected first vice-president and was reelected the following year.

At the local level, he became a member of the board of directors of the Taos Chamber of Commerce and director of the New Mexico Indian Voter Education Project under Arrow, Inc., of Washington D.C. He also served as a member of the Platform Committee of the State Democratic Party.

However, Rainer's involvement did not end there. He was elected a member of the Taos Municipal School Board in 1969 and served as its vice-president. His school board membership was made possible by state legislation enabling minority groups in local school districts to have representation on boards of education. In addition, as executive director of the New Mexico Commission on Indian Affairs, Rainer was extremely active in getting this legislation enacted. Once this was done, he set to work on the Taos Municipal School Board first. Six Indian candidates were recommended by the Taos Pueblo governor, and Rainer was the unanimous choice of the school board.

Other organizations in which Rainer has been an active member include the board of directors for American Indian Development, of Denver; the United States Civil Rights Commission Advisory Board for the State of New Mexico; Futures for Children; and Development Associates of Washington, D.C. He also has been an advisory board member for the American Indian Service and Research Center at Brigham Young University; for the Public Health Program for Native Americans at the University of California, Berkeley; for the Small Business Administration of New Mexico; and for the Institute of American Indian Arts in Santa Fe.

At Taos Pueblo, Rainer has served as secretary-treasurer of the Taos Pueblo Cattle Growers Association and most recently was appointed chairman of the tribe's golf course feasibility study committee and vice-chairman of the Tribal Financial Usage committee.

One of the top honors bestowed upon Rainer was his appointment by President Richard Nixon to membership on the National Council on Indian Opportunity (NCIO). Of the nine American Indians on this council, Rainer was elected head member. Non-Indian members included Vice-President Spiro Agnew. The council served as a direct communications link between American Indian people and the top echelon of the United States government.

The NCIO had four principal functions: (1) to encourage full use of federal programs to benefit Indians; (2) to encourage interagency coordination and cooperation; (3) to measure impact and progress of federal programs; and (4) to suggest ways to improve such programs. Rainer's involvement with the NCIO entailed considerable traveling from coast to coast to meet with Indian groups.

In August 1969 Rainer began working out of his AIS office in Albuquerque, located in a trailer on the University of New Mexico campus. The organization grew, becoming too big for the trailer. Subsequently, a new building was found, and Rainer returned to Taos on weekends when he could. After five years of traveling back and forth, Rainer expressed his wish to resign, but the board suggested that the office be moved to Taos so he would not have to commute. Consequently, for nine years AIS was headquartered at Taos Pueblo, until Rainer retired.

Because Rainer himself spoke only his Tiwa dialect until he was thirteen, when he began his schooling, he became an ardent advocate of good education for American Indians, exemplifying his beliefs by encouraging his own children to further their education. As a result, a daughter, Ann Rainer, received her bachelor's degree from Stanford University. After subsequently spending two years as a Peace Corps volunteer in Colombia, she entered Harvard University to earn her master's degree in anthropology. Later, Ann spent a year in premedical studies at Stanford. However, her studies there were interrupted by the demonstrations of the time, and she enrolled instead at the University of Colorado Medical School in Denver and from there transferred to the University of California medical school at Berkeley.

While Ann was at Berkeley, her health began to fail, and she returned home to recuperate. Unfortunately, she was never able to regain her health. After years of struggling to obtain higher education, she died at the Santa Fe Indian Hospital on Sunday, March 22, 1987.

John Rainer, Jr., earned both his bachelor's and master's degrees from Brigham Young University in Provo, Utah. Following completion of his degrees, he was employed at Brigham Young University as a counselor of Indian students; there he also directed an outstanding choral group of Native American students.

After marrying Veranda Dosala, a San Carlos Apache, John Rainer, Jr., and his family moved to San Carlos, Arizona, where he worked with the school system on the Apache reservation. His family now includes three sons and two daughters, and he currently works full time at what formerly was a hobby—flute making. The instruments he makes represent several Indian tribal styles, and he also records music on these flutes, marketing both the tapes and the flutes nationally.

Rainer's other son, Howard, also received two degrees from Brigham

Young University and currently is employed by the university as assistant director of the Institute of American Indian Services in the Department of Continuing Education. During the last sixteen years, Howard has devoted much of his work to motivating Indian students and adults through workshops on Indian reservations at schools and churches throughout the United States and Canada. He is married to Becky Diehl of California, and they have two girls and two boys.

John Rainer, Sr., has continuously updated his education and knowledge of Indian affairs by attending and participating in conferences, workshops, and institutes—well beyond retirement age. Rainer's unceasing devotion to the progress of the Indian people has been a blessing; he was endowed by the Great Spirit with great leadership abilities: Rainer has been able to utilize his talent, education, and experience for the benefit of all Indian people. Thanks in part to his efforts, there will soon be many more young Indian people with an American education who can help improve the complex lives of Indians throughout the country. As for Rainer himself, he has found happiness and satisfaction through serving in many demanding capacities and setting an example for all Indian students.

Living in retirement today, Rainer can reflect on his personal struggle to arrive at his goals for himself and the Indian people. His large adobe house is filled with mementos of the Indians' recognition of his accomplishments. There are plaques, trophies, flutes, tanned hides with drawings, and ceramics, together with certificates that this Indian leader has received through the years.

On one such plaque is a red apple, courtesy, he says, of the militant American Indian Movement (AIM), given to him at a time when the organization was very active. The apple, he explains, is to indicate that the recipient is red on the outside, white on the inside. According to Rainer, AIM discriminated against Indian people who were not in favor of the type of activism they engaged in. Despite this, it is clear that Rainer is 100 percent Indian. He was initiated as a young boy, and most pueblo Indians were not considered completely Indian unless they had been initiated according to their particular pueblo's rituals. By contrast, many of the AIM members during that period of controversy were "born again Indians" from the urban communities and had never been initiated.

During his life Rainer has rubbed elbows with persons in high political office in the state as well as in Washington, D.C. He has worn three-piece suits as his working clothes. Today, he wears high-topped work shoes or boots and Levis as he tends his one hundred cows and two buffalos. He has offered his buffalos to the Indian students at Brigham Young University to supplement their available food, but they have not come to claim them.

John C. Rainer (center) with New Mexico Governor David Cargo (left), and Indian Commissioner Robert L. Bennett (right). Photograph courtesy of Blue Lake Committee.

Among the many honors that have been bestowed on Rainer was a banquet at Brigham Young University on March 19, 1983, when he was acknowledged for his thirty years of unselfish service to Indians throughout the nation. At this affair, which took place during a conference of the National Indian Leadership and Agricultural Group, Rainer was recognized as the chief Indian member of the National Council of Indian Opportunity and instrumental in helping to reclaim the McQueen strip of land from the federal government for the Warm Springs Affiliated Tribes in Oregon; Mt. Adams for the Yakima tribe in Washington; and the sacred Blue Lake for his own people in Taos.

In his home state, Rainer received the New Mexico Distinguished Public Service Award in June 1983 from Governor Toney Anaya. The plaque presented with the award read, in part, "John has been one of the nation's leading advocates for the rights of Native Americans."

Rainer has also received recognition from other tribes, including the Comanche Tribe of Oklahoma, which honored him in appreciation of outstanding service to Indians; the Blackfeet tribe of Montana, which made him an honorary adopted member of the tribe; and the Navajo tribe, which honored him for his support of Navajo education.

In addition, Rainer also has a certificate signed by President Harry S. Truman in recognition of aid and support given the Selective Service System during World War II. And the state of Utah gave Rainer a state flag and an honorary citizen certificate in 1981. Moreover, in January 1994 the University of Redlands Alumni Association Board of Directors honored Rainer with its Alumni Career Achievement Award. Finally, as a special honor two Indian horse breeders have named their favorite horses after Rainer. With all of these honors naturally Rainer is listed in *Who's Who in New Mexico*.

In addition to the many forms of recognition Rainer has received from organizations, tribes, and officials, there are also scores of young Indian men and women all over the country who are grateful for Rainer's help. Although he believed he was only helping them in minor ways, he managed to affect their lives in major ways. One example is the two young boys from San Juan Pueblo whom Rainer took to a 4-H Club conference in Estes Park, Colorado, in the summer of 1957. Just out of high school and with no prospects in life, Herman Agoyo and Alfonso Ortiz made the trip with Rainer. It was their first trip outside New Mexico. Later, Agoyo became chairman of the All Indian Pueblo Council and Alfonso Ortiz was a renowned professor of anthropology at the University of New Mexico. Ortiz recalled that he saved most of the spending money Rainer had given him to buy a briefcase in Denver. The case survived the many years of college teaching and was still at the anthropologist's home, stuffed with papers, at the time of his death.

Likewise, this writer was selected by Rainer to accompany him to Towaoc, Colorado, to work with the Ute Mountain Ute Rehabilitation Program and was thereby given the prospect of greater and different work experience. And when the Graduate Scholarship program needed board members, this author was selected and served with Rainer for fourteen years.

At his retirement dinner, Rainer was asked, "What would be your advice to young Indian people?"

He replied, "Get the best possible training you can. Be like Allan Houser in sculpture, or like Scott Momaday and Leslie Silko in their novels, be an authority in your work. Be a Wendell Chino, he knows what he stands for."

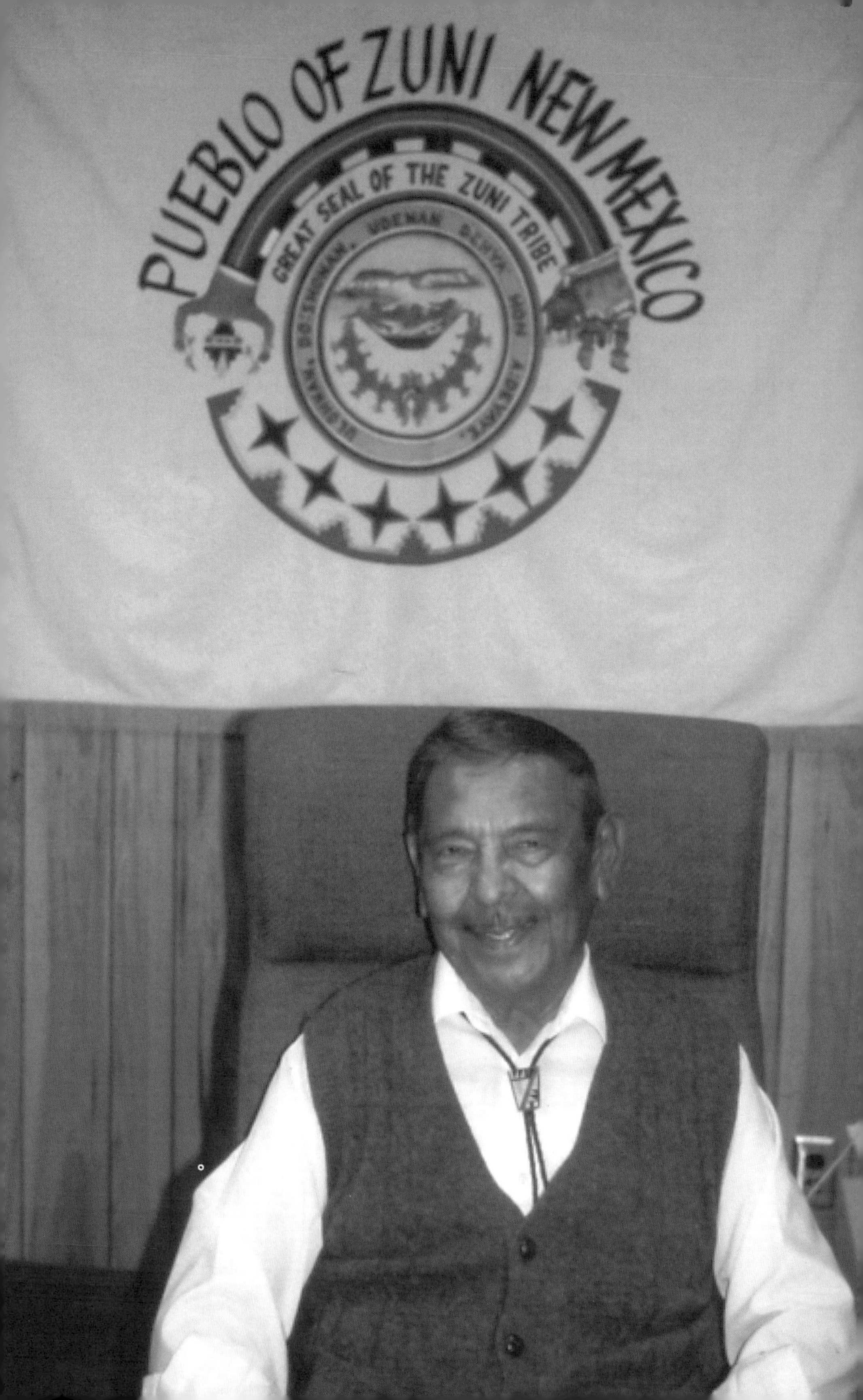
PUEBLO OF ZUNI NEW MEXICO
GREAT SEAL OF THE ZUNI TRIBE

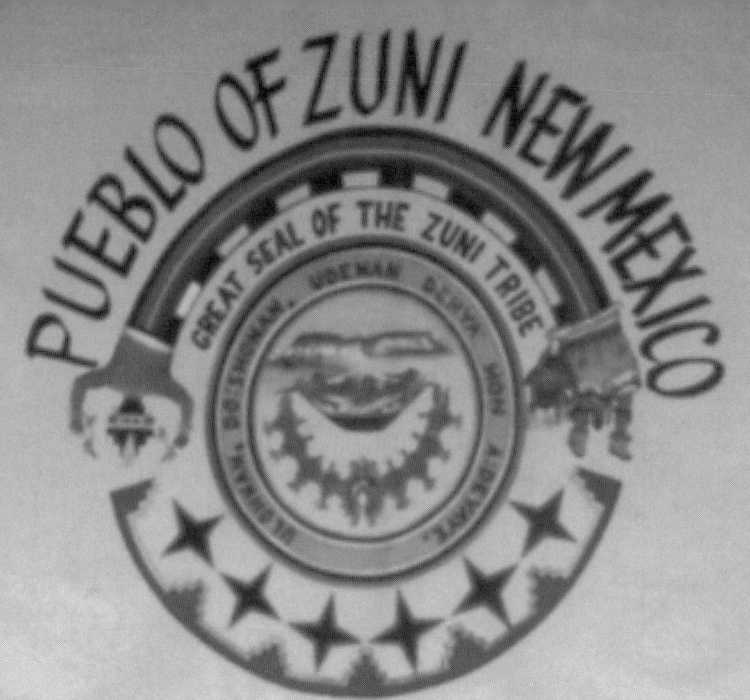

CHAPTER 13

Robert Edward Lewis
Zuni Pueblo

Into your care we entrust our land and our people. Regardless of whether you are poor or lack the oratory to express yourself fluently, you will to the best of your ability be the protector, impartially, for your people. The stranger who comes into our land will become as one of your people regardless of race, color, or creed, and you will give unto him the same protection and rights as you would your own. You will cherish and protect all that contain life, from the lowest crawling creature to the human. By hasty word or deed you will refrain from hurting the feelings both mentally and physically of your people. .

The above is a portion of the creed, read by the cacique, which the governor of Zuni Pueblo must swear to uphold when he is sworn into office. Others who are sworn in are the lieutenant governor and councilmen, who are elected to serve for four years.

Those words were as familiar to Robert Edward Lewis as the headline in the Gallup, New Mexico, newspaper every few years which reads "Zuni Pueblo Reelects Lewis." And he took them to heart each time he repeated them. First elected Zuni governor in 1965, Lewis was elected to four-year terms three times after that, beginning in 1970. Many changes occurred while Lewis was in office, with him frequently being the catalyst. That first election not only marked Lewis's ascent to pueblo leadership, but it also was the first time voting was by secret ballot and the first time women participated fully in the election of the Tribal Council.

Zuni, at the west-central edge of New Mexico, is the largest pueblo in population, with between 7,500 and 8,500 persons enrolled as members of the Zuni tribe. It also has the second largest landholdings among the nineteen New Mexico pueblos.

The Zuni Reservation was first established by executive order in 1877. Since then, the size of the reservation has grown from the original grant of 17,000 acres to more than 419,430.12 acres, with 10,085.70 acres in Arizona, according to the Albuquerque area office of the BIA.

It was at Zuni that the written history of New Mexico began, with the arrival of a black Moor named Estevanico, born in Azamore, Morocco. He came upon the pueblo accompanied by a few Mexican servants, as an advance party for what was known as the Fray Marcos de Niza Expedition of 1539. This initial contact was followed by the arrival of Francisco Vásquez de Coronado in 1540 and his small army on their historic march from Mexico across parts of what are now New Mexico, Texas, Oklahoma, and Kansas.

The Spaniards were looking for the fabled Seven Cities of Cíbola, said to be literally paved with gold. It is ironic that the Spaniards and later historians noted that only six villages were found: Halona (Zuni), Matsakya, Kyakima, Kwakina, Kechipbowa, and Hawikuh. One of history's best-kept secrets is that the seventh Zuni village was west of Silver City, New Mexico, near the present-day town of Cliff. The village is called "Kwilleylekia," which in Zuni means "seven." The Spanish called the land "Cíbola" ("buffalo"), a corruption of the Native word *shi'wona*. A Spaniard, Antonio de Espejo, first recorded the people as "Zuni," a corruption of a Keresan Pueblo word, *su'nyitsa*, the meaning of which has long been lost.

Most American Indians today are the product of two cultures, and in many situations they have the option of using the best aspects of each. In the case of Zuni Pueblo's election of officials, the pueblo has chosen to use the American system of popular vote. The Zuni constitution, which has an American-style charter, was ratified in 1970 and established the terms of office for the governor and council at four years. Although Zuni Pueblo uses an American system of popular vote to elect officials, after the ballots are counted and the winner determined, the winning candidate for governor is sworn into office by the religious leaders. A part of that ceremony is the ritual creed that Robert Lewis and other governors have always sworn to uphold. When the governor agrees to this statement, he gives his promise to the pueblo's religious leaders and makes a commitment to serve his people with justice. The head cacique of the pueblo sets the calendar for all annual religious activity. After the oath is given by the cacique to the elected council members, it becomes their duty to serve their people in all tribal civic affairs.

Robert Edward Lewis was born at Zuni Pueblo on August 24, 1914. His father was William Jones Lewis of Zuni, governor of the pueblo five times during his lifetime. Lewis's mother was Margaret Alberty, a Cherokee who came from Oklahoma to teach at Zuni in 1899. She learned the Zuni language so well that she became the tribal interpreter and, had to take the same oath that her husband and later her son would repeat as governor.

Lewis began his education at the Zuni Day School. After the third grade, he was transferred to the Santa Fe Indian School because his mother had been assigned to serve as a field matron, or nurse, on the Jicarilla Apache Reservation at Dulce, New Mexico. In her position as nurse, Margaret Lewis visited the Apaches on horseback, caring for the sick and delivering medicine. After he had spent one semester at the Santa Fe Indian School, Lewis's parents obtained a place to live at Dulce. Lewis then moved home and attended the Christian Reformed Mission School for three semesters, through the fourth grade.

That summer—1925—Margaret Lewis was transferred again, this time to Yuma, Arizona, and Lewis was enrolled in the Phoenix Indian Vocational School, where he remained until graduating from high school in 1933.

After graduation, Lewis returned to Zuni. Because of the Great Depression there were no jobs so Lewis helped his father with the farm work. The Great Depression actually had little effect on the Zunis, who continued to live as they always had, raising their crops and livestock and supplementing their diet by hunting game, such as deer and rabbits. The only tangible sign of the Depression was the government stamps that were needed to buy certain supplies.

In 1941, Lewis got his first salaried job with the Bureau of Indian Affairs at a gas station, where he serviced vehicles for the Soil Conservation Service. After six months Lewis entered the navy in October 1942 during the dark years of World War II. He was sent to San Diego for boot training, after which he was assigned to Submarine Division 41 for further training as a torpedo man. Lewis completed this training in March 1943 and a month later was stationed on the USS *Salmon*. Following one patrol in enemy waters in the Pacific, the *Salmon* returned to Pearl Harbor, Hawaii, where she was transferred to Submarine Division 44.

Lewis was reassigned to the submarine tender USS *Bushnell* but served on this ship only a few months before being transferred in April 1944 to the USS *Tuna*, which was assigned to special missions operating out of Perth, Australia. While he was on this ship, Lewis had the responsibility of seeing that all the torpedoes in the rear section were in operating condition and the tubes ready for action.

Lewis remembered that the *Tuna* was underwater in Subic Bay in the Philippines when the Pacific war ended. He was discharged as a Torpedo Man First Class on September 26, 1945. As a navy veteran, Lewis maintained his ties with fellow veterans. He was a charter member of Teddie Weakie Post 98 of the American Legion at Zuni. He also was a life member of Submarine Veterans of World War II. Two of Lewis's older sons saw military service in the Vietnam War, and returned home safely as well.

After his discharge, Lewis returned to the sunshine and tranquility of

Zuni and to his wife, the former Virginia Panteah, whom he had married on April 14, 1945, while on leave after one of his arduous patrols in the Pacific. Home once more, he began to work with silver jewelry, making rings, bracelets, necklaces, and other items. After three months, however, Lewis and his wife moved to Arizona, where he took a job at a trading post on Highway 66 at Leupp Junction. They remained there for seven years, until Lewis was hired by the famous Hubbell Trading Company and the Lewises moved to Winslow, Arizona. Lewis worked for the Hubbell Trading Company for three more years before returning to Zuni.

By that time, Lewis had been away from his home village, as an adult, for the better part of thirteen years as a student, then in the military, and in the business world getting a practical education. Then he was ready to settle down at home—he thought.

However, despite his satisfaction at being at Zuni Pueblo once again, in June 1975, six months after losing the gubernatorial election to Edison Laselute, Lewis received a federal appointment as a commissioner of the Hopi-Navajo Relocation Program and with it, assignment to Flagstaff, Arizona. In this new job he worked with the Hopi tribe and eleven Navajo chapters (governing districts) to help move members of both tribes from the lands which belonged to the other tribe. He commuted from Zuni to the Hopi or Navajo reservations to explain the relocation mandate by Congress to the tribes. His work on the relocation project lasted until January 1979, when he resigned after being once again elected governor of Zuni.

The Lewises raised a family of six boys and four girls. Tragically, their oldest daughter, Phyllis, died in 1953 from rheumatic heart disease. Their other children are James, Roberta, Margaret, William, Hayes, Robert Rex, Stuart, Jean, and Allen. All of the children married, and there are thirty-two grandchildren.

Grand Central Station in New York is well known as a hub of activity. Governor Robert Lewis's office was called "a second Grand Central Station," reflecting the energy Lewis generated at his work. Change continues to take place at the pueblo under Lewis's aegis. He explained the situation when he spoke at inaugural ceremonies for the sixteenth president of New Mexico State University at Las Cruces early in 1971:

> Not only are the Zunis busy with the task of building a new economic base in our home community, but the community itself is undergoing a face lifting.
>
> Our tribal government and our people were quick to take advantage of federal funds designated for home improvement. Some measure of Indian interest along this line is reflected in the fact that about five hundred new homes have already been completed and five

hundred fifty are under construction. An additional eight hundred fifty are programmed for construction in the near future.

In a later interview in his office, Lewis said:

In the past, homes in the village were constructed of adobe and native rock. More recently, the construction material is concrete or pumice block. In 1971, approximately 98 percent of the homes had running water and 75 percent had sanitation facilities. The homes are quite large; however, many of them are crowded because of a tribal marriage custom that results in the newly married couple moving in with the wife's mother. Generally when this occurs, another room is added to the home, but the cooking facilities continue to be used by the extended family.

Lewis spoke about the changes that occurred as Zuni developed a new economic base:

Whereas in the recent past a good part of the Zuni economy was dependent on [forest] firefighting, a call in May 1971 for manpower to fight fires in New Mexico and Arizona produced only eight available men. In the past, as many as two hundred had responded or stood by, available for duty. Now the majority of Zuni men and women are employed on the 408,000-acre reservation.

Industrial development at Zuni began during Lewis's second term. Early in 1967 Zuni Pueblo made plans to establish an industrial park. The Economic Development Administration and the Federal Water Pollution Control Administration eventually approved a grant of $275,000 to help encourage industrial growth on the reservation. Two companies moved to Zuni to begin operations that same year: Dittmore-Freimuth of Milwaukee and Aircraft Mechanics of Colorado Springs. A new company, AmiZuni, also was formed and later sold to Ampex.

In July 1969 the Zunis launched a five-year comprehensive development plan based on the needs of the Zuni people according to three perspectives—past, present, and future. During the ceremonies for the start of the comprehensive development plan, Lewis stated:

We live in accord with the Zuni Pueblo concepts and, in the past, have asked or expected little of those not of our pueblo. Now we want to achieve a level of living such as other Americans enjoy. We have a long way to go in a short period of time.

Zunis want to retain their identity—not the moccasins and feathers image—but the cultural and historical identification any man uses to reflect pride of his forefathers and their accomplishments and contributions to society.[1]

A grant for airport development was received that same year, and construction was begun on a 4,000-foot paved and lighted airstrip, which was completed in 1970.

Progress in the making and sale of crafts was made possible through the construction of a community building that allots space for sales and through the Zuni Craftsmen's Cooperative Association, which was organized in 1967 and incorporated under New Mexico State law. Its objectives, Lewis said, were to protect the interests of Zuni craftspeople; promote the highest standards of design and workmanship; and market Zuni work for the best possible return to those who produce it.

Among other new developments achieved by the tribe during this period of growth were radio station KSHI, which went on the air in 1977, and a new fifty-bed hospital at Blackrock completed in February 1976. Other programs, which have met with varying degrees of success, include a rental business for tools, machinery, and equipment commonly found in any American city; Zuni Air Corporation; the Salt Lake Enterprise; the Conservation Enterprise; the Candle Company; the Recreational Vehicle Campground Enterprise; and the Forestry Enterprise.

The Salt Lake Enterprise operates on a 619-square-acre salt reservoir on the site of a prehistoric volcano. The site holds cultural significance for Native Americans of the Southwest for it had been the focus of pilgrimages to obtain high-quality salt. Under Lewis' administration the tribe obtained a lease on the location in 1972 from the state of New Mexico. And in 1976, commerical salt production, primarily for livestock use, was begun by the Zuni people. Two years later, through an act of Congress the salt reservoir property was restored to the Zuni tribe. This action made it possible for other peoples such as the Hopi and the tribes of Acoma and Laguna to resume their traditional salt pilgrimages.

More than 1,850 new housing units were developed during Lewis' administration, all with modern facilities, as part of the housing development project. With the new houses and plans to renovate older tribal homes came improvements in housing for federal employees and personnel of the Zuni school system.

Lewis was reelected governor in 1979 for a second four-year term after being out of office for four years. As he began his new term, high on his priority list was an independent school district for Zuni. Historically, the Zuni public schools had been under the wing of the McKinley County School system. In this system, the Zunis felt they had been treated as stepchildren when it came to budgets and facilities. In 1979 the tribe petitioned for its own independent school district. After much debate and analysis, the McKinley County School Board consented to the creation of the Zuni Public School in January 1980. The first election for tribal school board members was held, and, beginning that fall, the system was totally under the control of the Zuni School Board.

The record of accomplishments of the tribe under Lewis's administration as well as under the man who served as governor between his terms, included a wide array of projects—street paving, reservation roads, bridges, dams, the radio station, a bank, the Zuni Public School District, a land claim presented to the United States Court of Claims, a jewelry cooperative, and many others. Lewis accomplished many important things for Zuni Pueblo and its people as governor. Of course, there are others with whom the credit is shared, but Lewis was the decisive influence in Zuni development efforts in the late decades of twentieth century.

While Lieutenant Governor Chancey Simplicio was completing the four-year term of Governor Quincey Panteah, who died in office in July 1983, there was a period of turmoil in Zuni Pueblo over succession of leadership. Consequently, the leaders turned to Lewis; the cacique appointed him governor under the old, nonelective system of selecting officials. This left the Zunis with two governors, one elected, the other appointed. The BIA opposed the dual governorship, because the Zunis had, in 1970, adopted a constitutional form of government calling for elections. In the end, the BIA persuaded the pueblo to stay with the popular vote system.

When Simplicio's term ended in 1986, Lewis was again elected governor by the tribal voters, with his term extending to 1990. Following this term he was elected for another four-year term, which ended in December 1994. In 1993, he declared that he would not run again due to health problems.

Lewis described both the change and continuity characteristic of the modern Zuni Reservation:

> A people's way of life is never stagnant. It may change slowly, but it changes. If there were such a thing as a written chronicle of events in New Mexico stretching back to the time when the first people came into the area, we would no doubt be struck by the many changes that took place in their way of life across the years as conditions changed. This was true in prehistoric times as it has been since the coming of the Spanish and later the Anglo-Americans. For a long time the tempo of change was slow and gradual in Zuni, as well as the rest of New Mexico, not only as it affected the Indians, but as it touched our Spanish and Anglo-American neighbors as well. Here at Zuni, agriculture and stockraising were, like bread, the staff of life, until very recent times.
>
> It was a peaceful existence, one in which we consumed many of the products of our own labor and sold or traded the surplus for commodities that we did not make ourselves. Our neighbors did likewise.

Robert Lewis circa 1965. Photograph © by Marcia Keegan.

The tempo of change remained slow until the 1930s and 1940s when the national Depression, the outbreak of World War II, and other events of major proportions set in motion a series of rapid changes in the life of the Zunis and other people in New Mexico. The population increased rapidly, and, to support it, industries began to spring up in the cities.

New highways were built, REA [Rural Electrification Administration] supplied us with power, and the automobile expanded the trade area from the trading post to the urban areas in search of industrial employment. Indians chose to stay in their own homeland but searched for a means whereby they could remain together and, at the same time, generate the income necessary to share in the prosperity and higher living standards of their fellow Americans. This is the reason, when the Zunis demanded employment and industry on the reservation, we of the council had to act and attract industry to locate here.

Not only do my people feel a strong attachment to the land upon which they have lived for so many generations, but they feel a strong attachment to the language, the religion, and the cultural life of the tribe and community to which they belong. They are willing to exchange the old economy for a new one to secure the benefits other people enjoy, but they are unwilling to do so at the cost of losing their identity as Indians. For a time, my pueblo faced a dilemma. We wondered how we could participate in the cultural and economic life of the state and nation without forfeiting our own tribal values. We attacked the problem by identifying some prerequisites to success—a higher level of education, for example, and by taking stock of local natural and human resources that might be converted into income, both collective and individual.

This was how we started. We were isolated and we had to move industry to Zuni to help our people find employment while they enjoyed security and practiced the way of life they were familiar with and knew best.

As the end point in this series of changes that have been taking place here at Zuni, we anticipate a day in the not too distant future when our community will be pointed out, not solely for the charm attaching to the distinctive culture of the Zunis, but because this community occupies a position of leadership in rural development. Our contribution to the state will increase and become ever more valuable while we succeed in maintaining our identities as Zunis and by our accomplishments in bettering our economic level. We Zunis desire to be an asset to ourselves, our state, and our country, not a liability.[2]

One attempt by Lewis to spur change proved controversial. In 1988, a federal law authorizing the establishment of the Zuni-Cíbola National Historical Park was introduced and sponsored by three New Mexico legislators, Representative Bill Richardson and Senators Jeff Bingaman and Pete Domenici.

Lewis had been pushing for the creation of the park for more than twenty years "in order to boost the pueblo economy while protecting historical and religious sites from vandals and pot hunters," he said.

Several religious leaders and other tribal members criticized the plan for the park, which they reasoned would endanger the religious ceremonies and spiritual life of the pueblo. Consequently, the governing officials decided to hold a referendum on the issue. The Zunis voted on the issue on January 30, 1990. Those who opposed the park won, with 863 voting against it; 125 were in favor. Lewis said afterwards, "That is water under the bridge, and it's time to move on to other things."

And the Zunis did move on under Lewis's leadership. On December 4, they celebrated the passage of the Zuni Conservation Act of 1990. This came about as a result of President George Bush's signing a bill authorizing a $25 million appropriation for a Zuni trust fund. This money was to be used to restore Zuni land harmed by erosion and other factors. To restore their damaged land, the Zunis had filed a lawsuit against the government for building dams that failed, for timber clear-cutting, and for overgrazing in areas of their watershed which were under the supervision of the federal government. Once the trust fund was set up, the Zunis agreed to drop the lawsuit.

Some months earlier, the Zunis had celebrated a victory that was significant not only for the tribe but for many other pueblos: the winning of easement rights to one of their holiest places, the sacred lake of Waynema, located in Arizona north of Saint Johns. It is also sacred to most of the traditional pueblos of New Mexico. There is hardly a Corn Dance song on a feast day which does not mention Waynema as the home of the deities who bring the summer rains from the southwest.

It is well known that Robert Lewis had originality, courage, and the willingness to stand alone in support of his beliefs. He may be aptly described as a man in motion—continually improving himself just as he brought progress to the pueblo and his people.

The walls of the governor's office were lined with honors. One certificate, signed by former New Mexico Governor David Cargo, designated Lewis as an honorary member of the state attorney general's staff. A handsome walnut plaque reads "Outstanding Citizen McKinley County," an award bestowed by the McKinley County Chamber of Commerce. There was an award certificate from the New Mexico Bankers Association for "conservative farming and ranching increasing production."

On the wall also hung a famous prayer that epitomized Lewis's philosophy: "God grant me the serenity to accept the things I cannot change, the courage to change the things I can, and the wisdom to know the difference."

Thinking that on a weekend Lewis might have more time to talk, this writer arranged to speak with the busy Zuni governor at his home. However, it was almost as busy there as at Lewis's office. If the phone was not ringing, there was someone at the door wanting to see Lewis. People came requesting to have their picture taken with Lewis outside the house. On this particular weekend, we had a few moments of privacy and then Lewis's wife, Virginia, reminded him, "Remember, we have to be in Gallup at 3:00 P.M. for the dedication of the new wing at Rehoboth Hospital." Due to his busy schedule, sometimes Lewis could not accept all the opportunities offered him. For example, in 1969 he was selected by the Ford Foundation to be one of ten American Indians to go to New Zealand in an exchange program with ten Maori tribesmen from that country, but his calendar was too full so he delegated the honor to Roger Tsabetsaye as representative of Zuni Pueblo.

In the years that I knew Lewis after his first term as governor of Zuni, and in more recent discussions with him, it has been obvious that he did not like to look back on past accomplishments, but to look ahead. He remarked: "I see that as giving in to temptation to rest on one's laurels and, therefore, slow down . . . with the timetable of the Zuni Plan there is much yet to be done. . . . One can only be impressed by how little one has accomplished."

In the autumn of his life Lewis developed cancer in his kidneys. During an operation one was removed at the Veterans hospital in Albuquerque and gave him life for a few more years. Unfortunately on January 8, 1996, the time came for Lewis. He died at the Veterans hospital. Thus a great Pueblo man returned to the place of his origin. Not only will his family miss him, but also the Zuni people and many others who knew Lewis during his lifetime. He accomplished much for the Zuni people.

NOTES

1. Personal papers of Robert Edward Lewis.
2. Personal papers of Robert Edward Lewis.

REFERENCES

Sando, Joe S. *Pueblo Nations: Eight Centuries of Pueblo Indian History.* Santa Fe, N.M.: Clear Light Publishers, 1992.

Handbook of North American Indians, Vol. 9, *Southwest.* Washington, D. C.: Smithsonian Institution Press, 1979.

CHAPTER 14

Tony Reyna
Taos Pueblo

Outstanding contributions and recognition are often achieved by several members of one family on a community or national level, like the Kennedys of Massachusetts. One such Indian family was that of Hilario Reyna of Taos Pueblo. There were six brothers, and two of them were outstanding achievers, John Rainer, Sr., discussed in Chapter 12, and his younger brother, Antonio (Tony) Reyna, the third son in the family.

Tony Reyna was born at Taos Pueblo on February 1, 1916. Soon after his birth he was given the name of Chu-tu which can be loosely translated as "Hunting Cry." As was common in those days, he spent his early years in the Indian environment of Taos Pueblo, entirely free from outside influences, such as radio, television, tourists, and American schools.

At age eight, Tony attempted to attend the Taos Day School, but his two older brothers, Jerry and John, kept sending him home. The following year he began his education, staying at the Taos Day School until he completed the sixth grade. The next year he went to the Santa Fe Indian School, which he attended through his sophomore year. Then he transferred to Santa Fe High School and graduated two years later—for Indians an achievement equivalent to attending college in those days.

Following high school graduation he enrolled at Bacone Junior College in Oklahoma, from which he was graduated in the spring of 1938. That fall he returned to the Santa Fe Indian School to serve as an assistant instructor of cabinetmaking and woodworking under George Blue Spruce. After a year, he was transferred to the Albuquerque Indian School, where he became an instructor of cabinetmaking and woodworking.

While at his new job, the clouds of World War II were gathering. On March 14, 1941, he volunteered for the service and was sent to Fort Bliss, Texas, for training; afterwards, he was assigned to the 200th Coast Artillery antiaircraft unit as a gun crewman.

On August 17, 1941, because of its high state of readiness, the 200th was notified that it had been selected for an overseas assignment of great importance. The units left Fort Bliss on August 28 and went to San Francisco where they boarded ships headed for the Philippines. Arriving at their destination on September 16, 1941, they went to Fort Stolsenberg, some seventy-five miles north of Manila. On November 23, the antiaircraft guns were placed in combat position for the protection of Clark Field and Fort Stolsenberg, and a training program was started to provide increased experience under simulated combat conditions.

As of November 30, 1941, the 200th had a strength of 1,723 enlisted men and 77 officers, making it one of the largest United States military units in the Philippines. When the soldiers of the 200th arrived in the Philippines, they did not know that they would have only ten weeks before war would erupt. However, at about 3:00 A.M. Manila time, December 8, 1941, the night radio crew of the 200th picked up broadcasts announcing that the Japanese had attacked Pearl Harbor.

The 200th was already in defensive positions as part of their exercise. Shortly after noon on December 8, Japanese bombers attacked Clark Field. The antiaircraft guns of the 200th were equipped with obsolete powder train fuses, effective only to about 20,000 feet, but the high altitude Japanese bombers flew above 23,000 feet. However, despite the unfavorable odds the 200th was equal to the task; when the smoke cleared, they had downed five enemy planes. For three months the 200th, along with the few other American military and the Filipino volunteers, endured continued Japanese air and ground attacks, as well as malaria, dysentery, and starvation. Finally, on April 9, 1942, with no relief in sight, the United States commander on Bataan, Gen. Douglas MacArthur, surrendered his forces to prevent further suffering and loss of life.

However, both suffering and death would continue. The surrender was followed by the horrors and atrocities of the infamous sixty-five-mile Bataan Death March from Mariveles on the Bataan Peninsula to the railhead at San Fernando. Entrapped in this "hell-on-earth," as Tony called it, were many young pueblo men besides Tony. These included, from Taos Pueblo Fernando Concho, Lupe Lucero, Jerry Lucero, "Big Jim" Lujan, Jimmy F. Lujan, Joe Lujan, Onofre Montoya, Mike Romero, and Santana Romero. From the Laguna villages were Pete Kasero of Mesita, Paul Natseway of Seama, Frank Romero of Casa Blanca, Frank B. Sarracino of Laguna, and Santiago Sarracino of Paraje. From Acoma Pueblo were Sam Antonio, Andrew Histia, Felipe Lorenzo, Thomas Charlie, and Clarence Ray. Also present were Manuel (Bob) Chavez of Cochiti Pueblo, Pablo Fragua of Jemez Pueblo, George Gachupin of Zia Pueblo, and Edward Beyuka of Zuni Pueblo. As of this writing, only five of these veterans are still alive: Beyuka, Chavez, Histia, Reyna, and Mike Romero. Of the

1,800 soldiers of the 200th who came from the New Mexico National Guard, only 900 returned.

The terrible Death March began for Tony and his group at Cab Cabin and continued up the Bataan Peninsula to the internment camp for American and Filipino soldiers established by the Japanese at Camp O'Donnell on Luzon Island. After arriving there Tony was assigned to the burial detail. There were many deaths caused by malaria (because of camp conditions in the tropics) and beriberi (due to vitamin B1-deficient prison camp food). At the internment camp the prisoners were forced to work continuously in dust and humid heat without sufficient food.

Years later, Reyna's daughter Diane remembered hearing her father constantly remind the children at the table, "Do not refuse any kind of food. Eat what you are served by anyone."[1] Reyna said that at the prison camp they were always hungry. All they got to eat at meals was thin soup along with a cup of steamed rice. The rice was dirty and full of worms and weevils, but it didn't kill them so they were thankful. "Being hungry, the stuff tasted good," he said. He continued, "An empty stomach is very discouraging. If one has never experienced it, one cannot imagine . . . what it means to be out of food and hungry. Most of us were skin and bones and very weak, but the Japanese made us work. One couldn't help but think about food all the time. We lost track of time and didn't even know what day it was. There was no such thing as time, just work."[2] Many have said that the prisoners there kept their spirits up by thinking of the families whom they knew were praying for them both in the Christian and Indian way and of their desire to return home.

After many months the prisoners were placed on ships, where they were crowded into small spaces with their baggage. Again it was a nightmare. They received one quart of water a day, but it was so hot and humid that they could hardly breathe. When a prisoner passed out, he was dragged up to the deck until he recovered. The ship Reyna was on headed first for Formosa then for Mukden, Manchuria.

Reyna had no idea how long the trip took from Formosa to Manchuria, nor did he know how long they were in Manchuria. He became aware that the Japanese must have surrendered, although no announcement was made. American planes began to drop supplies, which saved lives but also killed some prisoners running after them, who were crushed by falling cargo.

Soon after this experience, Reyna left Manchuria on a hospital ship bound for Okinawa and the Philippines; from there he was brought to Letterman Hospital in San Francisco. After a few days of having his papers processed and getting physical checkups, he returned home by train. Waiting at Lamy, near Santa Fe, for him when the train arrived, were his parents, his brother John, and other family members. Reyna said that this was unquestionably the happiest day of his life. Seeing his family made him realize that he was free at last from hunger, thirst, sickness, repression, and violence.

Reyna remained at the Bruans General Hospital in Santa Fe until June 1946, when he was discharged and returned home to Taos Pueblo. After three and a half years of near starvation, Reyna slowly began to regain his strength. He spent time in his boyhood haunts in the mountains north and east of his Pueblo. Soon he went into business for himself, starting a taxi service between the town of Taos and Taos Pueblo. However, the business did not do well. The unpaved road was hard on vehicles, and fares were not equivalent to what they are today. He chalked it up to experience.

In 1947, Tony started another enterprise, in Indian arts and crafts sales. In this business he was successful, eventually expanding it to include three shops.

As he regained his confidence living in a free and civilized world, Reyna began to notice a young school teacher at the Taos Day School, Annie Cata of San Juan Pueblo. She had received her degree and home economics teaching certificate at New Mexico State University in Las Cruces, New Mexico. In 1948, Cata and Reyna were married.

The next project for Reyna was building a home. Tony selected a spot along the Taos road about a third of the way from the town of Taos. Along with the living quarters the Reynas added a wing for Tony Reyna's Indian Shop, which opened in 1950. In 1960, the couple opened a second shop, which was to be managed and operated by Annie. This shop is located at Kachina Lodge, which is in town near the Taos Pueblo boundary. As business picked up, Tony even opened a third shop at the south side of the pueblo plaza.

The Reynas have four children. John Anthony, their oldest, is a graduate of Ft. Lewis College in Durango, Colorado. Diane, who received her degree from the University of New Mexico, is an experienced television news photographer and currently teaches video production at the Institute of American Indian Arts in Santa Fe. Another daughter, Marie, attended New Mexico State University for a while, but she returned home to Taos and is the mother of three girls—Marlene, Carly Aspen, and Anne Eva. The Reyna's fourth child is Phillip Hilario, who is currently managing the second shop, his mother's shop. In September 1993, Tony lost his wife Annie, who died at Taos and was buried at her birth village of San Juan Pueblo.

Reyna has a long history of public service. In 1948, soon after Indians in New Mexico had secured the right to vote, Reyna became the first American Indian in New Mexico to be on a federal grand jury. Governor Edwin L. Mecham also appointed Reyna to represent the governor at the unveiling of the Bataan Memorial in Santa Fe in the early 1950s. Since

Left to right: Tony Reyna, Bill Richardson, and Pete Concha. Courtesy of the Taos News.

then he has served as chairman of the Police Commission of Taos and on the advisory board of the Taos Day School, the Taos Municipal School Board, and the New Mexico Museum Board of Regents. In addition, he has been president of the Taos Kiwanis Club and was recommended for the Bacone Junior College Hall of Fame. Reyna was also selected to serve on the New Mexico Arts Commission, but he felt that would be a conflict of interest since his daughter Marie is director of an arts center at Taos Pueblo, which received funding from the State Arts Commission.

Reyna has also served Taos Pueblo in many capacities. In 1975, he was selected secretary of the Tribal Council, and in 1977 he was made lieutenant governor of the tribe. He was selected by the council to be governor in 1982 and 1992. And in 1991 he was chairman of the Twentieth Anniversary Celebration of the return of sacred Blue Lake (see Chapter 10).

During the years he was governor, Reyna kept the six canes representing the authority of his office at Taos. These canes were given to Taos and the other eighteen pueblos by various governments in recognition of their sovereignty.

Reyna sees considerable change at Taos Pueblo since Blue Lake was returned. According to him, the younger generation is better educated and therefore more assertive. He believes that as the tribe has increased in population, some disunity has developed—a very different situation than was the case when everyone was united during the struggle for Blue Lake. However, he feels that the new situation is a sign of the changing times and exists in every Indian pueblo.

In July 1992, Reyna's staff called a conference at Taos. On this occasion members of the Taos tribe who were employed by universities, private industry, and government offices were invited to join other tribal members in an economic development workshop for community brainstorming. According to the governor, this workshop resulted in a statement of longrange plans of action to benefit Taos Pueblo and its people.

Reyna has rarely taken long vacations, but he has done a lot of traveling for business to purchase jewelry and taken trips to meetings of the various organizations. He has judged jewelry at the Gallup Inter-tribal Ceremonial, the New Mexico State Fair, and the annual Indian Market in Santa Fe. As governor he has traveled to Washington, D.C., but he says he always dreaded the long airplane ride and crowds in the city. To him, Taos Pueblo is the only place for him—a place where family and friends come to visit him and where he entertains himself by singing Indian songs while beating his favorite drum.

Reyna's life, like that of many other American war heroes, exemplifies courage and fortitude. Also, like many war heroes, he rose from a humble origin to a position of eminence among his people and gained a will to survive the harshest treatment man is capable of inflicting on man. Reyna is the epitome of the Pueblo Indian—quiet, humble, loyal, ready to serve, and, as he has shown, to sacrifice if necessary. Recognized by both his pueblo and the neighboring town of Taos for his character and leadership, he was selected as a "Taos Living Treasure" in 1993. In 1997 he received the New Mexico Governor's Distinguished Service Award.

NOTES

1. Interview with Diane Reyna.
2. Personal interview.

REFERENCES

Jolly, John Pershing. *History of the National Guard of New Mexico,* Santa Fe Office of the Adjutant General, 1964.

Lee, Kenneth. *The American Soldiers in World War II,* Charles Scribners' Sons, New York, 1987.

Sando, Joe S. *Pueblo Nations: Eight Centuries of Pueblo Indian History.* Santa Fe, N.M.: Clear Light Publishers, 1992.

CHAPTER 15

Frank Tenorio
San Felipe Pueblo

San Felipe Pueblo is located twenty-nine miles north of Albuquerque and thirty miles south of Santa Fe, between the banks of the Rio Grande and the Black Mesa. The Indian name for the village is Katishtka; the name "San Felipe" was made official by the Spanish in 1591, commemorating a Jesuit martyr. Their Catholic church was first built by Fray Cristobal Quiñones in 1605 but destroyed during the Pueblo rebellion of 1680. It was rebuilt in 1706 by Fray Andres de Saballos.

The tribe, which numbers approximately 3,040 members currently, lives on a landbase of just under forty-nine thousand acres. While the Pueblo Center is on the west bank of the Rio Grande, pueblo homes are located on both sides of the river. After migration from the Four Corners area the people of San Felipe are said to have first established a village on the mesa overlooking the Rio Grande before descending below to their present location in the Rio Grande Valley. Here they raise corn, chile, alfalfa, fruit, and other crops. They celebrate San Felipe feast day on May 1 annually and Candlemas Day on February 2 in elaborate, colorful ceremonies. The people of San Felipe speak the Keresan language as do their neighbors to the north, the people of Santo Domingo, and the people of Santa Ana Pueblo to the south.

During World War II the American military outsmarted the enemy in many ways that helped to shorten the war. One was the top secret use of the Navajo Code Talkers, who communicated in their native language, confounding the Japanese, who had no way of deciphering the communication system. While secret communications were extremely important strategically, more standard ways of communicating were vital to the smooth operations of the military. The United States Navy continued to rely on signal flags and flashing light beams. This was the system with which Frank Tenorio worked.

Tenorio enlisted in the United States Navy Reserve in November

1942. After going through boot camp at San Diego Naval Training Center, he was sent to Navy Signal School for sixteen weeks. The actor Henry Fonda was in one of his classes at the combination signalman and quartermaster school. There, Tenorio finished at the top of his class and was assigned to a special secret unit in the South Pacific. One of the duties of his unit was to "degauze," or neutralize, the magnetic field of United States ships. A strong magnetic field was dangerous because it attracted Japanese magnetic mines and depth charges. Soon his unit was transferred to Sasebo, Japan. When the European war ended, Tenorio served for a time in the Fiji Islands and then in New Caledonia and the Philippines as the Pacific war advanced toward Japan. Tenorio was discharged as a Signalman First Class on November 10, 1945, and returned home.

Tenorio was born at Isleta Pueblo on December 31, 1922. His mother was Mary Jiron of the Isleta White Corn Clan, so Tenorio is also a member of that clan. His father was Candelario Tenorio of San Felipe Pueblo. When Tenorio was a week old, he took his first train ride from Isleta to San Felipe on the Santa Fe Railroad. He began his education at the local BIA Day School in 1929. Since his parents spoke different Native languages, English was often spoken in the home. Because Tenorio learned to speak English at an early age, his education was accelerated—he was advanced to the next grade three times during his initial school years. However, by the time he reached fifth grade, he was not allowed to advance again because of the age difference between him and his classmates.

During those early innocent but blissful days, Tenorio herded cattle with his grandfather. He said one time they spotted two covered wagons on the road now called the Turquoise Trail between Santa Fe and Cedar Crest. They went over to speak to the people, and after a few greetings, were invited to share the people's lunch, a tasty white meat. Acting as interpreter, the younger Tenorio asked what kind of meat it was. A man took him behind a bush and told him, "There is the rest of what you ate." Under a juniper tree was a snake skin. Tenorio told his grandfather what they had just eaten; his grandfather was shocked and asked Frank to promise never to tell anyone about it. In the pueblo world, snakes have a spiritual significance and are not eaten.

Tenorio had another encounter with a snake once while alone tending cattle. When watching the herd, because of the presence of snakes, his parents always told him, "Never lie down on the ground while you are herding." But like most children, one time he got bored and lay down to rest. When he woke up, he thought he felt something crawling on top of him. He literally froze as a big bull snake slithered over him and away. He was grateful it wasn't a rattler.

In 1933, Tenorio enrolled at the Albuquerque Indian School as a ten-year-old seventh grader. He finished high school at fifteen in 1938.

Because Tenorio felt his knowledge was limited when he graduated from high school, he enrolled at St. Catherine's in Santa Fe. After a semester in Santa Fe, the Sisters recognized his aptitude for learning and transferred him to the Lourdes High School south of Albuquerque. However, when Tenorio realized that it was a seminary for future priests, he dropped out.

That fall, Tenorio joined the labor force in the Albuquerque area since there were no college scholarships at that time. There was, however, a war raging in Europe, and America was building ships and planes, preparing to defend itself if the country became involved. Consequently, Tenorio went to Texas for a two-month course at an aircraft school to learn welding and riveting. And from there he went to California to work as a sheet metal worker.

After America entered the war, Tenorio volunteered for the navy and served for three years. When he returned home, he worked in Albuquerque as an apprentice boiler maker for the Santa Fe Railroad shops from 1945 to 1948. In 1948, he began working for the Eidel Manufacturing Company in Albuquerque. When the Korean War began, he joined the navy again and he was assigned to the USS O'Bannon, anchored at Vallejo, California, where he became acting chief petty officer.

It was at this time that Tenorio married for the second time. He had been married at Isleta and had two boys, Joseph R. and Michael Tenorio, from that marriage. Frank and the former Angela Sanchez Small of San Felipe were married by a justice of the peace in Vallejo in the church at San Felipe in 1951. Angela, who had also been married before, had two children, Ruby Small Harte and Simon Small. Later, Esther and Linda Tenorio were born. The Tenorios also have six grandchildren—Ruby's children, John and Tina Harte; Simon's Letty and Scott, Sr.; and Esther's Howard and Katrina Humetewa. Three great-grandchildren came from Letty (Christopher and Aaron) and Scott (Scott, Jr.).

While in the navy aboard his ship Tenorio took a fleet test for a warrant officer quartermaster rating, but he had an emergency at home. So he applied for and was granted a hardship honorable discharge.

After his return home in 1952 he went to work for the Timpte Brothers in Albuquerque as a steel welder, where he stayed until 1958. That year marked a major change of direction in his life—from that point on he began to focus his energies on the pueblo and devoted himself to service work on behalf of the Indian people.

First, he took the position of instructional aide in adult education at the San Felipe Day School. With this employment he could be at home and have more time for farming as well as participate in the political and spiritual life at his pueblo. He held this job until 1965, when he moved to the Branch of Land Operations at the Southern Pueblos Agency in Albuquerque, where he served until 1970.

Tenorio was elected governor of San Felipe in 1966 and became a member of the Tribal Council. Since 1968 he had been on the All Indian Pueblo Council (AIPC) water rights Committee as a special liaison on water rights between the AIPC and the Bureau of Indian Affairs. As governor he was automatically a member of the AIPC board. He became a permanent member of the AIPC staff in 1973 under Chairman Delfine Lovato. Then in March 1975 he was elected secretary-treasurer of the AIPC, serving until December 1982. He attended water rights hearings and water-related workshops in the state and reported to the AIPC general meetings in order to keep the pueblos informed about what was happening in water rights cases. He was also called upon to testify before the legislature in Santa Fe and in Washington, D.C., on pueblo water rights and education issues. During this time he was chairman of the Water Rights Committee and the Education Committee, the Albuquerque Indian School Board and the Albuquerque-Santa Fe Indian School Board.

In addition, Tenorio was on the Board of Directors of the Middle Rio Grande Conservancy District from 1974 to 1978 and again from 1982 to 1985. From 1982 to 1984 he was on the Federal Clean Waters Act Policy Committee. Other memberships included the National Council on Aging and the National Council of American Indian Litigation Committee.

The seventies were ushered in by a message from President Richard Nixon affirming the policy of self-determination for Indians. As a result, on June 23, 1972, Public Law 92-318 provided funds to Indian schools for curriculum development, teacher training, and mandatory parental participation; it also established an office of Indian Education Title XI of the Act Amendments of 1978 that set up a means by which Indian parents and tribes could have greater involvement in and control of education at the local level.

Another Indian Self-Determination and Education Assistance Act (PL. 93-638), signed by President Gerald Ford in 1975, gave tribes the right to contract with the BIA to administer programs. So when the All Indian Pueblo Council applied to administer its own school in Santa Fe, the bureaucrats in Washington wanted signatures from other tribal groups throughout the country because they envisioned the Santa Fe school as another Haskell national Indian Institute rather than an institution under the control of the AIPC. As secretary-treasurer of AIPC, Tenorio visited Indian reservations throughout the United States to obtain the approval of the various tribal chairmen and presidents in order to contract the operation of the Santa Fe Indian School under the Self-Determination and Education Assistance Act signed by President Nixon in 1970. The Council succeeded in bringing the school under Indian control in accordance with the Act.

During this busy period of activity on behalf of Indian education and the Nineteen Pueblos, Tenorio's own pueblo made him governor again in 1985. In the late 1980s, he was also selected for the second time as the advisor to the Santa Fe Indian School's "First 100 Years Project." As part of this project, he helped train students in interviewing techniques and worked with elders from the Nineteen Pueblos, as well as with the Navajo, Jicarilla Apache, and the Mescalero Apache reservations. During the project fifty oral history interviews were also conducted and over one thousand photographs collected that documented the history of the school from the point of view of the students and staff as far back as the turn of the century. This project resulted in the creation of a traveling exhibit that has been shown in many pueblos and tribal museums; a video documentary; school archives; curriculum materials; interactive multimedia videos; and a book entitled *One House, One Voice, One Heart: Native American Education at the Santa Fe Indian School,* by Sally Hyer, published by the Museum of New Mexico Press in 1990.

At the same time that he made the project possible, Tenorio continued to speak locally and nationally on pueblo water rights, education, sovereignty, self-determination, and other vital Indian issues. Through frequent visits to classes at the Santa Fe Indian School, he served as a role model for many young people and in 1988 was honored by the school, which named a special honors dormitory after him—Tenorio Hall.

Despite all these accomplishments, Tenorio has had no time to rest on his laurels. After retiring from work outside his pueblo, he was selected to serve as governor again from 1992 to 1993. The last term was especially difficult since during that year he had coronary bypass surgery.

Now in retirement he continues to farm at his ranch on the outskirts of the pueblo, where he has for years raised corn, chile, and watermelons. Over the years he has traded with and sold his produce to the Navajos during the Shiprock Fair and at Taos Pueblo during the San Geronimo feast. Tenorio's numerous accomplishments and his service to many sectors of society make him admired and beloved by all.

CHAPTER 16

James Hena
Tesuque Pueblo

"Wake up, wake up!" someone was saying. But in the drowsiness following a deep, sound sleep, the young boy was not sure if he had heard it. "Wake up, wake up, son, it is time for you to go to the kiva," he heard this time and recognized his mother's voice. It was 4:00 A.M., and the young boy felt as if he had just gone to bed. It was Christmas morning. He knew he had to get up and run over to the kiva, where other young boys and men would be gathering before they went together into the hills beyond their village. There was still no sign of daylight—the stars flickered brightly, and although the moon was about to disappear beyond the Jemez Mountains in the west, it was still casting rays on the snow-covered mountaintops of the Sangre de Cristos to the east.

The boy put on his trousers, his moccasins, grabbed a blanket, and disappeared to join the other men and boys at the kiva. Here they would dress for the animal dance of Christmas Day. Most of the young boys would be antelopes with two or three young fawns. The older men would be deer and mountain sheep. Two men would be buffalos with a female partner each; these women would be the mother figures of the forest creatures as they performed that day. After dressing up to represent the various forest animals, all the dancers left the kiva before daylight, before many of the villagers were awake. In the hills the war captain had built fires for them to warm their hands.

As streaks of dawn began to appear over the Sangre de Cristos, the men and boys could hear drums in the village. The drummers were coming toward the game animal dancers gathered in the hills, and they sang a few songs before the animals made their appearance. In one column there were the young antelopes chasing their leader; in another column were the deer and the mountain sheep. The four buffalos appeared from another direction. Soon they were all approaching the drummers-singers as they stood on the outskirts of Tesuque Pueblo, just over the hills from New Mexico's capital city, Santa Fe.

One of the little antelopes that day was James Hena, who would later become executive assistant to the commissioner of Indian affairs in Washington, D.C. and chairman of the All Indian Pueblo Council. Young Hena emerged from the hills to perform as an animal dancer many other Christmases also. Often this dance is also performed on November 12 during the annual Tesuque Pueblo feast day. While he was growing up, young Hena participated in all the dances and activities of his small tribe, which has approximately 400 members.

James Hena was born at Tesuque Pueblo on February 9, 1930. His mother was Dolores Duran, and his father was Louis Hena of Zuni Pueblo. His paternal grandfather and great-grandfather were known as traders to the Rio Grande Pueblos, coming from Zuni to trade salt, turquoise, and Zuni-manufactured jewelry. It is believed that his great-grandfather first acquired the name Hena, which comes from the Keresan word *he-nah*, meaning "let's go." As a trader, he was always going around exchanging goods, so the Keresan-speaking pueblos gave him an appropriate name. The Henas were traditional leaders of Zuni Pueblo, but during a trip James's father met the woman he would marry and settled at Tesuque Pueblo.

Tesuque Pueblo is ten miles over the hill north of Santa Fe about a mile west of U.S. 84-285; the land base of the tribe is about 16,800 acres. A small stream flows by the village down from the majestic Sangre de Cristo Mountains a few miles east. Like its neighboring Indian villages to the north, it is a Tewa-speaking village. Tesuque runs a gambling casino along the highway near a well-known local landmark—the natural formation known as Camel Rock.

Young James began his education at the Tesuque Day School when he was six years old and remained there for two years. From the third to the ninth grades he attended St. Catherine's Indian School in Santa Fe. Then he transferred to Santa Fe High School, from which he graduated in May 1949.

That fall Hena enrolled at the New Mexico School of Commerce in Albuquerque, which he attended for a year. The following year he went to Haskell Indian Institute at Lawrence, Kansas, but because of the Korean War, he was drafted into the Armed Services before he could complete the school year. First stationed at Fort Bliss, Texas, he went overseas with an Ordnance Corps to Anguleme, France. Here he was engaged in a warehouse operation, storing tanks, guns, and other ordnance items for American forces in western Europe. "After two years, two months, and twenty-eight days," he said, he returned to the States and was discharged at Fort Bliss on December 6, 1953.

After his return home he began looking for a job and in March 1954 found work with the Thunderbird Construction Company in Santa Fe, which manufactured nursery supplies out of redwood. Hena traveled extensively for this company, and by the time he transferred to another job after two years, he had become a foreman.

From 1956 to 1964 Hena worked for the Los Alamos National Laboratory in the graphic arts department, where he learned the printing trade. During this period he also began to attend night classes at the College of Santa Fe.

In both 1959 and 1961 he was appointed by his village leaders to serve as lieutenant governor. In 1963, he was once more selected for that post, but this time, after one month, the elders appointed him governor, since he showed great leadership ability even at the young age of thirty-three. The following year, Hena set a precedent in Tesuque by being selected governor of his village for two years in succession.

In 1963, during his first year as governor, Hena was selected as the Outstanding Young Man of New Mexico by the Junior Chamber of Commerce. A few months later another honor was bestowed on Hena. He was given the Distinguished Service Award by the United States Junior Chamber of Commerce.

The following year he was appointed by President Lyndon Johnson to the National Indian Task Force for the War on Poverty. As a member of this task force, Hena toured the Indian reservations of the Southwest explaining Office of Economic Opportunity (OEO) programs.

From 1965 to 1967 Hena was employed by Arizona State University as the Arizona field representative to assist the Indian tribes in Arizona in writing proposals and to initiate OEO programs on the reservations. The Indian tribes he worked with were Navajo, Havasupais, Walapais, Quechans, the Colorado River tribes, and the various Apache tribes of Arizona. He was appointed project director for technical assistance in 1966. As a result, his field of operations was increased to include tribes in California, New Mexico, Colorado, Mississippi, North Carolina, and Florida. He traveled around the South and Southwest, giving technical assistance to Indian tribes needing help with OEO programs.

In 1967, Hena brought his family back to Tesuque. He had been selected by the Governing Board of the Eight Northern Pueblos Community Action Agency to serve as its director. His village of Tesuque is a member of the Eight Northern Pueblos corporate body. At the beginning of his third year as director, he was again called upon by his tribal leaders to serve as governor of Tesuque Pueblo, and he resigned as director of the Community Action Program in order to serve his people.

However, in April 1969 he was hired by the Economic Development Administration in Washington as its program analyst specialist. He was able to convince his tribal leaders that this position was as important as being governor and that in this capacity he could serve all Indian people.

Consequently, Hena moved to Washington, D.C., but did not take his family with him since his children were in school in Tesuque. But after Hena had been working in Washington for eight months, he received a job offer from the Navajo Community College in Arizona. Hena considered the possibility for a few months and decided that since Arizona was not as far away or as humid as Washington, he would accept this position in Many Farms. By August he was employed by the Navajo Community College as director of development.

Seeking construction funds, Hena contacted private foundations and government agencies such as the Small Business Administration; the Department of Health, Education and Welfare; the Department of Housing and Urban Development (HUD); the Economic Development Administration; and the Office of Economic Opportunity. "The most significant effort," he says, "was to convince HUD to approve a 300-student dormitory in the amount of $1.5 million . . . and a 500-student dining hall for $500,000." He also was able to persuade the Navajo tribe to contribute $1,000,000 for construction of these two buildings.

When Nixon became president, he appointed a new commissioner of Indian Affairs, Louis Bruce. Bruce declared that he would appoint Indian men and women to as many high-level positions as he could find qualified Indians. As a result, Hena was asked to consider yet another position—executive assistant to the judiciary commissioner—after working at a new job for less than a year. When Hena became convinced by the commissioner that this job would benefit Indians all over the country as well as the vast number of Bureau of Indian Affairs employees, he accepted. Hena's special responsibility was in Equal Employment Opportunity, initially, but expanded into all BIA program areas until the American Indian Movement (AIM) takeover of BIA offices in Washington, D.C. In his position Hena was responsible for equal employment in all eleven BIA areas from Florida to Alaska and from California to Minnesota. The job demanded constant travel throughout the country to consider and settle the problems of BIA employees. Hena was also involved in special projects for the commissioner whenever his own assignment was not too demanding. Examples of these special projects are $65,000 seed money he was able to obtain for the Eight Northern Pueblos in New Mexico; $50,000 for a feasibility study for an Indian tribe in California; and $19,000 for continuing an Indian interns program in the Albuquerque area office. Hena also worked on the transfer of responsibilities for the care of Blue Lake to the BIA. The lake now belongs to Taos Pueblo following an extended legal and legislative battle with Congress that began in 1906 (see Chapter 10).

Because Hena traveled constantly, he maintained two offices, one in Washington and another in Albuquerque. Thus, his family did not have to move to Washington and was able to live at the family home at Tesuque Pueblo, which Hena had built when he was employed at Los Alamos. This arrangement afforded his children the opportunity to learn their pueblo culture and participate in the activities of the tribe, as Hena did when he was a young boy.

Hena traveled throughout the Indian country on behalf of the Bureau of Indian Affairs. Besides performing his own duties as an arbitrator of employee-employer relations and other special projects, he was assigned to fill speaking engagements for the commissioner when he was unable to attend events.

On January 9, 1971, Hena was honored at the state meeting of the Inter-tribal Council of California. At this ceremony he was awarded a certificate of recognition and appreciation for his role in aiding the establishment of the Inter-tribal Council and also for writing their first proposal to the Office of Economic Opportunity, which subsequently helped make their ideas become a reality. In 1979, the Navajo Tribal Council also gave him an award of commendation.

In 1972, while in Washington for nine weeks Hena attended the Federal Executive Management School sponsored by the United States Civil Service Commission at Charlottesville, Virginia.

Although it was a sacrifice for Hena to be away from his family so much over the years, he was compensated by the knowledge that he was furthering the progress of the American Indians. Undoubtedly, many people were aware of the good work being performed by Hena, since he understood their particular problems and had the ability to work with various individuals for solutions. Often he felt he could do more, but the politics of Washington did not permit it.

Other personal compensations for Hena were the friendships he made and trust the people had in him—perhaps the biggest rewards in the American Indian world, where material wealth is not valued as highly as the opportunity to serve as a leader in the community.

Louis Bruce resigned as commissioner of Indian Affairs in August 1973, when the American Indian Movement launched what it called the "Trail of Broken Treaties," invading the central office of the Bureau of Indian Affairs in Washington, D.C., and seizing the building where the commissioner's office was located. Since Hena was an appointee of Commissioner Bruce, he also resigned.

Hena then returned to his former position with the Navajo Community College, which was now at Tsailee, Arizona. There he served as a development specialist for a year and then became the director of development for four years, working in the position of special assistant to the college president before he resigned.

This time Hena took his family with him—his wife Sophie Vigil, his son Louis II, and daughters Barbara, Charlet, Thelma, and Diane. All of his children are married now and have their own families, with a total of fifteen grandchildren. Because of the housing shortage at the college the Henas had to live in Farmington, New Mexico. Life in Farmington was simpler for Sophie, who had spent many years chauffeuring the five children to different parochial schools in Santa Fe—St. Michael's, St. Catherine's, and St. Francis. When the children had been in Tesuque, they always maintained the family farm land and garden, where they grew alfalfa and vegetables, as well as assisting their maternal grandfather Martin Vigil with chores until he died in 1973.

While at Farmington the family enjoyed fishing in the nearby rivers and mountain streams of Colorado. Before the move, young Louis had always accompanied his father on hunting trips to the mountains east of Tesuque and on fishing trips to lakes and streams in northern New Mexico and southern Colorado.

After eight years with Navajo Community College Hena resigned and returned to Tesuque. Soon he was employed by the All Indian Pueblo Council in Albuquerque as an education specialist for two years. Next, he returned to his pueblo to assume duties as the business manager of the Pueblo Enterprises for two years. Then until 1989 he became the general manager of the pueblo and all its business activities connected to bingo, including the operation of a trailer park and a recreation vehicle campground, as well as a few other smaller business operations.

For the next two years, Hena ran his own consulting firm for investments and economic development for American Indian tribes, known as Te-Zu Limited.

Hena was voted in as chairman of the All Indian Pueblo Council in January 1991, to serve until December 1994. After the end of his term, he served as Chief Executive Officer in the Tesuque Pueblo Office, retiring from that position in 1996. In his sixties, Hena is still young as American Indian leaders go, and there are many things he can still do for the pueblo people. For instance, Hena was president of the Indian Pueblo Federal Development Corporation, a development arm of AIPC. One of the corporation's plans is to develop the site of the old Albuquerque Indian School, an approximately forty-four acre site across from the Indian Pueblo Cultural Center. Hena also lends his expertise to the Tribal Operations Committee of the Environmental Protection Agency in Washington, D.C., as well as to the Restructuring Work Group of the Indian Health Service in Rockville, Maryland.

Since 1992 Hena has been a member of the Board of Directors of the Association on American Indian Affairs in New York City. He has also been chairman and vice-chairman of the National Indian Council on Aging and on its Board of Directors since 1988. Other organizations for which Hena has been a board member of a group organized to recommend changes to the Public Law 638 Amendments; the National Indian Advisory Committee; and the Joint BIA-Albuquerque Area Tribes Indian Priority System Task Force.

Hena has been a member of the National Congress of American Indians (NCAI), and in 1968 and 1969 served as vice-president of the Albuquerque area of NCAI. NCAI is the largest American Indian organization in the country and a paradigm of American Indian unity.

Hena, who was born at tiny Tesuque Pueblo, has accomplished much for his people since the day he first got up before daybreak to perform the Christmas Day animal dances. And when he is not traveling because of work, he continues to participate in the cultural traditions of his people—as he did when he was a boy. He has proved an outstanding leader of American Indians. Hena has established many friends among the various Indian tribes who respect and trust him.

CHAPTER 17

Benedito Atencio
Santo Domingo Pueblo

Santo Domingo Pueblo is located on the east bank of the Rio Grande midway between Albuquerque and Santa Fe, four miles east of Interstate 25. Like their neighbors at San Felipe to the south and Cochiti to the north, the people of Santo Domingo speak the Keresan language. The population is approximately 3,770, and the land base is a little over 71,000 acres. At one time Santo Domingo was closer to the river, but a flood caused the residents to move further east. Santo Domingo Pueblo played an important role in the early history of New Mexico. It was here that Governor Juan de Oñate first met with thirty-eight pueblo leaders in 1598 to obtain their consent to establish a colony. For a time the pueblo also served as an ecclesiastical headquarters of the province for the Franciscan missionaries. Today, it might be called the capital of the pueblos, since the initial meeting of the year is held there by the newly appointed or elected governors of the Nineteen Pueblos.

Santo Domingo Pueblo is often mistakenly considered to be the largest of the nineteen New Mexico pueblos. Actually it is fourth or fifth in population, depending on which United States census report is consulted. One reason Santo Domingo could be considered big is that at festivals dance performances are very large compared to those of other pueblos. Santo Domingo has perhaps the largest plaza, or dance arena, at least five hundred yards in length and about fifty yards wide. On their annual feast day, August 4, in honor of their patron saint Santo Domingo or Saint Dominic, at least three-quarters of the plaza is filled by dancers and singers. This is only possible because the people of Santo Domingo are patriotic, cooperative, and enthusiastically support their traditional culture, which remains strong and meaningful to them. The people of Santo Domingo are recognized nationally as expert jewelry makers and traders. They make *heishi* (turquoise and shell beads) and silver jewelry as well as pottery, which they sell and trade for other Native American crafts.

Santo Domingo Pueblo is the home of Benedito (Benny) Atencio, who was born on May 15, 1929. His parents were Rafael Atencio and Dolores Aguilar. He began his education at the day school and after sixth grade went to the Santa Fe Indian School. Atencio was involved in many activities at the school, including athletics, and served as a class officer. Like many Pueblo Indians, Atencio has seen active duty in the armed forces. In 1948, before he graduated from high school, he joined the Marine Corps and served four years during the Korean War. After his return to the States he was stationed at Camp Pendleton Marine Base near Oceanside, California. Here he took advantage of his spare time to further his education. After obtaining his G.E.D., he attended the Oceanside Community College to take accounting and business courses, subjects he had begun to study at the Marine Corps Institute at the base.

Following active duty, he remained in the Marine Corps Reserves for twelve more years. Returning to civilian life, Atencio first served a four-year apprenticeship as a baker and worked in that trade for two years in Albuquerque. About this time he also began to attend night classes in management and accounting at the Western Business College. Next, he studied tribal business management at the University of New Mexico. With these courses behind him, he was accepted for graduate work at St. John's College in Santa Fe. Due to his many activities he has not had the time to complete the course of study, but he says he is listed as an alumnus.

Soon after he attended the business school at the University of New Mexico he opened up both a trading post and a curio shop at "Little Beaver Town," the latter on East Central in Albuquerque. Later, he worked for the American Car Foundry, a contractor with the Atomic Energy Commission.

About this time, however, he became involved in tribal affairs. In 1959 Atencio was appointed spokesman of the Santo Domingo Council and the following year tribal secretary. Since that time he has served in this position while performing other functions at Santo Domingo. In fact, he was perhaps the first director of the Indian Community Action Program (CAP) to lead the Head Start program, which is still continuing under a different administrator. During his years as CAP director, Atencio took a six-month course in managing CAP programs at the Massachusetts Institute of Technology in Cambridge. He was also tribal director of the Office of Economic Opportunity.

During a meeting of the All Indian Pueblo Council with his own Tribal Council, the AIPC elected Atencio to serve as its treasurer for six years, from February 1964 to January 1971. Following this, he served a two-year term as chairman of the AIPC.

While treasurer under Chairman Domingo Montoya, Atencio was involved in the negotiations and the planning stages of the Indian Pueblo

Cultural Center, located in Albuquerque. There were many meetings with congressional delegates, BIA personnel, and the architects, Harvey Hoshour and Andrew Acoya. Once the 11.6 acres was given trust status, and ownership of the future cultural center was secured by the pueblos, it was up to then chairman Atencio and his staff to secure funding from the federal and corporate sectors. Construction of the Indian Pueblo Cultural Center began a few years later under the chairmanship of Delfine Lovato.

Working to improve the lot of the pueblos has always been Atencio's priority. For his work, he was honored by the National Congress of American Indians during its annual conference in Washington, D.C., in 1992. For many years Atencio served this organization as secretary. He also served on the Santa Fe Indian Service Unit and he was on the State Alcohol and Mental Health Board. In 1967, Governor David Cargo appointed Atencio to the State Movie Commission; in 1971 Governor Bruce King selected him for the New Mexico Bicentennial Commission; and in 1983 Governor Toney Anaya assigned him to the State Fair Commission. In addition, Atencio was on the Martin Luther King Commission and the Advisory Board of the popular television program "Sesame Street." He continues to serve on the board of the Southwestern Indian Polytechnical Institute. While continuing to serve other groups outside the pueblo, Atencio has been selected to serve as an aide to the traditional governing system as well as the secular governing system of Santo Domingo. He was also vice-chairman of AIPC under Chairman Hena.

Atencio is known for his persistence, reliability, and honesty in "telling it like it is." Because of his concern that the younger generation remain involved in pueblo life, Atencio is active in Indian education. He is often called on to speak about pueblo government systems, the pros and cons of tribal constitutions, and other important issues, to high school students of Santa Fe Indian School. On November 18, 1994 Atencio was invited by the South Korean government to come to South Korea as an "ambassador of peace." At that time he was given a medal as an American war veteran of the Korean War and a proclamation plaque for helping to restore South Korean freedom and independence.

Atencio is married to Sofie Cruz of San Juan Pueblo. They had three sons, Steven, Benjamin, and Timothy—the one still living. Dr. Benjamin Atencio, is superintendent of the Southern Pueblos Agency day schools. The Atencios have three grandchildren, Saine Mae, Ralph Irwin, and Jannica, and one great-grandson, Steven Atencio.

CHAPTER 18

Clarence Acoya
Laguna Pueblo

The young boy sat at the crest of a hill as he watched a flock of sheep below. A greater part of the time he looked into the skies and observed the white clouds as they formed fantastic shapes like castles, such as those in the stories his teacher read aloud, or tall buildings, such as he saw once when his father took him to Albuquerque.

The boy's world in this sunbaked country of eroded dry washes, piñon-covered hills, and flat-topped buttes included seven small adobe villages that comprised the Laguna Pueblo Tribal Reservation over fifty miles west of Albuquerque. Near the reservation to the west was another town called Grants. A few miles west was a bigger town called Gallup, where his uncle John had lived and worked on the railroad. Young Clarence Acoya could sit for hours on a hill or around a campfire as he listened to Uncle John talk of the world beyond while they tended sheep together. Often as he studied the horizons he wondered where the clouds went and whether someday he would also venture that far.

Uncle John had gone to the camp while young Acoya was left alone to tend the sheep. All he had to do was stay nearby while the flock had their noontime siesta. As soon as the hot sun moved farther west, the sheep would begin to stir and move out from under the shade of the piñon trees, then Uncle John would be back.

A gentle breeze stirred the piñon trees and the noisy blue jays flew away as they saw Uncle John approach. After the flock of sheep left the shade, they scattered onto the flatlands. In order to keep them from wandering away, young Acoya went in one direction around the sheep while Uncle John circled in the opposite direction.

Near sunset, the two shepherds headed the flock toward camp with the help of their dog. The sheep bedded down immediately, and Uncle John built a fire while young Acoya searched for more firewood for the night. A good fire would keep the coyotes away and also made the stories more interesting.

Because of his stories, John Sarracino was one of Acoya's favorite uncles. He had been away from the reservation, but on returning he was elected governor, the top post of the Laguna tribe, and afterwards he became a member of the Tribal Council. In the Pueblo Indian tradition of government, at some pueblos once a person serves as governor, (or in some cases even lieutenant governor) he becomes a councilman for life. Lately that has changed at seven pueblos, where the ballot system is now used to elect officials. At these pueblos councilmen are voted in or appointed by the winning officials.

When they were not herding sheep together, Uncle John took young Acoya to the council meetings at Old Laguna, the site of the government, which was only a few miles south of their home at Paguate. They traveled by horse-drawn wagon, taking along alfalfa for the horses to eat while the two men were busy at the meeting.

Because of this early experience with Uncle John and the council, Acoya began to think of being a governor or councilman one day, or being a councilman and serving his people; and indeed he did go on to serve his community and Indian people of the state and nation.

Clarence Acoya was born at the Albuquerque Indian Hospital on October 20, 1930. His mother, Ruth Howie Paisano, belonged to the Turkey Clan, while his father was a member of the Young Corn Clan. Consequently, in the matrilineal system of the pueblo people Acoya is of the Turkey Clan.

Acoya began his formal education as a five-year-old at the Seama Government Day School on the Laguna Reservation. Like many Indian parents, Acoya's parents encouraged him to attend class consistently, knowing that the sooner Acoya started learning about the white men's world, the more he would benefit in later life. Since his parents, grandparents, and relatives all conversed in the Keresan language of Laguna, Acoya knew the language as well as any young student of his age. Although he was much younger than most students at the Day School, he was accepted without any problems from the older boys. He loved to clean the blackboard erasers for his teacher, and after school, walked the three miles to his home.

When he finished the sixth grade at Paguate, Acoya went to the Albuquerque Indian School. After a few homesick weeks he adjusted to the life of a boarding school student. To pay for his room and board he at first worked as a messenger for the boys' advisor. Later, he swept sidewalks before classes and worked in the kitchen washing pots and pans.

As he moved to the upper grades, he began to participate in school activities and met many interesting people. One person whom Acoya credits with influencing his future was William Shultz, a social studies teacher at the Albuquerque Indian School. According to Acoya, Shultz saw things as they were; he knew when to compliment you for a deed and when to censure you. Acoya learned to admire Shultz and often visited his home, where Acoya would read the newspaper, listen to the radio, and play records of Indian songs. Among other accomplishments, Shultz had written about Indian songs for an album and designed its jacket. Acoya listened as Shultz often talked about higher education, its purpose, the cost, and the different kinds of colleges and universities. Since there were no counselors in the Indian schools at that time, it was teachers like Shultz who prompted many Indian students to consider higher education. At the time Acoya was in high school, Indian men and women veterans of World War II were completing college studies, and he realized he wished to follow in the footsteps of these pioneers in higher education.

Acoya was graduated from the Albuquerque Indian School in May 1949. That fall he enrolled at Bacone Junior College in Muskogee, Oklahoma. After completing his junior college courses, he enlisted at the Marine Corps Training Center in San Diego.

With the commencement of military action in Korea, Acoya soon was sent there with the First Battalion of the First Marine Division. In Korea he was a squad leader of a machine gun platoon that went on patrols and his division received the Presidential Unit Citation. After Korea, Acoya was transferred to Alaska, where he served the remainder of his three years in the Marines. Today, Acoya is a member of the Veterans of Foreign Wars at Laguna Pueblo and the American Legion in Albuquerque.

After his discharge from the Marines in 1954, Acoya returned home and enrolled at the University of New Mexico. During this time he worked for several years with A. P. Quinn and Company, an investment advisory service.

While living in Albuquerque, Acoya began to participate in Indian affairs, particularly those of his own tribe. In 1960, he was first elected chairman of the Laguna Colony in Albuquerque, a group composed of Laguna tribal members who lived in the city and met to discuss the problems of the tribe on the reservation. The Laguna Colony participated in reservation government and stayed in close contact with tribal officials. Whenever there was an election of new tribal officers on the reservation the Laguna Colony voted in Albuquerque and took their ballots to the reservation. In addition, many times the colony hosted Laguna tribal officials when they came to Albuquerque to talk with tribal members living in the city.

Laguna is perhaps the only pueblo tribe that maintained colonies in several cities along the route of the Santa Fe Railroad. When the railroad was first planned, tribal officials requested that their members be employed by the system as part of the agreement allowing the railroad to use Laguna land. As a result, numerous Lagunas were employed by the railroad and lived in Albuquerque and Gallup, New Mexico, as well as Barstow and Richmond, California. Although many of these workers have retired and the railroad has been downsized since its heyday, the Lagunas living in Albuquerque have continued to maintain their colony.

In 1964, Acoya was elected Laguna tribal treasurer and he served in this position for two years. During his term he worked with Laguna tribal officials and attended monthly meetings of the All Indian Pueblo Council. His talent and ability were soon recognized by the Pueblo council, and he was appointed to serve on the Board of Directors of the Bernalillo County Medical Center—presently called the University of New Mexico Hospital. Acoya served on this board and represented the Pueblo Indians for four years.

As his integrity and ability were further recognized by other Indian tribes and non-Indians of the state, Acoya was selected as the first Indian to serve as executive director of the New Mexico Commission on Indian Affairs in 1986 under New Mexico Governor David Cargo. From his office in Santa Fe, he served as liaison between the Indian people of the state and the New Mexico governor's office, voicing the needs of New Mexico's Indian people to state legislators. In this position, Acoya had many responsibilities, including frequently speaking at conventions on behalf of the Indians of the state as well as representing the governor at Indian gatherings.

After Acoya left this position he served as business consultant for the National Congress of American Indians (NCAI), aiding the smaller tribes not recognized by the BIA. In this program, which was funded by the Ford Foundation through NCAI, he traveled throughout the United States. This employment came about through his membership in NCAI, which he joined when he first became involved in Indian affairs.

In 1969, Acoya received an Urban Program Fellowship at Yale University, sponsored by the National League of Cities and United States Conference of Mayors and the Ford Foundation, where he studied city administration. After completing courses at Yale, Acoya was sent to Tucson, Arizona, to work with the city's mayor. While he was in "mayor training," Acoya returned to his former hometown to attend the annual convention of NCAI in Albuquerque. At this convention in October 1969, he was selected to chair the meeting during the time when Vice-President Spiro Agnew and Secretary of the Interior Walter J. Hickel were in charge of the program. That same year the Republican administration began to search for a new commissioner of Indian Affairs. As a result of his experience and excellent record as executive director in Santa Fe, Acoya was recommended by the Republican governor of the state, David Cargo, for the post of commissioner of Indian Affairs. Consequently, Acoya moved to Washington, D.C., where he was interviewed by the Republican Interior Department hierarchy and considered for the high position. Acoya quickly convinced Lawrence Dunn, secretary for administration of the Interior Department, that he was capable and although he was not selected commissioner of Indian Affairs he served as assistant to Commissioner Louis Bruce.

When I interviewed Acoya at that time, he spoke of what he hoped to accomplish for all Indian people. He hoped to help Indian people achieve self-determination. Acoya believed that Indian people had the capability to shape their own future and attain progress. He thought good communication and cooperation at all levels among Indian people, the local Indian Bureau officials, Washington officials and congressional delegates would lead Indian people to improve their lives. The idea of Indian self-determination was a topic of casual conversation at that time, but it became a reality in 1975 when the United States Congress passed legislation known as the Indian Self-Determination Act. President Gerald R. Ford signed the Indian Self-Determination and Education Assistance Act that same year.

Although Acoya wanted very much to help Indian people he learned the hard way how Washington bureaucracy often undermined social and economic progress for the tribes. Consequently, after two and a half years of frustration and overwork, he left Washington and moved west to be near his home. The closest place he could find a suitable job was in Denver where he worked with the Equal Employment Opportunity office. Although this job allowed him to be closer to home, in this agency he no longer had the opportunity to work with and for Indians. Acoya remained with this office until April 1986, when he retired and returned home to Paguate.

Acoya has accomplished a great deal for the American Indians. Today, although he no longer has sheep to herd, after having broadened his horizons considerably with work and life in the country's capital, Acoya is once again enjoying fresh air, the open blue skies, and the chance to study the clouds as they sail overhead.

PART V

The Arts, Education, and Cultural Renewal

CHAPTER 19

Maria Montoya Martinez
San Ildefonso Pueblo

Pottery has always provided some of the important tools and utensils of the Pueblo Indian people. Potsherds have been studied through the years by social scientists to trace the history of Pueblo Indians. The earliest potsherds identified in relationship to the ancestors of present-day Pueblo Indians have been reliably dated around 300 B.C.

Although pottery has always been an essential part of Pueblo Indian life—traditionally made for use in homes and for bartering with other pueblo tribes—it was only in the last century that it began to be accepted as a decorative item by non-Indians. At that time it achieved status as an art form to be entered in fairs and art shows by individual potters. The concept of pottery as an artistic sale can be credited to the work of one person and to some unusual events that occurred in her life.

The name Maria Montoya Martinez is a household word among the potters of the world. She is probably the Pueblo Indian most renowned internationally as a superb craftsperson as well as an outstanding personality. She became better known after the publication of Alice Marriott's book *Maria: The Potter of San Ildefonso* in 1948. Since it was first published it has been reprinted at least a dozen times, and numerous other books and magazine articles have been written about Martinez.

Actually Martinez did not attain her fame alone. At the beginning of her career she was assisted by her husband Julian, who painted the pots she had created. When Julian died in 1943, her son Popovi Da took on the responsibility of painting Maria's pots. Tragically, in 1943 Popovi Da also died.

Martinez always remained unassuming and, in accordance with pueblo tradition, tried to avoid standing above the other women of her tribe. Nevertheless, she became internationally recognized as a major American ceramist and Pueblo Indian artist. Besides her unique contribution to pottery as an art form, Martinez together with her family, brought about major changes in the development and sale of pueblo pottery. The pottery was so outstanding that it attracted widespread attention and created a market for pueblo pottery in general.

In late summer 1970, I went to San Ildefonso Pueblo with the idea of interviewing Martinez for my first book. I knew where the family lived since I had gone to school with two of her sons. Also, my sister, who had taught weaving and embroidery at the Santa Fe Indian School in the late 1930s, knew Martinez. I entered her home, which turned out to be a Mom and Pop-type grocery store, and when Martinez greeted me, I introduced myself as the brother of Lupe Sando from Jemez Pueblo. I felt an instant rapport with Martinez, who, after I explained my mission, immediately told me that I should talk to her son Popovi Da. "He knows my story as well as I do," she said. "Just so you get my birth date right," she added.

Consequently, I went to their curio shop, located on the southwest corner of the north plaza of the pueblo, where I found "Po," as he was called. According to her son, Martinez was born at San Ildefonso Pueblo in April 1887, the child of Tomas Montoya and Reyes Peña, also of San Ildefonso. She attended the local day school for two years and then spent another two years at St. Catherine's in Santa Fe, where she won first prize for her craftsmanship—in sewing.

After these four years of education, Martinez secured a job as housekeeper at the pueblo day school. She found her job, Po explained, when she visited the teacher there one day. The teacher, Miss Grimes, asked Martinez about her plans for the future, to which she replied that she would probably do what most young ladies do—get married, have a home, and take care of babies. Grimes then suggested that because of her intelligence Martinez could continue her education and become a teacher if she wished. "We can help one another," Grimes said. "You can be the school housekeeper, if you like, and help with the sweeping and cleaning up, and I'll give you lessons in return." Martinez then went home to tell her parents about her discussion with Grimes.

Times were hard, and her father Tomas needed all the money he could possibly get to buy necessities for the family. Since continuing to pay her tuition at St. Catherine's and travel expenses to Santa Fe would have been very difficult, Martinez's parents approved of her proposal to work for Grimes in exchange for being tutored.

Martinez's housekeeping work went smoothly, and Grimes also tutored her as promised. At home, Martinez helped her father harvest corn, wheat, and garden crops in the fall. Ceremonies were held in the village as well as the Corn Dance in September. San Ildefonso was host to other pueblos and neighboring Spanish villages and they in turn went to other communities as guests during fiestas. Martinez's life continued like this until one day it changed radically.

In order to help the teacher and Martinez with the physical labor at the school, a young man of the pueblo had been hired to chop wood. The young man soon began to report to his work daily and worked so diligently that the teacher asked him not to chop any more wood for a few days. However, the young man insisted on coming to the school anyway to see if there was anything more he could do to help. Even when there was no work for him he was there to walk the housekeeper home after she finished her work. The young woodcutter was Julian Martinez.

In 1904, there was a World's Fair in St. Louis and Julian was part of a group that was to dance at the fair, giving Americans the chance to see live Indians off the movie screen. This opportunity provided a good way for Julian to surprise his love by asking her to marry him and accompany him to St. Louis. Since pueblo people do not go on honeymoon trips, it is doubtful that the journey was seen in that light.

Maria was married to Julian, and the two boarded a train in Lamy, near Santa Fe, for the journey to St. Louis. After their arrival in St. Louis Maria sometimes performed Indian dances with Julian but mainly she made traditional San Ildefonso pottery as a part of the American Indian life exhibit. She made simple pieces such as little bowls and ollas without designs, since the fair visitors preferred the plain polished red San Ildefonso bowls.

Thus, unknowingly, the world began to see a couple who would soon become famous. Hereafter, Maria and Julian became like the double-spouted wedding vase that they were given at their wedding—one could not be an entity without the other. Although they did not know it yet, one day the combined names of Maria and Julian would command a fortune from collectors of pottery.

After the fair the newlyweds returned home to San Ildefonso, where Julian became an apprentice to Martinez's father at the family farm while Maria began to work with her aunt Nicolasa, who gave her advice on making San Ildefonso pottery. Now and then Julian found a job that would pay him some cash to buy a pair of shoes, a little flour, or some other necessity. This was the way of life for most Pueblo Indians at the time.

In 1907, the School of American Research under Dr. E. L. Hewitt and Dr. Kenneth Chapman of the Laboratory of Anthropology at Santa Fe began excavating the ruins on the Pajarito Plateau beyond San Ildefonso. One of the first men hired to assist was Julian since he was young and most of the older men had to tend their fields. Julian was employed for three months that summer and returned home only when the rainy season started and digging could not continue at the ruins because of the mud.

It was after Julian's return from the excavations that Maria first noticed he was sick—that he had been drinking. When she told her father about Julian, Tomas said he did not want Julian to go back to the dig alone since he surmised that the white men had given Julian liquor.

It was Julian's connection to the excavations that eventually led to the couple's fame as pottery makers. One day Julian brought home one of his white friends. When the friend saw Martinez making pottery, he was surprised to see her doing what he thought was a lost art. Martinez told him pottery was still made for functional use by Indians, to which the white man replied that it could also be sold. Dr. Kenneth Chapman, an older white man, also came. Dr. Chapman suggested that Martinez go with her husband and make pottery at the camp near the excavation site. Martinez preferred to work at home, and although she tried to talk her way out of it, finally she agreed to go.

Once at the camp Dr. Chapman came to Martinez's tent one day with a potsherd that had a design on it. He asked her if she could duplicate the old pottery by using polishing stones that they had found at the dig. Martinez examined the potsherd and told the old man that she would try but that she could not draw designs. Dr. Chapman then suggested that Julian draw the designs since he had been seen drawing during his stay at the excavation site. Maria protested again, saying that pueblo men did not work with pottery, but in the end Maria and Julian began to work as a team as Chapman had suggested.

Some time later a young white man came to San Ildefonso in a government car looking for Maria. He said that he had come to see the famous potter he had heard about when he was on the Arapaho Indian Reservation in Wyoming. He remarked that since arriving in Santa Fe, he had seen her pottery for sale and wanted to meet her. He wanted to know if she was the only one who made pottery at San Ildefonso and was told that several women at the pueblo made pottery. "How can you tell your own pieces?" the man asked. He was told that each woman made the pottery differently. The man then said that many people didn't know other women at San Ildefonso made pottery and assumed it was all made by Maria. The white man then made a suggestion, saying: "When a white artist paints a picture, he signs his name to it. Then people who buy it know who made it. I think you ought to sign the pottery the same way," the man told Maria. She said she would not know where to sign it and the man suggested the bottom. Consequently, Martinez began to sign "Maria" on some of her work, and later the team began to write "Maria and Julian" on their products. The pottery with the latter signature is now mostly in museums and collectors' display rooms. As a result of this incident, today the pottery of other pueblos bears the signatures of the craftspeople who made it. Martinez continued to make pottery, and white people continued to come to San Ildefonso Pueblo to buy it. Indeed, her pottery became so popular that people came at all hours of the day to purchase it—even during mealtimes or when she was crafting pottery. And no matter when the people came, she had to take care of them. As a result, one day Maria told Julian, "I might as well have a grocery store. The white people are always coming to buy pottery, and I may as well be selling groceries also to our own people of the village."

"If you can manage the time, and if you think you can do it, I can help in some ways," Julian answered. They talked about the idea a few times before they went into the family business of groceries and pottery.

Maria and Julian did well with their business; however, every now and then Julian would not show up, and Maria knew he was out somewhere drinking. By now Maria, as well as other people of the village, knew where Julian was getting his wine. As she thought about the problem, Martinez kept wondering how to stop the man who sold the wine to Julian. One day she had an idea. With her scissor blades, she dug open a covered niche in the bedroom wall, where she had stored some money from her savings. She took out two big rolls of bills, tied the rolls in a handkerchief, picked up her shawl, and left the house silently.

Martinez went straight to the home of a Spanish family living near the pueblo. The man was known to be a bootlegger, but even the law officers were unable to do anything about his illegal activities. Martinez found the couple at home and after the exchange of a few nice words, she told them she wanted to buy their house. The Spanish man indicated they did not want to sell, saying they liked it there since their family had lived in the place for years. "You got to go," responded Martinez. "You can't stay here anymore. There is too much drinking. I have tried to be a good neighbor, and I want to keep on that way. I'll buy your house. How much do you want for it?" Martinez asked, trying to keep calm.

"A thousand dollars," the Spanish man said defiantly. "You pay me a thousand dollars now, this minute, and we will move," he said.

Martinez took a deep breath. Silently and quickly she calculated in her mind the amount she thought she had brought along. She unrolled the handkerchief, gave him the first bundle, and asked him to count it. Slowly, one at a time, the Spanish couple counted and laid the bills down on the kitchen table. They counted ten one-hundred dollar bills.

"A thousand dollars it is, *comadre*," the man said.

"Yes, that is your money," Martinez replied. "Now you can go, tomorrow morning."

In 1933 there was a World's Fair in Chicago called the Century of Progress. As the best known and most popular Pueblo Indian couple, Maria and Julian were asked to attend by the Indian agent in Santa Fe. Although they were reluctant at first, their background and experience at other fairs and their fame as potters meant that they would be very much in demand so they went. At the fair many people flocked to their booth to meet them, and they sold numerous pieces of pottery.

Amused, Po told how Martinez had kept their earnings safe. At the fair Martinez saw a woman she knew who lived in Santa Fe leaning over the guardrail and watching them work. Martinez asked the lady if she would do something for her. "If I can," the Santa Fe lady replied. Martinez went to her worktable and took a sack of money that represented four months of their earnings at the fair. Martinez had kept it to herself and never told Julian how much there was. "Send this to Adam, please," Martinez told the stunned fair visitor. "Adam can take care of it and use it for the farm."

"But Martinez," the lady protested, "you can't do this. You can't just give your money away like this."

"No," Martinez said, "I'm not giving it away. You send it to my son, Adam, please."

A few days later a letter came from Adam in San Ildefonso telling his parents that he had the money and would put it in the bank. Adam, who is also a potter, is the only member of Maria's family still living.

A few months after the Martinezes returned home from Chicago the agent from Santa Fe was back to see them at San Ildefonso. This time he announced that he had been asked to take a group of Indians east, to Washington, D.C., and then on to Atlanta, Georgia, where the commissioner once lived. After a short discussion the couple told the agent they would go. Although President Roosevelt was not at home when the Indian visitors went to the White House, one of the highlights of the Washington trip was meeting Mrs. Eleanor Roosevelt, who shook hands with everybody and then made a speech. Maria said she congratulated the First Lady on the speech, and Mrs. Roosevelt in response told her, "You are one of the important ones. We have a piece of your pottery here in the White House, and we treasure it and show it to visitors from overseas." Maria thanked her again.

From Washington the Indian visitors went to New York City, the fascinating city Miss Grimes had told Maria about many years ago. There they visited the Statue of Liberty, the Empire State Building, and Rockefeller Center.

In 1939, there was another World's Fair in San Francisco. Not surprisingly, the Martinezes again received an invitation to attend as artists. Although Maria's first reaction was negative, since she thought there was more security at home, she finally agreed. Julian had been drinking again since they returned from the trip east, and she thought that if they were together at the fair his drinking would stop. So when Alfreda Ward, from the arts and crafts department at the Santa Fe Indian School, approached them for a second time, they agreed to go for a month.

In San Francisco the couple lived on one island and worked on another, Treasure Island. Maria had seen the Pacific Ocean in San Diego during that fair, and when they went to Washington and New York she saw the Atlantic Ocean. So much water had seemed wasteful to her when it was needed at other places, like San Ildefonso Pueblo, she told her family when she returned home.

In 1940, Julian was made governor of San Ildefonso Pueblo. The tribal leaders' selection of Julian as governor was heartwarming to Maria. He was aware of his responsibility and served his people well. Now people not only came to buy pottery but also on official business. During this time Maria became concerned about the poverty in the world due to wars. Remembering the time when she herself was poor before her pottery began to sell, she decided to help people in other parts of the world. She gave a little roll of bills to Julian and said, "Send this to the people overseas to buy food. I don't want to think about children not eating."

"Which people?" Julian asked.

"I don't care, anybody that's hungry. They all need it over there."

"All right, I guess we'll send it to the Chinese," said Julian. "They look like Indians," at which they all laughed.

"Some people say that the Indians were Chinese once," Martinez said. "Go ahead, send it to them."

The next government employee who came to see the governor was assigned the task of sending the donation to the Chinese. Some time later the couple received a letter from the United China Relief Association thanking them for their generosity. Maria saved the letter, which was decorated with beautiful Chinese designs all around the edges.

The year when Julian was governor Maria did not worry about her husband's drinking as much. He was always busy with meetings and other responsibilities. As a result, that year was an especially happy one for Martinez. As in the past, she participated in the Comanche Dance during the annual fiesta of San Ildefonso on January 23; and on Easter Sunday she also took part in the Corn Dance and was placed at the front, behind the lead male dancer. During the Corn Dance there are two rows of dancers. Behind every male dancer there is a woman. The number of dancers depends on the size of the village and the total population.

After one year as governor, Julian started drinking again. All Maria could do was pray for him. Then one cold October morning in 1943 Julian did not come home, as sometimes happened when he was out all night. Martinez and her son looked for Julian at all the places he often stayed when he was away from home, but there was no trace of him. Finally, after four days, two young boys found his body up on a hill. This was the end of the team. Maria was devastated; it was like the wedding vase having only one spout.[1] However, with her character and strength Maria found a way to continue without Julian.

Fortunately, Martinez had her four boys and their families to help her through these times. Adam had his own family. Juan had completed his studies at Stanford University. Popovi had married during the San Francisco World's Fair, and was looking for a career. The last son, Phillip, was just finishing high school. Soon after Julian's death, Martinez teamed up with her son, Popovi, and this team also became famous. Whereas once the names Maria and Julian on pottery had made it highly desirable, now pottery with the names Maria and Popovi Da was sought after by collectors. During the 1970s, Martinez continued to make pottery, but she limited herself to working with clay during the summer and warm seasons. Many people continued to come to San Ildefonso Pueblo to see the famous potter.

In May 1971, Martinez was honored at the New Mexico State University at Las Cruces, which awarded her an honorary doctorate of fine arts during graduation exercises. Jokingly, she told of her first award—for sewing—when she was a young woman at St. Catherine's School. She does not recall how many pottery awards she has received or when her first was awarded. While still grateful for any recognition, after so many honors, both personally and with her late husband, Julian, she now considers any honor bestowed upon her as a recognition for all Indian potters. As she said, "Pueblo Indians have been making pottery for hundreds of years. I am just doing what other women from this pueblo and other pueblos are doing. They also need recognition, and when I get an award I think of them as I receive it."

Martinez continued to use the same workroom that she and Julian used to make pottery since the early years of this century. Since her death on July 20, 1981, many of her works continue to be displayed in a handsome curio and jewelry shop in the west end of the north plaza at San Ildefonso. In a corner of the sales room is a separate room that contains the private collections of Martinez and Popovi Da. In her private collections are some of her earlier works, decorated by Julian. Some of these collections have been bought by persons who are willing to sell or from heirs of the original buyers. Also included are some special collections of work done by her husband, Julian, son, Popovi, and grandson, Tony Da. None of these are for sale.

This same room contains framed certificates of awards, plaques, and medallions that Martinez has received, among which were the Craftsmanship Medal from the American Institute of Architects; the Symbol of Man Award from the Minnesota Museum of Art; the Presidential Citation from the American Ceramic Society; the University Recognition Medal from the University of Colorado; the Catholic Art Association

Medal; and the Jane Addams Award from Rockford College. Martinez is also included in *Who's Who in America* and *Indians of Today*.

Martinez looked like a typical Tewa woman in her Tewa costume. Knowing about her fame and talking with her inspires respect and admiration: respect for her art and her contribution to bringing Pueblo Indian pottery the recognition and appreciation it has today, and admiration for the way she retained her unassuming personality and character as a typical Pueblo Indian woman, despite her fame and honors. Although Martinez experienced much unhappiness in her life, she did not allow it to crush her spirit or interfere with her work. In fact, it may have motivated her to strive ever harder toward perfection and beauty in her art. Pottery had a special meaning to Maria. First, it was a necessity for the household; then it became an art form, bringing fame and recognition from throughout the world to the former day school housekeeper. It was this recognition that made it possible for other pueblo potters to develop and become successful in their own art.

NOTES

1. The traditional wedding vase has two spouts so that husband and wife can drink from it together.

CHAPTER 20

Cora L. Durand
Picuris Pueblo

There is the story that tells about two young people walking the streets of New York City looking for Carnegie Hall. At one point they ask for directions to Carnegie Hall. The answer they receive is, "Practice, practice, and practice."

It was a similar method that Cora Lopez Durand of Picuris Pueblo used when she was growing up. Her grandmother was a potter who made the beautiful and functional micaceous Picuris bean pots. Until recently, such micaceous bean pots served as the only bean pots in the pueblos, before pressure cookers became available. However, as many people will testify, use of a pressure cooker does not result in pinto beans as flavorful as those cooked in a micaceous bean pot.

Eventually Durand also mastered the art of making bean pots, water jugs (or ollas), and other functional kitchenware.

Durand was born at Picuris on August 23, 1904, to Crucita and Miguelito Lopez, both of Picuris Pueblo. Located in a picturesque Shangri-la nestled in the Sangre de Cristo Mountains, Picuris Pueblo is fifty-seven miles north of Santa Fe. The people speak the Northern Tiwa dialect like their neighbors to the north, at Taos Pueblo, twenty miles away. Although Picuris is a small community today numbering approximately 340 people, it was originally larger.

Picuris played a part in the Pueblo Revolt of 1680, and one of the leaders, Luis Tupatu, replaced the original leader Popé, soon after the revolt. When the Spaniards returned twelve years later in 1692, Tupatu was still the leader, and de Vargas acknowledged his position, giving him a horse with a saddle. It is said that the early Spanish expeditions did not know of the existence of Picuris until Gaspar Castaño de Sosa first visited the isolated pueblo in 1591 on a cold day in January. Their reports described the pueblo as having buildings seven to nine stories high occupied by at least 3,000 people. It is also written that having heard of prior Spanish treachery in the pueblos to the south, the Picuris would not let de Sosa enter any of their buildings, driving his army away with hurled stones.

Cora Durand in her home in Picurís Pueblo. Photograph © by Marcia Keegan.

Today, the people of Picuris continue to maintain their traditional way of life. Their annual feast in honor of their patron San Lorenzo is on August 10, at which time they celebrate the Pueblo Corn Dance or the Basket Dance. On their feast day there is also pole climbing by the koshares, similar to an event at Taos Pueblo. As on most pueblo feast days of today, the one at Picuris Pueblo is packed with friends and visitors. San Lorenzo, patron saint of the poor and sick, was martyred by the King of Spain in A.D. 275 when he stood up for the rights of poor people.

Though Picuris is still an isolated pueblo, it was even more so during Durand's childhood when it was connected to other settlements only by wagon trail. It was on this trail that Durand was taken to the Santa Fe Indian School as a youngster where she completed the eighth grade. During Christmas breaks the trail was often covered with snow, and visiting home was difficult at best.

As Durand was growing up, the Tewas from the Rio Grande area would come and trade garden crops for pots. Since Picuris was located along the foothills of the Sangre de Cristo Mountains, fish were abundant in nearby streams, and the forest furnished a variety of game animals. Consequently, the family was well supplied with food by her father.

In time, Durand married Roland Durand of Picuris, and they had four children—one boy and three girls. Durand outlived all of her children except Isabel D. Guydelkon of Mescalero, New Mexico. The other children were George, Melinda, and Katherine. Durand is survived by fifteen grandchildren and numerous great-grandchildren.

The Durands lived at Picuris Pueblo their entire lives except during the time when Roland was employed as a night watchman at the Santa Fe Indian Hospital in the late 1930s and early 1940s. In the 1950s, he was employed by the Indian Bureau at Towaoc, Colorado, with the Ute Mountain Ute tribe. During this time Roland served as the vice-chairman of the All Pueblo Council under Popovi Da of San Ildefonso and Martin Vigil of Tesuque.

Perhaps Durand would be better known today if she had not lived in a very isolated pueblo and done her work during a period when being near a market was important. As a result of this isolation, her work is less well known than that of many other gifted potters, although her classic micaceous pottery is prized by those lucky enough to know about her. Her pots have become very rare, almost all having been sold to collectors over the years.

Cora Durand died on January 21, 1998, at the age of 93. Picuris has lost a distinguished artist in whose work a precious but now rare tradition of pottery making is preserved.

CHAPTER 21

Agnes Mary Shattuck Dill
Isleta Pueblo

Pueblo Indians of New Mexico are among the most traditional tribes in America, especially when selecting tribal leaders, who are traditionally men. However, despite this tendency, in recent years there have been two pueblos which have had women governors, both elected under the American system of popular vote. By contrast, governors in more than half of the nineteen pueblos are selected by the religious leaders under the traditional system of the Cacique Society.

Isleta, just south of Albuquerque, is one of the two pueblos that have had women governors—amidst some dissent by some traditionalists. For example, Verna Olguin Williamson was elected governor of Isleta Pueblo in 1987 for a two-year term. It was Agnes Mary Shattuck Dill who made female leadership visible at Isleta Pueblo and throughout the country.

Dill served as president of the New Mexico Indian Council on Aging (1986–1988), was national president of the Native American Women's Association (1973–1975), and in 1980–1983 was president of the New Mexico chapter of that organization. She also has done volunteer service in national, state, and local Indian-related health, social service, and educational organizations. To her way of thinking, these volunteer services were "employment" of her talents for the benefit of others. In addition, she has been appointed by United States presidents, governors of the state, and by various organizations to many committees and conferences as a delegate or speaker.

Dill was born at Isleta Pueblo June 23, 1913, the daughter of Maria Beatrice Abeita of Isleta and Paul Shattuck of Paguate on the Laguna Reservation. Dill has had many Indian names given her on various occasions. One of them is Kee-tu-shuree—the first two syllables are the name given to the traditional Isleta universe symbol, and the last syllable means "blossom" or "flower."

Dill's mother, Maria, or Bea, attended a local mission school up to the fifth grade. She became multilingual, speaking her native Tiwa as well as

German, Spanish, and English fluently. This linguistic proficiency came about because she was raised by the German family (Seis) that started the Tiwa Weavers shop at Isleta and later moved to Albuquerque. She learned Spanish through association with her friends and neighbors; and she learned English, the language she spoke at home, in order to talk with her Keresan-speaking husband. Maria was of the Sun clan, so everyone in the Shattuck family, the father included, was a member of that clan. Shattuck became a member of the Isleta tribe and the Sun clan when he relinquished his Laguna membership.

Dill's father, Paul, had gone to the famous Carlisle Indian School in Pennsylvania with a few other youths from Laguna. But he had to return home after his junior year in high school to help his father and grandfather with the ranch, where they had many cattle, sheep, and horses. Ownership of large herds in those days was a sign of wealth; money was not so important as trading or bartering.

Later Paul told his children that during long days in the saddle he had visions of running away from home to return to Carlisle. He put this notion aside, however, when he reflected on the commandment: "Honor thy father and thy mother." But he vowed that if he ever had a family he would see to it that his children would have the best education. Consequently, all of the Shattuck children went to college.

Isleta Pueblo is contiguous to Albuquerque, the plaza and church being just a few miles south of the city. Among the nineteen pueblos, it is both fourth in population with approximately 3,500 residents, and fourth in area at 211,026.31 acres.

The complex history of the pueblo was influenced by its proximity to Spanish settlements and by its location on the Rio Grande. In 1675, the pueblo gained a few new members when the Abo and Quarai Piro survivors of the Saline Pueblos east of the river came to Isleta as refugees. The Piros had been decimated by Apache raids and diseases introduced by the Spaniards. Later, in 1708, some Tiwas who had settled in Alameda in 1702 following their return from the Hopi country to the west were moved to Isleta by Fray Juan de la Peña. They were placed in an area southwest of the plaza called "Oraibi" by the refugees. The Tiwas had fled to Hopi land in 1681 when Governor Antonio de Otermín returned to the pueblo country and torched some Tiwa villages, including Isleta. Another group of refugees, some Lagunas, were also resettled in the Oraibi sector in the 1880s.

The population of Isleta dropped substantially following the Pueblo Revolt of 1680. Many of the villagers, it is believed, followed the Piros from the Saline Pueblos who traveled south with the fleeing Spaniards. Because of the presence of a Spanish garrison at the pueblo, the Isletans who left probably did not do so out of choice. When the Spaniards were retreating southward they very likely coerced some Tiwas to become servants. These Indians were allowed to settle and build a church about fifteen miles east of present-day El Paso and are known today as the Tigua Indians of Ysleta del Sur (Isleta of the South). In September 1987, the Tiguas gained federal recognition and receive services under the Southern Pueblos Agency. Now they are eligible to receive federal funds and to join the prestigious All Indian Pueblo Council.

At some time during her childhood, Dill moved with her parents to Winslow, Arizona, where her father had a job as a boilermaker with the Santa Fe Railroad. There she spent her early childhood with other Indian children—Hopis, Acomas, Lagunas, Navajos—as well as with Hispanics, Blacks, and other neighboring ethnic groups.

When she was six years old and ready to start school, Dill's parents sent her to Paguate to live with her grandparents. She may have had an advantage over other Laguna children when she started school in Paguate since in Winslow her peers spoke English as did her parents.

In the grade school at Paguate, Agnes had two Indian teachers—Mrs. Susie R. Marmon and Rachel Paisano—whom she thought were the smartest women in the world. These two women were the role models who influenced her later decision to become a teacher.

Dill's early days at Paguate with her grandparents were happy and carefree. She especially enjoyed grinding corn on the stone metate, a skill she learned from her aunt. She was enthralled by the beautiful songs the men sang as the women ground the corn and she enjoyed watching her grandmother make bread—paper-thin corn bread that is unusually delicious. Learning how to make it herself was difficult, however; the blue corn dough had to be spread by hand very lightly over a hot stone. Only Pueblo Indian women know how to prepare this delicate type of corn bread; neighboring Spanish and Navajo women who frequented pueblo communities never learned the art. Paper bread is still made in large quantities for pueblo religious and public feast days.

Another happy memory Dill recalls about her time in Paguate is of her uncle holding her on his lap and recounting legends or singing Keresan songs. She also looked forward excitedly to sheepshearing and calf branding on the ranch. She and her cousins would stand on the fence and watch as the men wrestled the calves down to be branded and then slit the animals' ears for identification.

When Dill was nine years old and in the fourth grade, she was enrolled in the Albuquerque Indian School, where she lived with children from several other Southwest tribes. It was her home for nine years except for summers when all students went home to their parents.

Dill remembers her days at the Albuquerque Indian School with great emotion. The school was run like the military.

"It seemed like an army post," she says, "and one of the activities was to get up early in the mornings to drill for the Sunday parades. On Sunday afternoon all the companies lined up for inspection with their nails polished, shoes shined, wearing uniforms of white blouses with blue skirts and red ties all in place By the time I became a sophomore, I was captain of Company B."

Competitive drills were held among the companies on the last Sunday of the school year. During her senior year, 1932, Dill's company won the grand prize—a gold bust of George Washington given in honor of the bicentennial of his birth. As captain of the winning company, Dill was permitted to keep the trophy. Today, it remains with her prized possessions among many other special gifts and memorabilia in the living room of her home at Isleta. A chapter of the National Honor Society was formed at Albuquerque Indian School in 1927 and Agnes was selected as a member, maintaining her membership throughout her time at the school.

Graduating from the Albuquerque Indian School in 1932, Dill took a test to qualify for a Bureau of Indian Affairs college loan. (There were no scholarships at that time through the agency.) She obtained her loan and enrolled in New Mexico Normal University, now New Mexico Highlands University, at Las Vegas, New Mexico. Dill attended the University of New Mexico in Albuquerque during the academic year 1935–1936 but returned to Highlands her senior year, graduating in 1937 with a bachelor of arts degree in education. After leaving college, Dill was employed by the BIA in Oklahoma, at the Cheyenne-Arapaho Indian School in Concho. She served her first year as an apprentice teacher for which she received $700. Out of this small salary she had to repay her loan and support herself. The following year Dill was transferred to the Fort Sill Indian School at Lawton, Oklahoma and completed her apprenticeship there.

Beginning in the fall of 1939 Dill taught at the Sequoyah Indian School in Tahlequah, Oklahoma, where she remained for five years. As a result of her success in the classroom with Indian students in the lower grades, she was promoted and assigned to the Chilocco Indian Boarding School at Chilocco, Oklahoma. That became her home base for another four years.

In her teaching job, Dill was able to visit many students' homes and meet many Indian parents with whom she formed lasting friendships. At Concho she traveled with the school's sports teams and met other students, many of whom still correspond with her and to whom she is known as "Aunt Agnes" or "Grandma Agnes."

Dill had completed eleven years of teaching in Oklahoma when she resigned to marry "the right man," Clarence Arvin Dill of Huntingdon, Tennessee. Soon after the marriage, Clarence Dill experienced a surprise.

"Well, you've gone back to your people," one of his uncles said to him. Clarence asked his uncle what he meant.

"You've married an Indian girl, and one of your grandmothers was an Indian. Didn't your papa ever tell you?"

Clarence had never heard the story, and consequently he and his new wife went to ask his father about it.

Dill's father explained that he didn't think there was any need to tell Clarence of his Indian background. In those days it was not the "right" thing to be an Indian. Because of the Indian Removal Act after the Civil War, many eastern Indians were forcibly moved to Indian Territory, now Oklahoma. Dill's Indian grandmother had been a Powhatan from Virginia; as a young girl she had been sent to Tennessee to live with a family there and had married into the Dill family.

In 1948, Agnes and Clarence Dill established a trading post at Edmund, Oklahoma, later opening another at Vinita—the Fort Cherokee Indian Museum and Trading Post. This second business included a restaurant and service station. As with any Mom and Pop operation, the two entrepreneurs managed all facets of the enterprise. They were curators of the museum as well as wholesalers and retailers, especially in Indian arts and crafts; and they kept the books for the business. Unfortunately, Clarence Dill became ill in 1963, and the couple began to talk about selling the business and moving to Isleta. This they finally did in 1965. Clarence Dill died five years later.

When the couple returned to Isleta, community affairs became one of Agnes's prime concerns.

"I always had a desire to come back and work here," she explained. "Sometimes, though, it's awfully difficult for Indian women, because of their traditional feelings, to want to become involved.

"But I guess I've always been pretty much involved," she continued. "In school I was always president of this group or that club. It's a natural inborn thing. I've always been interested in people. I guess the fact that I like people has made me get out and do things."

Though she was with her husband throughout his illness, Dill found time to teach at the pueblo in addition to serving as assistant director for the Isleta Community Action Program. During this period she established a local office at the pueblo to design, implement, and administer programs for the improvement of living conditions, educational advantages, and cultural awareness of the residents. In 1969, she organized a tutorial program in which high school students volunteered to help day school children who were having difficulties. Two years later, Agnes was appointed tribal court clerk and worked in this position to amend tribal voting rights.

The following year Dill formed a state chapter of the North American

Indian Women's Association (NAIWA), which had been founded in 1970, and has been a member ever since. The NAIWA focuses on the unique problems and concerns that confront Indian women throughout the country. Agnes was elected national president of the NAIWA in 1973 and held that office until 1975. As president, she traveled on speaking tours to various parts of Canada and the United States.

This busy woman from Isleta also found time in 1973 to serve on the steering committee for the first Southwest Regional Women's Conference in Albuquerque. Largely through her efforts, a representative from the United States Department of Labor met with Indian women to discuss the problems confronting Indian women in marketing arts and crafts and in finding employment.

A call from President Gerald Ford in 1975 placed Dill on the National Advisory Council on Women's Educational Programs, which was formed as a result of the Women's Educational Equity Act to overcome gender bias in American education and help achieve educational equality for women. One of her first requests to the council was to invite Indian women to each of its conferences. As a member of the council's Special Committee on Rural Women, Dill toured the main regions of the nation to study and recommend ways in which to improve educational opportunities for farm, rural Black, and Native American women.

"It involved a great deal of work," Dill said, "but we found that the needs of all women are pretty much the same, especially . . . women in isolated areas. I think there's a great consciousness among women that too many times they have been shortchanged in many phases of education, employment and political life.

"Those problems are even more acute among Indian women," she contended. "We're a specialized minority. Many of us lack the training necessary to find employment suited to our individual interests and abilities. A question repeated to me many times has been, 'Why are you always interested in women's causes?' My standard reply has been, 'Because in my youth I could only find work as a domestic and so have many other Indian women.' In my speeches, I repeat the theme over and over."

Dill was a member of the Isleta Constitutional Amendment Committee, which she herself organized with the hope that the committee would rewrite the Isleta Constitution. She is well aware of tribal traditions, particularly with regard to women. Of the women's involvement at Isleta, Dill said, "Wanting to become involved doesn't mean we want to take over the reins of the government, which men have had traditionally all these years. But I think the one thing we do want is to be able to provide help in areas where we have a sensitivity to certain problems like in health, education, and family roles. We have a lot of capable and intelligent women who can be sought out by organizations like the All Indian

Agnes Dill, 1997.

Pueblo Council or our tribal officials and who would be very glad and willing to give any assistance they can."

Dill's work on behalf of Indian women was validated when Verna Olguin Williamson was elected governor of Isleta in 1987 under the pueblo's constitutional form of government for a two-year term. In addition, another young woman from Isleta, Christine Zuni, was made president of the New Mexico Indian Bar Association.

Dill has been honored for her work on numerous occasions. In 1974, she received the Headline Award from Albuquerque Women in Communication for her work as a consultant to the Albuquerque Public Schools. Brigham Young University honored her in 1975 with its American Indian Agriculture and Home Management Award for Distinguished Service to the Indian people. She was given a New Mexico Distinguished Public Service Award by New Mexico Governor Jerry Apodaca in 1977. Dill was also recognized by her university in 1979 with the New Mexico Highlands University Distinguished Alumnus Award for years of "outstanding service" in a wide variety of fields. Another award came from Brigham Young University in 1985, when Dill received the Spencer M. Kimball Award for Devotion and Support to the Indian Cause during the annual Indian Leadership Convention in Provo, Utah.

Among other volunteer activities, Dill has served as announcer at the Indian Village of the New Mexico State Fair for nine years, explaining Indian culture and the meaning of Indian dances to all people in attendance. She also arranged for Albuquerque meetings for non-Indian organizations with which she was associated in order to introduce conferees to New Mexico culture and history. In spite of all these acknowledgments, Dill said, "My greatest reward is not in awards received but the satisfaction and fulfillment of service rendered for the cause of all people, especially our Indian people."

I once asked Dill whether she gave credit for her success in life to anyone besides the grade school teachers who became her role models. She replied, "I give much credit to my parents for what I have come to be in my life. The training, advice, and support my three sisters and two brothers and I received at home gave us the incentive to try to amount to something and to be good citizens. My father often quoted a sentence from the poem, 'The Psalm of Life'—'Be not like driven cattle. Be a hero in the drive.' This has stayed with me throughout my life."

For the benefit of Indian youngsters I asked Dill what she would suggest for them to do to become leaders. Her reply was, "In my case, I searched for the career and activities that I wished to be involved in. Secondly, I tried to do my duties as best I could and always tried to do a little more than was expected. Thirdly, I like people in general and get along with them regardless of color, creed, or race. Fourthly, I try hard to be myself—friendly, courteous, polite, and honest with everyone I come in contact with. I never 'talk down' to our Indian elderly who may not be as proficient in English. And, lastly, I try to share my God-given talents and knowledge with my fellow man."

She added, "I don't know if you were going to ask me, but I am proud of my Indian heritage. In fact, I have been a member of the Albuquerque Council for International Visitors, and I entertain and talk with visitors from around the world about New Mexico and about our Indian culture and traditions."

My last question concerned her Indian school education. How did she feel about it?

"The BIA schools have been criticized for many reasons," she told me. "But I . . . say if it weren't for those schools I might not be what I am today, as well as many other Indians throughout the country. I am the oldest of seven children. How hard it would have been for my parents to educate all of us if we had had to go elsewhere.

"It's usually the young activists who damn Indian schools and government programs. They don't understand how much those programs have helped Indians. Most of the militants are urban Indians. They haven't lived the hardships of reservation life," Dill said.

Dill has been an unofficial ambassador for the state of New Mexico in Washington, D.C., and all over the country, representing the tribes and Indian pueblos at national conventions across the United States and Canada. Perhaps one of her most important accomplishments is that she has opened the door for other Pueblo Indian women to come forth and play a role in leading their people.

CHAPTER 22

Pablita Velarde
Santa Clara Pueblo

The art of the Pueblo Indians has blossomed from utilitarian roots and fiber. The pueblos were among the ethnic groups that did not devise an alphabet or a system of writing in order to communicate or record their lives. However, they did develop a system whereby the people were able to pass on information through drawings—of people, animals, and scenery. They brought life and color to them with natural dyes made from plants and minerals. And they learned this process well; hieroglyphics or hieratic symbols are found both in present-day kivas and in excavations of the ancient ones, indicating that this practice of drawing has been continued over many centuries by the pueblo people.

Today, American Indian art is widely acclaimed here and abroad for its beauty, vitality, and distinctiveness. In this modern era of specialization, there are many Native American artists of renown, among them numerous Pueblo Indians. However, perhaps the best-known pueblo artist is Pablita Velarde, whose style is strikingly unique; her works are in museums, libraries, civic centers, and in the homes of private collectors and connoisseurs throughout this country and the world.

Born on September 19, 1917, at Santa Clara Pueblo, Velarde—her Tewa name is Tsa Tsan (Golden Dawn)—was surrounded by the natural beauty of the Rio Grande Valley set against the backdrop of the Jemez Mountains. Santa Clara, called Ka-'p-geh in the native Tewa language, is one of six Tewa-speaking villages and is located approximately three miles south of Española. The life-giving Rio Grande flows to the east of the pueblo, and to the south is San Ildefonso Pueblo. The Jemez Mountains begin to rise west of Santa Clara in a series of steps from the valley to broad, flat-topped mesas and then to blue peaks that seem to spring from the mesa tops. The mountain range is dominated by Tsi-kumu, the sacred mountain of the Tewas.

Velarde's mother, Marianita Chavarria, died when the little girl was only three years old, leaving her father, Herman Velarde, with four daughters—Pablita, two older sisters, and a younger one. Under these circumstances, the family had to depend on Velarde's paternal grandmother to help raise the children.

The future artist was approaching her sixth birthday in September 1924 when, early one morning, her father hitched his team of horses to a wagon, loaded up his three older daughters and headed for Santa Fe. "Four young girls are just too much for your grandmother, so the three of you older girls are going to enroll at St. Catherine's," their father explained. "Grandmother can pay more attention to Baby Jane at home."

"Where are we going to live?" asked Velarde.

"In a big red house with many other girls of your age," her father replied. "Your sister, Legoria, will look after you and Rosita," he assured them.

"Who will look after all of us?" Velarde insisted, with an air of uncertainty.

"Oh, don't worry about that, little one, I will come down in my wagon once in a while, and there will be the good sisters to look after you every day," their father replied.

After a long day's ride, the Velarde family arrived in Santa Fe. Herman had brought some alfalfa along, and he tied one of the animals to each side of the wagon so they could feed and water them. Afterwards, he ate supper with his daughters in the school dining room and, after bidding them Songe-de-ho, walked back to the boys' dormitory, where he would sleep for the night.

The two older girls had been to the pueblo day school, so they knew what to expect in the classroom. But everything was strange for Velarde. She was put in a room with a few other girls who did not understand the language of the kind lady in black who held her hand and stroked her hair. But then the teacher drew squares on the floor, and she jumped, hopped, and danced over them across the room, asking the girls to do likewise. When they had done this, they watched as the lady bounced a little rubber ball and picked up stones while she did so. They learned this game, too, and soon were playing jacks and hopscotch by themselves, too busy having fun to be homesick.

Velarde attended St. Catherine's Indian School, a private Catholic institution, until she completed the sixth grade. From time to time during the school year Herman came to Santa Fe to visit his daughters, but he could only stay for a short time because it was a long wagon drive back to Santa Clara. The girls stayed at the school from September until the term ended the following May, when their father came with his wagon to take them home for the vacation period.

During the summer, the girls lived with their father in a log cabin in the mountains while he hunted. The game he sought included mountain lions, fox, and eagles; the pelts and feathers were used by his people during their dances and ceremonials. He also trapped coyotes and other predators that killed small game the pueblo boys liked to hunt. Occasionally, he brought home a deer or turkey. On these occasions Velarde tanned the deer hides and made moccasins for the girls and himself.

At the summer cabin, the elder daughter did the cooking, while the younger girls helped as much as they could. Sometimes their father asked them to go to the river for water—enjoyable trips for the youngsters because after the water containers were filled, the girls could play in the mud beside the river. There they would build houses and fashion pottery as they saw the women of the village do. Sometimes they drew outlines of their bare feet in the sand of the riverbank so the kachinas, who were watching the girls from the clouds and mountaintops, could see the size of their feet and make them moccasins. In the evenings their father told stories as they sat around a fire outside the cabin. Velarde especially loved to hear stories about the beginnings of their people and about the antics of Spider Woman.

During the years the girls were at St. Catherine's, their father remarried. Tragically, their stepmother died two years later giving birth to a baby boy. Velarde's grandmother was able to keep the baby alive for three months before he, too, died.

The year that Velarde finished the sixth grade, the girls were transferred across town to the Santa Fe Indian School. Operated by the federal government, this was a bigger school with students from many different tribes. Because of the years she had spent at St. Catherine's, Velarde was more articulate than many girls her age at the new school and was placed in the eighth grade, skipping seventh. This meant she was in the same class as her older sister, Rosita.

Velarde considers 1932 her lucky year since it was then that a young woman named Dorothy Dunn came from Chicago to teach at the Santa Fe Indian School. Dunn, who was to have a significant influence on the development of numerous Native American artists, became interested in the Indian children's natural artistic abilities, encouraging them to draw the things that came most readily to their minds. Using no models, they generally drew scenes from their home life such as horses or dancers. Through their drawing the students began to focus on tribal symbols that they had observed but never thought much about before. Velarde was one of the students who drew easily and with much expression; most of her early work centered on the women of Santa Clara and their daily tasks.

After the 1932 Christmas vacation, Dunn announced to her classes that there would be an open competition Indian art show near the end of the school year. The news excited Velarde, and she determined that she would work hard to have some of her art entered. By the time Dunn began to look for exhibit material, Velarde had created at least three suitable pieces: one showed women baking bread, another depicted women husking corn, and the third was of a woman carrying an olla (clay jar) on her head.

The Indian art show drew many people from the artistic community of Santa Fe, including a well-known Santa Fe artist, Olive Rush, who at this time was beginning to draw some murals on masonite panels for the Chicago World's Fair, called "The Century of Progress." After seeing the work of the Indian children, Rush asked Dunn whether some of the Indian students would like to help her with the assignment. One of three students selected to work with Rush, Velarde's contribution was an oil painting on masonite of a pueblo girl. At the fair, thousands of people saw the work of the Santa Clara girl who was just finishing the eighth grade and her first year of art study.

That same year, 1933, the government bought some of the Indian students' artwork, including several works by Velarde: a mural in oil on masonite and a number of small watercolors—all scenes from Santa Clara. These works by Velarde and other students were shown in Santa Fe and Washington, D.C.

The Velarde girls returned home that summer to a new stepmother, since their father had married for a third time. His bride was a woman not much older than Pablita's sister, Legoria. For some reason, the girls did not feel close to the third Mrs. Velarde. Legoria married, and the other girls moved in with their eldest sister and her husband. However, the following summer, Velarde was asked to move back in with her father and his family. She was now a young teenager, and in the pueblo tradition it was up to her father to make decisions about her future.

Velarde no longer went up to the mountain cabin with her father, but she stayed in the village and helped her father with the garden, where the family grew chile, onions, squash, and corn. Although life was never easy for her, there were many joyous occasions, such as the June 13 San Antonio's Day celebrations at the pueblo. In addition, on June 24, her father would take the entire family by wagon to San Juan Pueblo for the annual fiesta and on August 12 there was the feast day at Santa Clara.

Many times Velarde took part in the Corn Dance during the annual August 12 fiesta at Santa Clara. She recalls the excitement of preparation for feast day events:

> *It was fun to be fitted with the headpiece, called the* tablita, *which all the women corn dancers wore,* she said with a twinkle in her eye, reflecting memories of the good old days.
> *It is a piece of board about a quarter of an inch thick, about ten inches wide and fifteen inches high. There is a round niche or cutout*

about five inches deep the size of a person's head with a soft padded round cushion fastened on the tablita, *which rests on the head. This then was tied at the bottom end of the* tablita, *and these strings meet under your chin tied in a knot to fasten the* tablita *securely to your head. Sometimes, when the wind blew during the dance, you could feel yourself being pulled. These dances were on saints' days introduced by the Spaniards through the Catholic Church. We didn't have any July 4th celebration, nor Memorial Days, nor Labor Days, which are white peoples' feast days.*

A few weeks before our feast days, the governor announces them from the rooftop as well as after Sunday mass. Then the people can prepare for weeks before the fiesta. New songs have to be made and dances rehearsed. The women have to bake bread and cook for all their friends who are expected on the day of the fiesta.

Many times during the summer when her father had some cash, the family went by wagon to Española. There they would buy clothes for Velarde to wear to school or tools for her father. Ice cream, candy, and chewing gum were unheard of luxuries, so Velarde did not crave them.

After two years at the Santa Fe Indian School, Velarde was not permitted to return to SFIS. Her father did not think much of her artwork and told her she would never be able to make a living painting pictures. He wanted her to attend the Española public high school to learn typing and bookkeeping.

Velarde was heartbroken to think that she could no longer paint in Dunn's class or participate in activities like ball games and movies. Nevertheless, she could not go against her father's wishes and thus stayed with the family and walked the two or three miles to the Española high school in all kinds of weather.

However, Velarde continued to miss her art teacher more and more as well as the students with whom she had enjoyed the art courses. Finally, after a year and a half she was permitted to return to the Santa Fe Indian School for the second half of her junior year.

Velarde was graduated from the Santa Fe Indian School in May 1936, the first member of her family to graduate from high school. Her father had left school after the eighth grade, and her sisters had left to marry.

Now it was time for her to earn her own living. Following her graduation from high school, Velarde went to work as a teacher's aide at the Santa Clara Day School, teaching arts and crafts and helping produce puppet shows. She held this job for two years.

In the autumn of 1938, Ernest Thompson Seton, the widely known naturalist who owned an estate south of Santa Fe, invited Velarde to join the Setons in a speaking tour of the eastern United States, providing her an opportunity to see more of the United States. Pablita had attracted the Setons' attention through her artwork displayed in Santa Fe. The four-month speaking tour took Velarde through Nebraska, New England, down the eastern seaboard, and back through the southern states. She was pleased to have seen more of the outside world. The streets of Boston were very much like those in Santa Fe, she discovered; and New York City reminded her of the cliff dwellings at Puyé.

Early in 1939, Velarde was offered another challenge by an admirer of her artwork. Olive Rush had been asked by a new arts and crafts shop in Albuquerque to supervise Indian artists as they painted murals in the lobby of Maisel's store. For this mural Velarde painted a Santa Clara scene, a group of women in colorful costumes standing in front of an adobe building.

When this assignment was completed, Velarde returned to Santa Clara only to be offered another by yet another person. Dale King, a supervisor at Bandelier National Monument, wanted Velarde to do a painting of the ancient residents of the Bandelier cliff dwellings for the Park Service museum in Frijoles Canyon, present-day Bandelier National Monument. Velarde again painted scenes from memories of her childhood since life of the modern Pueblo Indians was much like that of the ancient ones—men making drums and women gathering herbs and fashioning pottery. While she was painting, Velarde occasionally went home to Santa Clara to get information from elders about certain points to make sure her paintings were accurate. Many times the elders gave her good ideas to pursue.

While she was working at Bandelier, Velarde also began building her own house in Santa Clara. She was nearly twenty-one years old and did not want to be dependent on her father. She hired a man to make adobe bricks, and when they were dried her father delivered them to the build-ing site in his wagon. Velarde's brother-in-law also helped by building a foundation of rocks and mud. Her sisters assisted her with the plastering both inside and outside while their husbands laid adobes, set the windows and doors, and put the vigas in place. By the time the house was com-pleted two years later, everyone related to Velarde had helped with the construction. Their work was a good example of the cooperation among extended family members during that time. Unfortunately, such close co-operation among family members in completing work no longer exists as it did before in the villages, since most Indians have adopted the white man's philosophy of remuneration for any kind of work. When Pablita's house was finished, it was all paid for. All she needed were the furnishings.

Velarde was an unusually brave young woman for her time to build her own house, furnish it, and pay for all the things herself. Other women of her age got married and expected their husbands to build the home and buy the furnishings—if they had jobs.

Eventually the assignment at Bandelier ended, and Velarde had to find another job. The only thing she could find was a job in an Española Indian trader's shop decorating drums. Although the work was easy it paid poorly. So to help make ends meet, Velarde made small paintings during her free time, displaying and selling them under the portal of the Palace of Governors in Santa Fe.

Velarde says she often wonders whether the tourists who bought some of her early work at bargain prices kept it until it commanded a very high price. Between her Española job and her painting, Velarde got by, but she longed for a more challenging job with the promise of a better future.

One day a Bureau of Indian Affairs employee left information at Santa Clara that the BIA office in Albuquerque was looking for high school graduates to take jobs as telephone operators at the agency. Being a telephone operator was not the career Velarde wanted, but it was a better job. She was accepted, trained, and after a short period became a regular operator.

Occasionally, when another operator was unable to work, Velarde filled in. Thus it was that Velarde was working one night when a young night watchman at the agency came in to use the phone. His name was Herbert Hardin. He was friendly and struck up a lighthearted conversation with Velarde. After that, Hardin came by more often, finally asking her for a date. Hardin, who was a white man, courted Velarde for several months before proposing marriage. By this time, Velarde was twenty-three and independent. She had graduated from high school, had toured the United States, and had built her own home. There were many circumstances in Velarde's life that indicated she might not live the conventional lifestyle of the average Santa Clara woman. She had never attended the Pueblo Day School but rather had gone to school in Santa Fe from preschool through high school. She had not married young. And she had taken jobs that involved travel and living away from Santa Clara. It was not surprising, therefore, that she accepted Hardin's proposal.

Thus, on Valentine's Day in 1942 Velarde married a white man in the rectory of St. Francis Cathedral in Santa Fe. Since they had no money for a honeymoon, the Hardins went back to Albuquerque and moved into a small apartment. There they lived and worked at their jobs for two months until Hardin was drafted into the army.

After Hardin completed basic training, Velarde moved with her new husband to Texas, where he was stationed. They lived together for a while near his army post, but Velarde finally returned to Albuquerque to await the birth of their first child. On May 28, 1943, Tsa-sah-wee-eh ("Little Standing Spruce")—named after Velarde's beloved mother—was born.

Although Velarde and her daughter tried to follow Hardin wherever he was stationed, the constant transfer of troops during World War II made life too hectic so they returned to Santa Clara to await Hardin's return. Meanwhile, during the annual feast day, Tsa-sah-wee-eh was christened and received the name "Helen." She, too, would become a world renowned painter, not copying her famous mother's style but developing a powerful style uniquely her own. While Velarde was at home that summer, she also gave birth to another child, named Herbert, Jr.

In 1945, Velarde's husband was discharged from the army, and the family returned to Albuquerque, where Hardin sought employment. He wanted to be a policeman, but for the kind of police work he wanted to do, he needed a college education. Like millions of other World War II veterans, he could attend college on the GI Bill and consequently moved with his family to Richmond, California, where he enrolled at the University of California at Berkeley. In order to supplement the family income, Velarde continued to paint. Although they had to struggle on their limited income, they enjoyed life in California for a time. Then Velarde's health began to be affected by the California climate. Because she had grown up in dry, clear semidesert air, the Bay Area humidity caused her to be troubled by asthma. Finally, Velarde had to return to Santa Clara with the two children. There she continued painting to earn the money needed to cover some of Hardin's expenses at school and the family's requirements in New Mexico.

It was in the midst of these hard times that Velarde received an offer of more exciting employment. Dale King was superintendent of Bandelier National Monument, and with the end of World War II, he had more funds to build the displays in the museum. King offered Velarde another assignment at the monument—if she could move to Frijoles Canyon. Velarde wasted no time in accepting the offer.

This time at Frijoles Canyon Velarde had her two children with her. They moved into a cottage used in the summers by Park Service rangers. In many ways life at Frijoles Canyon was idyllic. Her children played with children from the resident rangers' families while Velarde painted. Squirrels darted back and forth up and down the pine trees, and the deer roamed among them.

In June 1947, Hardin received his bachelor's degree in criminology and after looking for work for four months, he took a job as a rookie policeman with the city of Albuquerque. At that time the Hardin family moved back to Albuquerque.

As Velarde continued to progress in her painting, she began to gain more and more attention. She entered her works in competitions throughout the western states and won numerous prizes, which, in turn, brought publicity in newspapers and magazines of the region. A turning point in her life came in 1948 when she won her first important prize from the Philbrook Art Center in Tulsa Oklahoma, one of the largest art centers in the Southwest. The prize-winning painting became her first big sale.

The family home in Albuquerque was pleasant but small. Velarde had no room for a studio—she had to paint in the kitchen. The painting technique she was developing, however, required more space for tools and materials. To produce her earth paintings, which today have become so famous, she collected clays and stones of various colors. Then she crushed the stone on a hard, flat rock called a metate, using a hand-sized stone called a mano. After the colored rocks were pounded and ground into powder, the powder was sifted through a wire screen. Then the powder and clay were stored in jars until needed. Velarde mixed these pigments with glue and water and painted on masonite before placing her works in painted wooden frames.

All these activities take up a lot of space and leave a room messy. Velarde's husband was irritated by the art materials in the house and asked her to move her work into the garage. Despite this, Velarde continued working in the kitchen and winning more prizes while Hardin resented the attention she was receiving and the time she was spending on her art. Eventually, this caused such friction that Hardin moved out.

One of the outstanding surprises in Velarde's life came about through an article written in 1952 by her former art teacher, Dorothy Dunn. The short article about Velarde was published in *El Palacio*, the magazine of the Museum of New Mexico in Santa Fe. Somehow this small publication found its way to England and into the hands of Mrs. Robert Aiken, who, after reading the story, recalled her own visit to Santa Clara Pueblo in 1910. At that time she had met Velarde's parents and had taken photographs of them. Velarde had never seen a photo of her mother, since her mother had died when Velarde was three years old. Consequently, it was a wonderful surprise for Velarde to receive a photograph of her mother from Aiken.

During the period when her marriage was floundering, Velarde became closer to her father again. Visiting him at Santa Clara, she remembered the times she had spent with him in the mountains and the tales told around the campfire. How wonderful it would be, she thought, to write down the stories so that others could enjoy them. At first, her father did not agree since he felt the stories were private, for the people of Santa Clara alone. However, Velarde argued that there were not many Santa Clara people who could carry on the tradition of storytelling—that the old ways of their people were disappearing and that she wanted to help save their culture. Finally convinced, her father became enthusiastic about Velarde's plan and agreed to help her. Thus, on Velarde's many visits, her father retold the tales he had remembered faithfully from his childhood, as he had done when she was a little girl.

Subsequently, Velarde began writing the stories, also painting illustrations for them. In the process, she painted *Old Father Story Teller,* which won the grand prize at the Gallup Inter-Tribal Indian Ceremonial in 1955.

Working on the stories from her childhood was a blessing for Velarde during this troubled time of her life. After Hardin left, she took her children on a trip to Arizona. On the way they had car trouble and had to stop in Globe, Arizona, where Velarde acted on a hunch and looked in the telephone directory to see whether her old friend and boss Dale King still lived in Globe, where he had moved after retiring from the Park Service. Velarde was delighted to find his name in the book, and after dialing she heard the familiar voice saying, "Hello. This is Mr. King."

"This is Pablita calling you," she said.

"Where are you?" he inquired.

"Right here in Globe, at a garage."

"Stay there," said King. "I will come and pick you up. You must stay the night with us."

The Kings wanted to know what Velarde had been doing recently and were very interested when she told them about the book of stories she was writing. And to her surprise, he said he had just gone into the publishing business and might publish her book. By the time Velarde and her children left the next day, King had given her added impetus to finish the book.

Velarde returned to Albuquerque to devote her full attention to the project. The hard work served to help keep her mind off the disintegration of her marriage. In July 1959, the Hardins were divorced; the book, *Old Father Story Teller,* was published the following year.

Velarde was not the kind of person to give up in the face of trouble. After her divorce she did not return to Santa Clara to seek her family's condolences nor did she go to the welfare office for assistance. Instead, she painted. She made plans carefully and then carried them out. She wrote to people who had expressed an interest in buying her paintings and invited friends and acquaintances to visit her when they passed through Albuquerque. In this manner she was able to make some sales.

She also built up a supply of paintings to sell, concentrating on an individual style that was easily recognized. She created a wide range of earth paintings relying on the ancient methods of her people and on the natural earth for pigments. The subjects of her paintings were frequently scenes of pueblo daily life, fiestas, and ceremonial dances, as well as petroglyphs and animals she had seen in Frijoles Canyon. Drawing on her Christian religion, she fused it with Indian elements, painting *Birth of Christ, The Three Kings,* and *The Flight of the Holy Family.* She clothed the holy family in familiar Indian costumes; for example, The Blessed Virgin Mary had straight black hair and wore a shawl, a *manta* (traditional Pueblo women's dress), and white buckskin boots. Joseph wore a head scarf and a *chongo,* hair tied back in a knot like a Pueblo Indian man. The three kings were dressed as a Plains Indian, a Navajo Indian, and a Pueblo Indian. Having seen her work, in 1960, *New Mexico Magazine* commissioned Velarde to do three interpretive Indian paintings of the nativity story for the Christmas issue.

Another fortunate experience for Velarde occurred soon after her divorce when she was most in need of companionship and assistance. She met a couple who became dear friends and business associates— Margarete and Fred Chase, owners and operators of The Enchanted Mesa, a store on Albuquerque's East Central Avenue. After viewing many of Velarde's paintings, the Chases asked if they could display her work in a room and serve as an outlet for her work. Velarde enthusiastically agreed, and since then The Enchanted Mesa has been a showcase for Velarde's work, the pottery of her sister Legoria, and the paintings of Velarde's daughter Helen. Since 1958, Velarde has had an annual pre-Christmas show at the store.

Many honors have been bestowed on Velarde by the Gallup Inter-Tribal Indian Ceremonial, the Philbrook Art Center, New Mexico State Fair, *New Mexico Magazine,* the Santa Fe Indian Market, and the New Mexico Arts and Crafts Fair. Velarde won her first prize at the Santa Fe Indian Market in 1939. Her first prize from the Philbrook came ten years later; she won the grand prize at Philbrook in 1953. Other awards from Philbrook were made in 1956 and 1957.

At the Gallup Inter-Tribal Ceremonial in 1954, Pablita was presented with the coveted French government award, Palme Academique, for originality and excellence in art. The following year, Velarde swept the entire Inter-Tribal Ceremonial with numerous awards. She won a first prize again in 1959 and was honored with a special award by the Ceremonial in 1965.

Velarde received special recognition from the Twentieth Century Art Club of St. Louis in 1955. And she was featured in magazine articles in *New Mexico Magazine* and the Inter-Tribal Ceremonial in 1960.

In 1957, Velarde was commissioned by Foote Cafeteria in Houston, Texas, to do a twenty-one-foot mural of the Green Corn Dance. This was followed by another mural for the old Western Skies Hotel in Albuquerque. This earth painting depicted the legend of *The Buffalo Who Never Dies.* In addition, a bank in Los Alamos commissioned a Velarde mural in 1959.

In 1964, Pablita won the Walter Bimson Grand Award at the Scottsdale National Indian Arts Exhibition in Arizona. That same year, she was honored at the Central Florida Museum of Orlando, where she exhibited paintings and lectured. She was invited to Palm Springs in 1966 to give a one-woman show at the Desert Museum. She also exhibited her paintings at the Heard Museum in Phoenix for many years, winning numerous awards.

In 1962, Velarde received one of her greatest honors when the Philbrook Museum gave her a special award for her outstanding contributions to Indian Art in America. Few artists have received this award, known as the Waite-Phillips Trophy. Of her many awards, perhaps Velarde has won more in the annual show in Tulsa than in any other show.

In 1972, the prestigious magazine *Carte Blanche* commissioned Velarde to do a painting of the Christmas Story for its December issue. The inspirational painting, *The Visit of the Wise Men,* is an Indian interpretation of the birth of Jesus. Also in 1972, Velarde, along with other celebrated Pueblo Indian artists, was commissioned to do a mural at the Indian Pueblo Cultural Center in Albuquerque. For this venture, she painted *The Santa Clara Herd Dance.* The buffalo woman in this painting is a true likeness of Velarde herself.

In 1974 and 1975, Velarde was commissioned to design three medallions for the Franklin Mint in Franklin Center, Pennsylvania, for their Medallic History of American Indians.

For the Museum of New Mexico in 1976, Pablita executed four large paintings for their "Sacred Path" show, which toured the United States, Canada, and Mexico. That same year she was invited to stage a one-woman show at the Governor's Gallery at the Capitol in Santa Fe.

With all her activity in the art world, Velarde received further recognition in 1975 when the Political Caucus of New Mexico gave her the Distinguished Woman of New Mexico Award. It was the first year that award was given, and she was one of fourteen women selected from different fields to be so recognized.

In 1977, Governor Jerry Apodaca presented her the Governor's Award for Achievement and Excellence in the field of visual arts. The following year, she received a rare distinction for an Indian when the University of New Mexico bestowed upon her an honorary doctor of letters degree in recognition of her work as a painter, writer, and illustrator. In addition, the New Mexico Folklore Society placed her on its roll of honor in 1979 for distinguished contribution to the study and presentation of New Mexican folk traditions.

In 1987, the Smithsonian Institution in Washington, D.C., honored Velarde and six other distinguished New Mexico women in a traveling exhibition titled "Daughters of the Desert," which opened in Albuquerque on October 10, 1987.

During an interview, Velarde spoke with typical candor when she was asked how she felt about the Smithsonian Institution exhibition. She said, "I guess I am a daughter of the desert, but I'm still just me. I don't think

Pablita stands in front of the mural she painted of the Buffalo and Deer Dance at the Pueblo Cultural Center in Albuquerque. Photograph © by Marcia Keegan.

of myself as being the most famous Indian woman artist. I define myself as a mama, a grandma and now a great-grandma. Most of the time I've been just the cook and bottlewasher around here."

Today, Velarde's unique paintings are on view around the world. Her works are in the American embassies in Ecuador and Spain and in the Department of the Interior Building in Washington, D.C. President Lyndon Johnson gave one of her paintings to the prime minister of Denmark as a gift. Museums in Tulsa, Santa Fe, and San Francisco also own her paintings, and her work is in scores of private collections.

After a life mosaic of good fortune occasionally interrupted by tragedy, Velarde looks back at the joyous occasions, such as the birth of her first grandchild, Margaret Terrazas on November 11, 1964. Helen Hardin and her husband Pat Terrazas were divorced when Margaret was five years old. Later, in July 1976, Helen married Cradoc Bradshaw. Velarde's son, Herbert, Jr., also married and presented Velarde with three more grandchildren—Ralph and his two sisters, Theresa and Pamela.

However, following these joyous occasions tragedy struck on June 9, 1986, when Helen died of cancer after a short but rich life. Helen Hardin's contributions to the world of pueblo art were important and unique. Deeply saddened by this event, Velarde nevertheless showed her indomitable spirit by saying that she was proud to have been Helen's earthly mother. As a counterpoint to this tragedy, on November 17, 1986, Velarde's first grandchild became Mrs. Gregory Tindel, and in August 1987 the Tindels presented Velarde with a great-granddaughter, Helen Christine.

During her life in Albuquerque Velarde has been active in various clubs and organizations, enjoying fellowship with Indians and women who have similar interests. From its inception, Velarde has been a member of the New Mexico Council of American Indians and has served numerous times on its board of directors. She also has served on its membership, scholarship, and Indian Village committees. The Indian Village, known as "O-Ween-Gay," has been for many years a favorite attraction at the Fairgrounds during the annual New Mexico State Fair, with the Council of American Indians directing its activities. In addition, Velarde has been a member of the Piñon Branch of the National League of Pen Women. One friend and fellow member, Mary Carroll Nelson, wrote a book about her, *Pablita Velarde,* which was published by the Dillon Press of Minneapolis.

In order to improve her communication skills, Velarde at one time joined the Kachina Toastmistress Club of Albuquerque. She also has been cast in a few movie and television roles. The TV roles were in the 1964 "Enchanted Sands" part of the *America the Beautiful* series, and the part of Mary Bluefeather in "Little Bear Died Running," in the *Name of the*

Game series in 1970. In addition, she played small parts in two movies—
Flap and *The City.*

Velarde's Indian background is strongly evident in her personality. She is modest, humble, and conservative. None of her achievements or honors has altered her modesty. Her Indian sense of humor and spirit remain strong despite the unhappiness she has experienced.

Today, Velarde continues to paint, although not as prolifically as in earlier years. Her eyesight has deteriorated due to age. She is visited often by her grandchildren, who bring cheer to her life. After many years of struggle and hard work followed by her numerous honors and awards, Velarde is still Tsa Tsan (Golden Dawn) of Santa Clara Pueblo. She is most deserving of the great success and fame she has achieved.

CHAPTER 23

Geronima Cruz Montoya
San Juan Pueblo

Geronima Cruz Montoya of San Juan Pueblo is a woman who has helped her community in many ways. Her life took numerous unexpected turns as she rose to the forefront in her field.

To gain prominence at San Juan Pueblo is no easy task, since San Juan has been in the limelight of New Mexico history since the arrival of the Spaniards in 1598. This modest pueblo early established itself as the home of Pueblo Indian leaders. The prolonged effort by the Spaniards to dominate a freedom-loving people brought to prominence the first leading figure from San Juan—Popé—who played a major role in the Pueblo Revolt against the Spaniards in 1680.

The leadership prominence nurtured in San Juan did not end with the colonial epoch. Well-known *Hámbios,* as other puebloans call citizens of San Juan, have continued to move across the stage of New Mexico history. Sotero Ortiz from San Juan was the first modern-day chairman of the All Pueblo Council, serving for twenty-four years, from 1922 to 1946. The next prominent figure from San Juan to become chairman of the renamed All Indian Pueblo Council was Delfin Lovato, who served from 1975 to 1984. Herman Agoya, elected chairman in 1987, is another leader from San Juan.

Within this milieu, Geronima Cruz Montoya, known as "Gerry," developed not as a governmental leader but as an educator and painter who inspired students—both children and adults—from her own and other pueblos. Born at San Juan Pueblo on September 22, 1915 to Pablo and Crucita Trujillo Cruz, Montoya spoke only her Tewa dialect until going to school and knew only her name, P'ot'súnú, Tewa for "shell."

Her first experience with formal education was not prophetic of her career. Montoya started school when she was about seven years old. Like many pueblo children, she spent the first two years in kindergarten and "pre-first," since she spoke no English. She attended the San Juan Day

School through the fourth grade, a period, she said, which left her with unpleasant memories.

The source of her unhappy experience was the tyrannical attitude of her two teachers. One wore a large turquoise ring, which she used to pound on the heads of the students when they did not properly understand lessons or commands. The other teacher had an "education board"—a paddle—which he used frequently, and he also threw chalk, rulers, and erasers at the students. It got so bad, Montoya recalls, that one day the entire class decided to "ditch" school, literally—they spent the whole day hiding in an irrigation ditch. Montoya was reluctant to attend school and happy when she could stay home.

There were no boys in Montoya's family—but five sisters, one of whom was adopted. They all had chores to do, including working in the fields with their father during the summer. While he guided the horse-drawn plow, one of the girls would follow behind him planting the seed corn. Typical of most pueblo children, the girls used mostly hand tools in the fields. They rose early to hoe the cornfields and garden before breakfast while it was cool. After breakfast they went back to the fields for more hoeing. The children enjoyed working together planting and tending the vegetables.

Her father, Pablo Cruz, was an experienced farmer who grew not only a garden but large fields of corn and wheat. Gerry Montoya recollects that the whole family was involved with the harvesting. "In August," she said, "we cut wheat by hand using a sickle and tying the wheat in bundles to be hauled to the threshing machine. In October we picked corn, hauled it, and husked it. When the chile turned red, we picked and hauled it and made *ristras*." Gerry recalls that there was no end to the farm work.

The Cruz family raised alfalfa, which also required hard work. After the hay was cut it was raked by hand with a pitchfork and put in small piles. Then it was loaded by pitchfork onto a wagon and taken to the corral, where it was placed on a rack above the barn and fed to the animals during the winter. Alfalfa and other legumes were stored in this way because there were no hay balers then.

Like all farmers, the family harvested crops in the fall and occasionally would travel to neighboring Spanish communities such as Ojo Caliente, La Madera, Vallecito, and Cañon to trade their produce, spending an exciting week there. Montoya remembers those times as part of "the carefree, happy days of my childhood."

Sometimes, the Cruz girls would go to the highway east of the village to sell their pottery. "Some days were very good," Montoya reminisces with a quick smile. Those were the days when the girls ran excitedly home to show their earnings.

But there was always school waiting. In the autumn of 1927, Montoya was sent to the Santa Fe Indian School, where she started fifth grade, apprehensive about the new school. Would it be as bad as the old one?

On this first day, her teacher, Miss Rae Seibert, saw Montoya sitting at a front row desk, homesick, with tears streaming down her face. Filled with compassion, Seibert came over and comforted Montoya. It was such a change from her previous experience at school that Montoya began to feel better. She soon forgot her loneliness and began to enjoy school. "Miss Seibert was a very good teacher, and I corresponded with her until she died a few years ago," Montoya said.

During her elementary and middle school years, Montoya did not stand out from the others in school. However, by the time she reached high school she had become active in extracurricular activities such as scouting, home economics club, Indian club, glee club, mixed chorus, archery, debating, and other groups. In fact, she was involved in so many things that the girls' adviser, Mary Bonn Gay, wrote to Montoya's parents telling them that their daughter was taking part in too many activities and suggesting that she drop some of the clubs for the sake of her health.

One of the teachers during Montoya's early high school years was Alvin Warren, a Chippewa. He often spoke to the students about their future education and vocations and had them write to universities for curricular information. Montoya was interested in nursing and wrote for a catalog in that field. This interest had been aroused by her school job, when she worked at the Indian Hospital. All the Indian students had work they had to do before or after class in lieu of paying room and board.

In the meantime, however, arts and crafts were introduced to the schoolchildren, and soon plans for nursing had a lower priority for Montoya. Her work in this new field of interest was of such quality that in the fall of 1934 she was selected to go to Atlanta, Georgia, to the Southeastern Fair at the invitation of Indian Commissioner John Collier. She was one of only a few individuals selected, all outstanding in their fields, chosen to demonstrate crafts at the fair as well as participate in Indian dances. Members of this select group later became well known in their fields. Among them were Maria and Julian Martinez of San Ilde-fonso; Martin Vigil of Tesuque; Velino Shije of Zia; Josephine Meyers (Wapp), a Comanche; and Manuelito, a Navajo medicine man.

After a week in Atlanta, the group performed dances in Washington, D.C. at the Department of the Interior building. The highlight of their trip was a White House visit during which they met Eleanor Roosevelt. For Montoya, the trip was especially exciting and educational since it was the first time she had been outside New Mexico. She considered the experience the highlight of her school days, although a senior class trip to Mesa Verde, Colorado, the following spring was also memorable.

In June 1935, Montoya graduated from the Indian School, and during the summer she attended a health school on the campus since she was still considering a career in nursing. However, instead she was offered a position assisting the Indian School art instructor, Dorothy Dunn. Montoya had earlier been her assistant for two years. The direction of Montoya's professional life was determined when she became director of the Fine and Applied Arts Department, a position she held until the school was reorganized into the new Institute of American Indian Arts in 1963. With this change, Montoya was transferred to her home pueblo of San Juan, where she initiated an adult education class and worked for another ten years until retiring in 1973.

During her career Montoya was not just a teacher of art; she became a renowned painter in her own right. Her paintings have been exhibited and won awards at such places and events as the San Francisco World's Fair on Treasure Island in 1939; the Gallup Inter-Tribal Ceremonial; the Brooklyn Museum; the New Mexico State Fair; the DeYoung Memorial Museum, San Francisco; the School of American Research, Santa Fe; the Philbrook Art Center, Tulsa; the New Mexico Fine Arts Museum, Santa Fe; the Millicent Rogers Museum, Taos; the Scottsdale National Indian Arts Exhibit; the Heard Museum, Phoenix; and many other museums and art galleries throughout the country. She has had one-woman shows at the Hall of Ethnology, Museum of New Mexico in Santa Fe; the Amerika Haus, Nuremberg, Germany; the Philbrook Art Center, Tulsa; and the Los Alamos Librar, and Espanola Valley National Bank, both in New Mexico.

For the show in Tulsa she was asked to include the work of her students. Thus, the exhibition became a "hall of fame" for some students, who were already outstanding artists. Included were works by Narcisco "Ha-so-de" Abeyta, Navajo; Gilbert Atencio, San Ildefonso; Harrison Begay, Navajo; Joe "See-ru" Herrera, Cochiti; Charlie Lee, Navajo; Eva Mirabel, Taos; Ben Quintana, Cochiti; Percy Sandy, Zuni; Theodore Suina, Cochiti; Quincy Tahoma, Navajo; Roger Tsabetsaye, Zuni; and Beatien Yazz, Navajo. Montoya's most recent show was with her sons Robert and Paul, in 1987 at the Legends Cafe in Santa Fe.

At the start of her career, Montoya was the only Indian member of the State Art Teachers Association. As such, she was called upon to give lectures on art during conventions of the New Mexico Education Association. While she was a teacher, Montoya also was a student, taking summer classes to earn a bachelor's degree. She started her degree work at St. Michael's College (now College of Santa Fe). She also attended Claremont College in California in 1947 and 1948. Despite a busy teaching schedule, raising three sons, and attending summer school, Montoya received her bachelor's degree in 1958 from St. Joseph's College (the University of Albuquerque). Some of the teachers she remembers most fondly, besides Dorothy Dunn, are Alfredo Ramos Martinez, Jean Ames, and Kenneth Chapman.

On August 26, 1939, Gerry married high school sweetheart Juan Montoya of Sandia Pueblo, a carpentry instructor at the Santa Fe Indian School, who worked side by side with her on many volunteer projects. The Montoyas had three sons, and today Montoya is the proud grandmother of one boy and two girls. The sons are Robert, an architect, who makes his home in Albuquerque; Paul, Police Chief of Laguna Pueblo, who lives at Laguna; and Eugene, a New Mexico juvenile probation officer, who lives in Santa Fe.

The Montoya children were brought up as "campus brats" at the Santa Fe Indian School until in 1960 the family moved into a house in Santa Fe. Located halfway between the San Juan and Sandia pueblos, it has remained the family home. Family members are active participants in the ceremonial life of both San Juan and Sandia. Today, Montoya's main contribution is helping cook at both villages on feast days. Until recently, however, she participated in the San Juan dances, the main feast day being June 24, when the Comanche Dance is performed. Other times, Montoya has taken part in the Basket, Spring, and Butterfly dances. She has also danced in the Corn Dance on San Juan's feast day in honor of San Antonio, June 13, and the Corn Dance at Sandia Pueblo.

Juan Montoya was for many years the sponsor and manager of the highly successful San Juan Hawks baseball team. In order to keep the team outfitted and fed, Gerry Montoya and her sisters, with help from team mothers and sisters, worked hard to raise funds, holding bake sales and raffles.

Today, there are many successful young men of San Juan Pueblo who were helped by their participation on the baseball team. Anthropology Professor Alfonso Ortiz, of San Juan Pueblo, asserted that there were many boys who might have fallen prey to alcoholism if baseball had not become a favorite pastime. Herman Agoya says Juan Montoya was a role model for many of the young ballplayers. After Juan's death, a building at the school was named in his memory for his many contributions to the school, its students, and Indian communities. A number of Juan Montoya's players, including Agoya and John Calvert, went on to become star athletes in high school. Much credit goes to the Montoyas and other families who cared for children in their community.

Besides her community service at San Juan Pueblo, Montoya was active in Santa Fe, where she belonged to the Community Concert Association and chaired membership campaigns for the organization.

Montoya's participation in dual cultures did not go unnoticed. Once a co-worker at the Santa Fe Indian School remarked to her, "I envy you because you fit in with the pueblo people and in Anglo society."

Geronima Cruz Montoya, 1996, Photograph © by Marcia Keegan.

Montoya's response was, "I don't have any problem. I get along with people. I have a lot of non-Indian friends. Before the woman told me that," Montoya said, "I had never given it a thought."

When Montoya came back to San Juan to begin an adult education program, she found the people were most interested in reviving their crafts, so she concentrated on that field. She started the program in an elementary school classroom, and participants held annual exhibits to showcase their works. But as more work was produced, Montoya was faced with a marketing problem. She dreamed of having a building at the pueblo, where there would be more work room as well as a sales outlet. She and San Juan Governor Frank Cruz discussed the idea with Senator Joseph M. Montoya, who helped them obtain a grant from the Economic Development Administration (EDA) for a building. Senator Montoya's help was critical in gaining EDA support for the project.

The adult education class was moved from a cramped classroom to its own $16,000 building in June 1973. The structure now houses organization, maintenance, and retail facilities. In 1968, the group had organized into a competitive business called Oke Oweenge Arts and Crafts Cooperative, which was incorporated according to the laws of New Mexico.

Montoya believes that establishing the cooperative was her most important contribution to her people.

> They wanted to improve and continue their crafts by involving their children; they needed an outlet for their products, and I felt that a coop was the best thing I could do to help them organize and get a building for their business. Some people have no other income except for the sale of their crafts. Many are now employed by the coop. Classes are held there also, and they are learning to operate a business. Furthermore, the people enjoy what they are doing and what they make. They are not interested in quantity as much as they are in quality.

Before she retired, Montoya spent most of her time at the coop, but now she only serves as a volunteer one day a week. In recognition of her work, she was elected lifetime chairman of the cooperative. She also serves as a board member of the Southwest Association of Indian Affairs (SWAIA), which stages a highly successful Indian Market in Santa Fe each August for Indian artists and craftspeople from throughout the Southwest.

Being a member of SWAIA, Montoya believes, gave her a chance to support her people through the Indian Market. During the many years she was on the SWAIA Board, she served on several committees—Standard, Nominating, Education, and Membership—and was chairperson for the clothing contest. When she resigned in 1992, Montoya received a plaque with the following inscription: "Geronima Montoya: In Appreciation for your dedicated service as a SWAIA Board Member."

She has been a board member and docent for the Wheelwright Museum in Santa Fe; served on the All Indian Pueblo Council Tri-Centennial Commission in 1980; and was chairperson for the Eight Northern Pueblos Arts and Crafts Committee. She also has been a member of the Smithsonian Institution in Washington, D.C., and the Millicent Rogers Museum in Taos.

Montoya has assisted in judging shows at the Heard Museum in Phoenix and at the Maxwell Museum at the University of New Mexico. At one time she also served on the National Endowment for the Arts National Task Force. In recent years she was selected to serve on the advisory committee of the Indian Museum of Art and Culture in Santa Fe.

A novel experience for Montoya was her role as an extra in the movie *Gambler III,* starring Kenny Rogers and Linda Gray, filmed in New Mexico in the summer of 1987. Because of her long involvement and prominence in art, she has been widely recognized and is listed in *Who's Who in American Art, Who's Who in the West, Who's Who in New Mexico, American Indian Painters,* and the *Reference Encyclopedia of the American Indian.*

Beginning in 1987, the Santa Fe Community Foundation established the annual Geronima Cruz Montoya Award for Arts and Humanities. The first award was made to Open Hands Arts with Elders Program, a volunteer project of professional artists, musicians, writers, and performers, giving elderly persons the opportunity to join in art experiences.

On December 17, 1991, the Museum of Indian Arts and Culture in Santa Fe honored Montoya with a full day award celebration for Artistic and Teaching Contributions to American Indian Art. She received a Nambéware plate with an inscription thanking her for sharing her vision and citing her "life-long commitment to encouraging education in the arts." Montoya's most recent honor was an award from the National Museum of the American Indian of the Smithsonian Institution in 1994, given in conjunction with the opening of the NMAI Museum.

Montoya belongs to the Women's Tewa Choir at San Juan Pueblo. She has composed hymns in the Tewa language, including "The Lord Have Mercy," "Gloria," "Gospel Acclamation," and "The Great Amen," which are sung regularly at Mass. The Mass and hymns have been recorded on cassette to be sold by choir members. Montoya is also a member of the Tekakwitha Circle in San Juan, an organization of Indian Catholics working to have Tekakwitha, a seventeenth-century Mohawk woman, recognized as a saint.

Montoya's life and work are the subject of a book titled *The Worlds of P'ot'súnú,* by Jeanne Shutes and Jill Mellick.

In Montoya's view, commitment to their people is a natural attitude among Indians:

Indian people in the communities are very close. They help one another any time there is a need. Indian people are very unselfish in their ways. Even if it's their last cup of coffee, they'll offer it to you. Any time it means help to the Indian people, I am willing to serve. Our parents have told us, "If you can help people, then help them." If I am able, then I'm willing to help.

Of her current artwork, Montoya says:

My people live in a landscape that stretches in all directions, even towards the sky. They have developed their way of life, their beliefs, and their ceremonies in accordance with the patterns and happenings on the earth and in the sky. They have created dances, songs, poetry and cultural phenomena. The veneration of all these features and forces has brought forth fine arts from the Indian peoples.

My style of painting is very simple. My subjects are mainly traditional dances, home scenes, and designs. My inspiration also comes from the Mimbres figures, pictographs, and petroglyphs. . . . I continually experiment with new forms and styles.

In response to a final request for comment on the scores of young Indian artists now at work, Montoya says:

The most important thing an Indian artist needs is the ability to relate feeling onto the canvas. It is much like being a musician. You have to have lived on a reservation to be able to paint Indians and their lives well. Many Indian artists do not know enough about Indians to do a good job of painting with that special spiritual feeling that can only be conditioned by living in the pueblo or reservation and participating in the various aspects of Indian life. This kind of contact with the Indian people, I believe, trains the painter to capture that spiritual feeling in his or her work.

An outstanding individual and artist, Montoya, P'ot'súnú of San Juan Pueblo, has helped many famous Indian artists and opened a way of making a living for her tribe.

CHAPTER 24

José Rey Toledo

Jemez Pueblo

Jemez Pueblo is located forty-five miles northwest of Albuquerque near the town of San Ysidro and has a population of approximately 2,800 on a land base of about 89,600 acres. The pueblo has few natural resources since a greater part of its forest land was declared United States Forest land by President Theodore Roosevelt in 1906.

The present pueblo, which is called Walatowa by the residents, has been occupied since the sixteenth century. Most of its buildings, however, date back to the period following the Pueblo Revolt of 1680 in which the Jemez warriors played a leading role. "Jemez" comes from the native name "Hemish," meaning "The People." Jemez is the only Towa-speaking pueblo, a dialect of the Tanoan language. It is known for its long-distance runners, since Jemez runners hold records to the top of high mountains like 10,678-foot Sandia Peak in Albuquerque and 14,110-foot Pikes Peak in Colorado. The Jemez people still make fine pottery and are the only Pueblo Indians who make yucca ring baskets. They also do weaving and embroidery, as well as make drums, moccasins, dolls, and stone sculpture.

Classroom teachers often say that drawing and painting appear to come naturally to the average American Indian child. Although this may be true, often other factors are necessary in order to excel—such as the opportunity to observe an inspiring model. This was the case for José Rey Toledo, commonly known at Jemez as Stia-na, short for Ha-stia-na. He was named by his grandfather after a song (perhaps from Tampiro Pueblo, to the east of the Manzano Mountains) sung by a men's society to which Stia-na belongs.

When Toledo was about five or six years old, his brother-in-law, John Shamon, painted watercolor scenes of Jemez, including animals. At the same time, his uncle, Juanito Moquino of Zia Pueblo, who painted deer and forests, used to visit and would sometimes sketch on the walls of the

Toledo home. According to Toledo, "This is where I got my earliest inspiration."

Later, when Toledo was in junior high school, a cousin from Zia Pueblo, Velino Shije, became a nationally known artist. Shije sold his work to art collectors, and Toledo was tremendously inspired; when Shije moved to Santa Fe in 1932, Toledo went along. At first he imitated his cousin's work, "in a humble way." But he showed enough ability that Frank Patania, of the Thunderbird Shop in Santa Fe, hired him to demonstrate Indian painting to tourists.

Toledo believes that he first became a professional artist in the 1930s, after he received recognition and prizes for his work at the Gallup Inter-Tribal Ceremonial art show and the Philbrook Art Center in Tulsa, Oklahoma. Since that time his work has been exhibited and purchased for permanent collections in many art centers and museums throughout the world.

Toledo was born at Jemez Pueblo on June 28, 1915, of mixed pueblo blood. His father was José Ortiz Toledo, part Pecos and part Jemez; and his mother was Refugia Moquino, part Hopi and part Zia, of the Tobacco clan. The Pecos people moved to Jemez in 1838 as the remnant of a once powerful tribe which the Spanish colonial government depended on for military assistance. The Pecos were eventually decimated by diseases brought by the colonists they assisted, as well as by tribal warfare with Apaches and Comanches. Consequently, many Jemez people have some Pecos blood, including Toledo's widow, Amelita Toya Toledo.

Toledo had two older sisters, Andrea T. Fragua and Angelita T. Shamon, and a younger brother, José Ignacio Toledo; only his sister Andrea is still living.

One way Hopi blood became mixed with Zia blood was when, as a result of droughts in the Hopi country in the nineteenth century, some Hopi youngsters were taken to the New Mexico pueblos until the drought was over.

The mixture of blood sometimes made life difficult for Toledo as a child, since other children would tell him that he was not one of them. Because of this treatment he would often become despondent and get into trouble.

During the time Toledo spent with his Zia grandmother, he learned the Keresan language. Toledo participated in Zia dances as well. Consequently, he was soon considered a member of Zia. However, at Zia Pueblo he was also considered "different," and the children called him "Jemez," which was calculated to hurt his feelings. As Toledo matured, he began to wonder why he had to experience so much pain because of his mixed blood. Nevertheless, he believed later in life that such difficult experiences made him stronger and more resistant to other things that he could not readily accept.

Like all Jemez children, Toledo began his education at the San Diego Mission School. And like most boys his age, he was an altar boy. The sisters liked him a lot, and he responded by being a good student.

During the fourth grade, he transferred to the Albuquerque Indian School. Everything about the school, including the dormitory living, the dining hall, and the pseudo-military environment, fascinated him. On Saturdays the students would scrub the rooms, hallways, and stairways. On Sundays the band would play and they would do precision marching drills, which people from the city of Albuquerque would come out to watch.

Speaking their native language was restricted, but often students forgot where they were and would unknowingly shout something in their own language while they were playing. For such outbursts the students received extra work, such as scrubbing stairways or halls. In the dormitory the matrons kept them busy with tasks like mending clothes or taking sheets to the laundry. Some students were bakers, shoemakers, or kitchen and dining room helpers. Others worked at the farm—students had their own crops to grow and took care of chickens and dairy cows. Everyone learned to be self-sufficient. "We didn't think we were mistreated," Toledo told me, "even though we were always under supervision and being hollered at." It just seemed natural, and he got used to it.

When Toledo was in the seventh grade, he was assigned to work at the repair shop, where students repaired shoes for their fellow students and harnesses for the school farm. Toledo was in this shop for three years and became proficient at this work.

Next, Toledo was assigned to the engineers, who stoked cinder blocks between the furnaces at night. It was hard work and they were always hungry while working. When he was in the tenth grade, the school started the art department, and that was when Toledo took his first art lessons.

After Toledo graduated from high school in 1935, he enrolled in the College of Fine Arts at the University of New Mexico. However, he had to drop out after two years due to lack of funds. When he later reenrolled, it was in art education and he received his bachelor's degree in art in 1951. He continued doing graduate work while teaching, and in 1955 earned his master's degree in art education.

Commenting on his experience with such teachers as Mala Sedillo Brewster, Edward Del Dosso, and Kenneth Adams, Toledo said, "I seemed to discourage my professors because I really was not conscious of perspective. I appreciated perspective, but I couldn't make myself draw angles and foreshortened areas of the human body as they would have desired me to. But I worked on it because that made for good grades."

With his master's degree he began to teach art at the Santa Fe Indian School. But this school was replaced by a national Indian art school called the Institute of American Indian Arts and Toledo was not entirely happy with the new school. Consequently, in the summer of 1956, he applied to a program offered by the Indian Health Service which trained health education specialists in Tuba City, Arizona. Following this brief course he was assigned to Fort Yates, North Dakota, with the Indian Health Service.

In 1959, Toledo was transferred again, this time to Pine Ridge, South Dakota, and remained there until June 1964. From there he was assigned to the Service Unit at Laguna Pueblo until 1971. While at Laguna he participated in many of the tribal dancing activities and easily learned many Laguna songs because he had already known the Keresan language from childhood.

At this time, in order to advance in his employment, Toledo went to the University of California at Berkeley to study for another master's degree—in the field of comprehensive health planning. He completed this course in 1972, receiving his third degree. With this accomplishment he was transferred to the Albuquerque Service Unit as a tribal liaison officer in health. Now he finally was able to live in his home at Jemez Pueblo.

Toledo was with this service unit until he retired in 1976, to devote more time to art and other activities. Toledo was always interested in many areas of culture. In 1960, when he was offered a small part in the movie called *Flap*, he began a new phase in his life and a different type of involvement with the general public. Following his retirement, Toledo began to work in movies. Along with his natural acting abilities were his distinct pueblo features with long hair and chongo—that attracted moviemakers. He appeared with Anthony Quinn in *The Man and the City*, in which Quinn played a mayor of a city with ethnic problems, and Toledo was a pueblo governor. This movie was filmed partly at Isleta Pueblo. Some of the other movies that he was involved in were *Bobby Joe and the Outlaws, The Legend of the Lone Ranger, Gambler 3, Nightwing,* and *The Trackers.*

Toledo also appeared in a well-known pizza commercial. Originally intended to be shown only in California, it was so funny and appealing that it was aired in many other regions as well. The scene showed him dressed in his pueblo costume eating a pizza, walking away, saying, "I am going back to my native country, Italy."

In addition to all his other accomplishments, Toledo became a well-known storyteller. As a pueblo person who grew up in a pueblo world with little Anglo-American influence, Toledo heard many pueblo legends and Coyote stories in his early years. As a result, near the end of his life Toledo and his wife appeared at conferences called "Coyote Gathers His People" where Toledo retold childhood stories of Coyote. These gatherings were organized and conducted by Larry Littlebird, Santo Domingo-Laguna, of Santa Fe to articulate interactions of ancient and modern lifeways. Toledo was specially honored at one of the gatherings.

Toledo, or Stia-na, and Amelita Toya of the Coyote clan, both descendants of Pecos Pueblo, were married at Jemez Pueblo on August 2, 1938, the feast day of Pecos descendants. The Toledos have been blessed with eight children, seven of whom are still living. Their son Steven tragically drowned in 1957. Their other children are: Jane T. Leonard; Angelina T. Defender of South Dakota, the eldest, who has three children and three grandchildren; Allen Rey, an attorney, who also has three children and three grandchildren; Wilma T. Tapia, a nurse; Mary T. Tang, a Ph.D. who has three children; Michael, a teacher, with one child; and James Ernest, the youngest, who has one child. Toledo and his wife have eleven grandchildren and six great-grandchildren as of this writing.

As an Indian artist, Toledo had a commitment to communicate a message to the younger generation, as well as to the non-Indian world, through the Indian life portrayed in his paintings. Because of his involvement in Jemez dances, Toledo vividly remembered the details of costumes and tried to portray the dance figures accurately in his art. The solemn expressions of his dancers convey the seriousness of the Prayer, or Thanksgiving, dance—prayers for rainfall in a desert environment, and thanksgiving for rain and harvests granted by nature. Because of his knowledge of the Pueblo Indian lifestyle, the meanings of dances and songs, and his ability in the English language, Toledo was chosen to serve as master of ceremonies for the Indian Pueblo Cultural Center and as an announcer at the Indian Village at the New Mexico State Fair.

Like many of the early Indian artists, Toledo is often imitated by the younger generation and even by non-Indian artists. Of all the murals that he has done, one of the most popular is on the east wall of the patio at the Indian Pueblo Cultural Center in Albuquerque; it portrays a Tewa Basket Dance.

During the tricentennial commemoration of the Pueblo Revolt of 1680, in August 1980 at San Juan Pueblo, Toledo had a heart attack. He was rushed to a hospital, where he underwent a coronary bypass operation. When he was released from the hospital, he resumed his usual pace of activity for the next ten years. After that, his health began to fail him, although he persisted in his work nevertheless. A few years later, after an evening Bible study session the family was returning to the village. Toledo wanted to be driven around the pueblo, and the family complied. Once they reached home Toledo went to bed and never woke up again. Thus, on April 1, 1994, the American Indian world lost one of its pioneers.

CHAPTER 25

Joe H. Herrera
Cochiti Pueblo

For many years it was the policy of the Bureau of Indian Affairs, dictated by higher administration and lawmakers, to eliminate the culture of the American Indians. Fortunately, the policy apparently did not affect the Pueblo Indians of the Southwest as much as it did other tribes. The Pueblo Indian people have been able to practice their native religion and live in the manner of their choosing.

People who did not grow up in a pueblo cannot fully appreciate the benefits of living within the pueblo culture. A pueblo man who has given expression to his cultural heritage in a unique fashion and thereby gained recognition and renown is Joe H. Herrera of Cochiti. Even as a young boy, he had begun to develop his own artistic style of painting pueblo ceremonial figures and dancers.

This style of artwork had its genesis in his village where he, like many pueblo Indian youngsters, longed to be a Koshare or a Kwi-reina member, the two clown societies. When Herrera was about nine years old, he was accepted by the Kwi-reina society and initiated into membership a year later. He participated with other society members in the dances of his people. Later, he drew on many of his childhood memories of ceremonies and costumes in creating his pictures of Pueblo Indian dancers. Eventually he achieved worldwide recognition for both the substance and the style of his paintings.

Herrera, or See-ru (meaning "Bluebird"), was born at Cochiti Pueblo on May 17, 1922. His mother, Tonita Peña, or Quah-Ah, meaning "White Shell Beads" in Tewa, from San Ildefonso Pueblo, was herself a well-known painter. From his mother comes See-Ru's clan identification, which is the Turquoise clan. His father, who died when See-Ru was one month old, was Felipe Herrera of Cochiti.

Herrera's mother had attended the Santa Fe Indian School, where she learned to draw and paint. When he was eight or nine years old, Herrera used to watch his mother paint, chasing flies away from her paintings. By the time Herrera attended the Santa Fe Indian School, he had his mind made up that he would be an artist like his famous mother.

Herrera began his education at the Cochiti Pueblo Day School. During the fourth and fifth grades, he attended St. Catherine's Indian School in Santa Fe. Because of an illness, he returned to Cochiti and was out of school for a year. Later, he reenrolled and finished the sixth grade at Cochiti.

The following year, he returned to the Santa Fe Indian School. After his two years at St. Catherine's, he was able to speak English, and boarding school life was no problem for him. Fortunately for Herrera, at that time the Santa Fe Indian School had an art program that was second to none. Dorothy Dunn was the dominant force behind many fledgling Indian artists and the paramount figure responsible for encouraging young artists to draw on their culture and develop the traditional style of flat art that is recognized as Indian. Such cultural emphasis on artistic style thrived under her supervision. Geronima Cruz Montoya of San Juan Pueblo, who had recently graduated from the same school, was assisting Dunn when Herrera became an eighth grader at the school. Today, Herrera credits both of these women with helping him develop his talent.

After several years of instruction in art, when Herrera was a sophomore in high school, a few of the promising student artists were commissioned to do murals for Maisel's Indian Trading Post in Albuquerque. Among the artists were Apaches, Navajos, and Pueblo Indians. Olive Rush in Santa Fe, a world-renowned artist, directed the painting of the murals. She also helped the artists, and, with Dorothy Dunn and Geronima Cruz Montoya, did so well in instructing that the majority of the mural painters eventually became recognized Indian artists. Today, those murals remain an outstanding attraction at this famous Indian Trading Post.

Besides the four women artists in his life, Herrera was highly influenced by his stepfather, Epitacio Arquero of Cochiti Pueblo and Reginald O. Downey, his advisor at the Santa Fe Indian School. Downey's technique, rapport, and charisma made him an outstanding advisor who was probably responsible for many students' success later in life. In addition to his focus on art, Herrera also played varsity basketball when he was a student at the Santa Fe Indian School. In addition, he served on the student council as a school commissioner.

Herrera graduated in May 1940 and joined the armed forces in October 1941. Once in the service he was sent to the Radar Operators Training School near Tacoma, Washington, and from there transferred to the East Coast for flight training. Afterward he was stationed in Brazil and later Puerto Rico. His squadron patrolled the Atlantic Ocean and the Caribbean Sea and also shuttled between Brazil and Africa.

After contracting a tropical disease, Herrera was transferred to Santa Monica, California, in 1944 for rest and recreation at the Delmar Hotel overlooking the Pacific Ocean. Following a month of rest, Herrera volunteered for overseas duty again. However, before he could be assigned to a squadron, he became ill once more and was hospitalized for a month. To his disappointment, he was rejected for further overseas duty and grounded because of the effects of the illness. He was then posted to a radar control center and later assigned to duty with Special Services and the USO, receiving his honorable discharge in November 1945.

After the war, Herrera returned to Cochiti, where he farmed and began to paint seriously. During this period, he married Julia Paisano of Old Laguna, and they had two children, Joseph and Yvonne. In the summer of 1947, Kenneth Chapman of the State Museum in Santa Fe asked Herrera to come to Santa Fe to work with him on Southwest pottery research. There Herrera was employed to draw exact reproductions of ancient Southwest Indian pottery, which was being studied intensively. After two years of this work, Herrera realized that his chances for a better life would be improved with a college education. Consequently, he took advantage of the GI Bill and enrolled at the University of New Mexico with the goal of a degree in secondary education.

After four years of hard work, Herrera received his bachelor of arts degree in May 1953. He was immediately hired by the Albuquerque Public School system to teach art at Highland High School. After three years at Highland, he was assigned temporarily to the State Department of Education in Santa Fe as a guidance and placement officer in the division of Indian education. Eventually, he resigned from the Albuquerque Public School System to work full time with Indian high school students throughout the state under the State Department of Education.

In May 1968 Herrera became an assistant director of the division of Indian Education. A month later he became chief of the Human Services Development Program of the State Employment Commission. In this position, he was in charge of twenty-one employees located throughout the state whose job it was to assist Indian people in securing jobs.

It is the dream of most American Indian college students to return to their reservations and help their people after graduation from college, and Herrera was no exception. After earning his degree in May 1953, Herrera was elected to serve out the unexpired term of Popovi Da, who had been secretary of the All Pueblo Council when he died. The following year Herrera was reelected and eventually served as secretary of the council for fourteen years, until February 18, 1967. He began serving during the tenure of the Chairman Martin Vigil of Tesuque Pueblo and also served with John C. Rainer of Taos Pueblo and Domingo Montoya of Sandia Pueblo. During those years, the All Pueblo Council did not have an offi-

Joe Herrera, circa 1942.

cial office, and Herrera had to work out of his home and visit the chairmen at their homes to discuss business.

Not only has Herrera been involved in work with the Pueblo Indian people, he has also been very active with the National Congress of American Indians. He was elected to serve as the Gallup area vice-president for NCAI on three occasions—in 1966, 1967, and 1969.

For three years, Herrera also served as chairman of the governing board of the Sandoval County Indian Pueblos Community Action Program. And for his pueblo, he was the chairman of the Cochiti Development Committee. This committee was an arm of the Tribal Council working with outside interest groups on economic development for the benefit of Cochiti Pueblo. An example of its work is the Cochiti Lake project on the Rio Grande near the village. In addition, for five summers Herrera was in charge of a Cochiti dance group that entertained in the Indian village at Disneyland in Los Angeles.

On the state level, Herrera was a member of the State Advisory Council for Vocational Education and the New Mexico American Revolution Bicentennial Commission. He was appointed to the latter organization by Governor David Cargo. The All Indian Pueblo Council appointed him to the board of the Southwest Indian Polytechnic Institute in Albuquerque.

On the local level Herrera served for many years on the Santa Fe Fiesta Council and for seven years was a newscaster of Indian news on radio station KTRC. Herrera carried all these responsibilities while working for the state—and continuing to pursue his art.

A special memento that Herrera is very proud of is a pen used by President Lyndon Johnson to sign Senate Bill 1648 of the 89th Congress, which created the Four Corners Development and Regional Planning Commission. As an officer of the All Indian Pueblo Council, Herrera had testified before Congress in support of S.B. 1648. The following is part of his speech to the legislators:

> The Regional Action Planning Commission will play an important part in the economic development of the Indian reservations. The rate of Indian unemployment is ten times that of the national average, and on some reservations it is almost total. Lack of opportunity, lack of sufficient education to take job training, and the lack of training so essential in these days of increasing technological advancement, cause the Indian to be unemployed and underemployed and result in a very low annual income.
>
> Federal financial assistance, including grants for the development of reservation facilities, establishing of industries and enterprises, particularly where there are self-help features, should do much to allevi-

ate poverty and to help the Indian people become self-sufficient. It will, indeed, as Section 2 states, "enable such areas to help themselves achieve lasting improvement and enhance the domestic prosperity by the establishment of stable and diversified local economies and improved local conditions. . . ."

We wholeheartedly support the view that such assistance should be preceded by and consistent with sound, long-range economic planning; and that under the provisions of this Act, new employment opportunities should be created by developing and expanding new and existing public works and other facilities and resources rather than by merely transferring jobs from one area of the United States to another.

Under the prior program of the Federal Public Works Administration, sufficient thought was not given to planning; it was a crash program, under which insufficient funds were granted for a project that had to be completed by a certain date. It was a case of too little too hurriedly, and because of this, comparatively few Indians were employed. Contractors "had to get the job done," and they brought in their own crews in the interest of speed.

That program, when it was before the Congress, at first didn't even include the Indian tribes; it was amended later so that Indians could participate. We hope that in this bill, due attention will be paid and consideration given to the needs of the impoverished Indians, whom the president has said are the neediest of all this nation's minorities. What is needed, therefore, is not stopgap legislation, but a law that will make it possible to recognize the economic needs of the tribes and put into effect a program that will not only develop the reservation economy, but enable the Indians to do things for themselves, to be trained so that they can take jobs on their reservations.

For too long it has been the practice to do the planning without consulting Indians, who are the ones most vitally concerned, and in too many cases, do the work for them and then hand it to them.

It is difficult for the Indian, whose education averages only half that of the rest of the population, whose health is only two-thirds as good, and whose economy is only one-fourth that of the nation at large, to bring to a job the comprehension and understanding of those who are more familiar with the English language.

There are some 650,000 Indians in the United States, but they are an important minority. They have a love for their country which is unsurpassed by any segment of our population, because this is (or was) their land, and they venerate it as a gift from the Great Spirit and from the Mother of all Creation. You find no subversives, no communists, among the Indians; their record of service to their country in time of war is one to be proud of, and just as they were numbered among those who were immortalized in the raising of the flag on Iwo Jima, so they are numbered among the great ones in American history. Too little is known of what the Indian has meant to this great nation. And yet, they have suffered more than any others at the hands of their government in the past. This Senate Bill 1648 makes us proud of our country, proud of its evident intention to improve the lot of its impoverished minorities, and we are grateful to the Congress for this consideration of the needy ones in America. . . .[1]

Soon after Herrera testified, President Johnson signed the bill, and the pen he used was mailed to Herrera.

As an artist, Herrera has won numerous awards throughout the country. He has won first prizes and grand prizes at the Philbrook Art Center in Tulsa, Oklahoma; the Gallup Inter-Tribal Ceremonial; art shows in Arizona and Wyoming; the New Mexico State Fair; and the Indian Market in Santa Fe. As the crown of all these art awards, in 1954 Herrera was presented the Palme Academique, the highest art award given by the French government, during the Gallup Inter-Tribal Ceremonial. His paintings have been exhibited in France, Spain, Germany, England, Italy, the Chicago Art Institute, and the National Gallery in Washington, D.C.

Herrera says that he did not paint seriously after 1967 because of the many other demands on his time. But after retiring in 1983, he took it up again and sold some new works. He found that his eyesight was failing, however, so he was forced to retire from painting also.

Now he has returned to his home at Cochiti Pueblo, where his grandchildren visit him. His daughter Yvonne lives in Santa Fe and brings her four children and sometimes Herrera's two great-grandsons who live at San Juan Pueblo. Yvonne is also an artist in her own right. She graduated from the Institute of American Indian Arts in Santa Fe while it was still on the Santa Fe Indian School campus where her father and grandmother took their art training.

Herrera's son Joseph graduated from the University of Colorado in Boulder and went to work with Honeywell. Recently he took a job with another company in Chicago, where he makes his home with his wife and a daughter, Kate, who is a student at Loyola of New Orleans, Louisiana.

In addition to becoming an outstanding artist, Herrera ultimately found satisfaction in serving his Indian people—locally, statewide, and nationally.

NOTES

1. Cited from the personal papers of Joe H. Herrera.

CHAPTER 26

Moses Peña
Nambé Pueblo

Although Moses Peña made many contributions during his lifetime as a Nambé Pueblo governor, he is remembered especially for his work with children and for passing the Tewa language and cultural and religious traditions on to younger generations.

Peña, whose Tewa Indian name was Ogatsa, or White Shell, was born in 1899, during a period when the number of people living at Nambé Pueblo had fallen to fewer than one hundred. Today Nambé numbers about six hundred people living on a 19,124-acre reservation less than twenty miles north of Santa Fe. The community is blessed with a year-round stream of water, a lake, and spectacular views of the Sangre de Cristo Mountains. It is said the word *Nambé* means "People of the Round Earth."

Moses Peña was the son of Alcario Peña, a farmer, and Perfilia Peña, a well-known potter whose work was sold and traded outside the Pueblo. Moses Peña grew up traditionally, learning all the Nambé Indian prayers, songs, and dances, and was active in religious observances throughout his life.

Interviewed in 1970, Peña spoke of what he remembered as a child and young man and about the many changes he had seen over the course of his life.

Nambé Pueblo, with its plentiful water and good farming and grazing land, had great value to the Spanish during the colonial era. Non-Indians who were given grazing privileges later claimed the land, and much Nambé land was lost as a result. Today the Pueblo retains some three hundred acres of land suitable for farming, with the rest divided between open grazing land and noncommercial forest.

Moses Peña recalled that in the early years of the twentieth century the main occupation of the Nambé was still farming. "We raised what we raise today," Peña said, "corn, wheat, chiles, beans, squash." Nambé farmers sold corn and wheat to their Spanish neighbors, particularly to a little store below the Pueblo where supplies such as coffee and sugar could be purchased.

In those days Nambé land covered a much larger area and deer and elk were still fairly plentiful. Nambé men occasionally hunted to help feed their families and the community. For the young boys and the elders, however, hunting had a different purpose. Moses Peña described expeditions to the Nambé waterfall when he was a child. "When we were young," he said, "we used to go together on Sunday. . . . We always enjoyed going with the old men. We used to go out there with bow and arrow to hunt rabbits. After a snow—about three feet [deep]—we would hunt rabbit right around the cedar bushes." Most of the old men and boys of the Pueblo participated in these hunts. "We all went out together, old men and the young boys," he said, "and cooked up there and ate the rabbit ourselves." The point of it was enjoyment, just to be together. "The old men's idea was to go out there and teach us how to hunt." Moses Peña remembers the rabbit hunts as a wonderful opportunity to learn from the elders. Because of the changes that later transformed Pueblo life, he felt especially fortunate to have had the chance to learn traditional Indian ways during his youth.

Peña remembers that during that period the traditional Nambé crafts were gradually dying out. His mother was one of the last potters to make the traditional micaceous Nambé ware. "She was busy with her pottery night and day," he recalled. "You have to work at the pottery night and day so it won't dry out." According to Peña, his sister Josefa was the last of the older potters working in Nambé. In recent decades younger Nambé artists have recovered the old methods and are working to revive traditional arts within the community.

Because both their parents were gradually losing their eyesight, Moses Peña and his brothers spent most of their younger years working the family farm, taking care of their home, and tending the livestock. When he was fourteen years old, Peña started his schooling, attending the U.S. Indian School in Santa Fe. Since he had spent all his early life at Nambé, he spoke Tewa and Spanish but not English and had to learn it quickly. In spite of this problem, his teachers apparently saw that he had ability and advanced him three grades in one day. Moses finished the eighth grade there, the highest level the school offered during that period.

The Indian School was poorly funded at the time. Although the school owned a very small farm, or garden, which the children worked, food was always scarce. The children did other work to maintain the school and were taught vocational skills. The school followed the usual policy of stripping Indian children of their culture in order to force them to assimilate. They were required to wear uniforms and march to classes and forbidden to speak their native languages. The boys' hair was cut short. Boys and girls were schooled separately, and the children were allowed to return home only once or twice during the school year.

Peña said that many children ran away from the school; others coped with these pressures and with isolation from their homes by gradually becoming indifferent to Indian culture. "At that time," he remembered, "we were not much interested in the Indian ways. We didn't know any better."

Peña had become active in Pueblo affairs by 1920, but also often spent part of the year working on ranches and farms in Colorado. In 1924 the U.S. government, through the Pueblo Lands Board, was trying to persuade Pueblo Indian tribes to accept allotments of land in exchange for cash. Peña said that a lot of the pueblo governors favored the idea because the government talked about reestablishing Indian rights to some of the lost land, but very little was recovered. Later, when Moses Peña was governor of Nambé, the government admitted it had wrongfully taken land from several northern pueblos, including Nambé. Peña attempted to recover the land, but the government claimed that legally and financially it could only reimburse the tribes for it.

Moses Peña served three terms as lieutenant governor of Nambé Pueblo between 1927 and 1931, and seven terms as governor between 1934 and 1949. Like other pueblo leaders, he worked hard for land and water rights and to preserve sovereignty. He also argued against hastily adopting programs that were new and strange to the traditional way of life. He believed that such developments as the American style courts, law enforcement, administration, and elections would allow both sovereignty and traditional values to be chipped away little by little.

In speaking of his official position in the Pueblo, Peña remarked, "Once you become governor, you walk on the edge of a knife and everyone is your child." He recognized how hard it was for the governor to pay enough attention to Pueblo affairs while working to support his family. Since he did not marry and have children, Peña felt he had more time to devote to the community.

As he grew older he became more and more concerned with the loss of the traditional Indian ways. He was especially concerned that young people were not being taught what they needed to know to carry on these traditions, and was encouraged to see young Indians becoming increasingly interested in traditional singing and dancing.

"The older you get the more you realize you are proud to be Indian," he said. "But I think today [it's] the young people [who] are more interested in going back to Indian ways." He felt they needed more advice and counseling in Indian values, culture, and secrets, however. "Then," said Peña, "it will be up to them to follow the way they choose." He himself was given the chance to learn at a time when the older men and women of the community gave tradition greater importance. "But," he said, "I should have listened more."

He did not mention that one reason many young people were becoming more interested in traditional culture had to do with Peña himself. He instructed Nambé children and teenagers in traditional dances, songs, and drumming and gave informal classes in the Tewa language. He used storytelling as a way of teaching both the language and the cultural traditions that had been passed on to him as a child. Word got around the other northern Tewa-speaking pueblos, and soon children were coming from Pojoaque, San Juan, San Ildefonso, and Santa Clara to learn Tewa, dance, hear the old stories, and enjoy spending time with "Uncle Mo," as he was affectionately called.

His nephew Gilbert Peña, who was born in 1947 and lived with his uncle until 1968, remembers that Moses always talked about the language and culture. He told the children stories about the emergence of the Nambé and instructed them in religious ceremony and the religious significance of the traditions that were a part of every aspect of daily life. Moses Peña also worked closely with teachers in the Pueblo after the day school was established, to make them more sensitive to the needs of the Pueblo. One of his major achievements in this area was to persuade school authorities to make attendance more flexible, so that children could be excused from school for the traditional family and community observances that are so vital to the life of the community.

Gilbert Peña would later be elected Nambé governor for seven terms. His uncle prepared him to take on the responsbilities of the office and instructed him in the traditional ways of dealing with state and federal government. Gilbert currently lives in Nambé, in Moses' parents' house, and named his son, Brian Moses Peña, now 21 years old, after the man who was his mentor for so many years. Gilbert Peña is now Dean of Students at the Santa Fe Indian School, which has radically changed since his uncle was a student there. Now owned and operated by the nineteen pueblos of New Mexico, it incorporates Indian perspectives, issues, and culture in a modern curriculum; encourages student involvement with home communities; and has achieved national recognition for academic excellence.

When Gilbert Peña was elected vice-chairman of the All Indian Pueblo Council in 1980 and chairman in December 1984 until December 1986, he benefitted from Moses Peña's experience and wisdom. His uncle asked him to remember that he would be working for the nineteen pueblos, not just Nambé. "The agenda you carry on is their agenda, not yours," he said. He advised Gilbert to get to know all the council people, govern with respect for all, and work for agreement and consensus.

Moses Peña died in 1988 after a lifetime of dedicated service. He is especially remembered for the joy he brought to young people and for his invaluable work in helping them reclaim their heritage.

He understood the difficulties facing young people who are educated outside the Pueblo and all those whose work takes them between the Indian and white worlds. "Be careful when you travel," he used to advise Gilbert. "Keep the tradition even when you leave the Pueblo. Always do your prayers and offerings."

CHAPTER 27

George Rivera
Pojoaque Pueblo

I t is said that, some years ago, a man on a fishing trip in northern New Mexico left Santa Fe early without stopping for his morning coffee. As he was passing through Pojoaque Reservation, he saw a fast food sign and pulled over. He had an idea he was in Indian country but was not sure just where. There weren't many signs of civilization. As he settled down at the counter, he asked the waitress, "What is the name of this place, and say it real slow?" The waitress answered, "Lot-ta-bur-ger."

Whether this story is true or not, it nevertheless illustrates what many small Indian villages have faced since the arrival of Europeans. When Coronado and his Spanish entourage first arrived in Pueblo Indian country, there were so many villages that the intruders could not visit all of them. Since that time many have died out, becoming part of an almost forgotten history. One of those that disappeared was Pojoaque Pueblo.

Pojoaque had been abandoned by 1700 and the land granted to two Spaniards by Governor Pedro Rodriguez Cubero. The Indians resettled Pojoaque in 1707 and bought back their lands, paying for it with corn, tanned buckskins, woolen blankets, chickens, and the loan of two horses. When another Spaniard occupied the land in 1715, the Pueblo appealed to the *Protector de Indios,* who decided in favor of the Pojoaque tribe, arguing that the land had long been irrigated and had belonged to the Pueblo since the Pueblo Revolt.[1]

The already small population of Pojoaque was nearly wiped out during the influenza epidemic of 1918. Some of the survivors journeyed to southern Colorado to work in the fields, while others apparently settled in nearby pueblos. When the Pueblo Lands Board began looking into the land rights of the various reservations, it found a Pojoaque Reservation with no inhabitants, and with only the walls of an old Catholic church. Notices were put in the newspapers asking Pojoaque tribal people to return and claim their land; otherwise it would be sold. Initially about a dozen people returned, some from nearby pueblos. Pojoaque was officially reestablished in 1932. A Tribal Council was elected, and the long process of restoration began.

The name "Pojoaque" comes from the Tewa word Po-Suwae-geh, which means "water drinking place." Pojoaque Pueblo is located approximately sixteen miles north of Santa Fe along Highway 84/285. Today, a population of about 250 people lives on the 12,000-acre reservation. Since 1932 significant changes have occurred, and the pueblo is enjoying a dramatic renaissance. The revitalizing of Pojoaque arts and crafts owes much to the artistic work and development ideas of a young man named George Rivera.

Rivera was born at the Indian Hospital in Santa Fe on March 19, 1964. His mother is Dora Viarrial from Pojoaque, his father, Joe Rivera from Santa Fe. His parents separated when Rivera was only a young boy. After living with his mother in Long Beach, California, for a while, he moved to Pojoaque, where he stayed with his aunt Josephina and attended the elementary school. In his early teens Rivera went to live with his father in Santa Fe and attended high school there, graduating in 1982. This school was where Rivera developed his love for art, in part because of his art teacher, Phil Karshis. Although Rivera had considered entering the military or finding work in the construction field, Karshis convinced him that art could be his vocation.

Subsequently, Rivera enrolled at the Institute of American Indian Arts (IAIA) in Santa Fe. In 1984 he received his associate of fine arts degree in three-dimensional design. Following this he went to Oakland, California, where he received his bachelor of fine arts in 1986, specializing in ceramics and drawing at the California College of Arts and Crafts. During 1985 he was also able to study for a semester at Lacoste School of Arts in Provence, France, where he concentrated on stone sculpture and drawing. The location of the school afforded Rivera an opportunity to travel to many of the arts centers of Western Europe: Rome, Florence, Madrid, Barcelona, Paris, and London. He spent many hours in museums and galleries, where he observed and studied intensively the paintings of the European masters. Rivera then returned to Lacoste in 1987 to accept a teaching apprenticeship in sculpture. During that time he took on a second job as an apprentice to a master carver. Rivera gives this teacher much credit since the apprenticeship gave him considerable experience in monumental sculpture and design. At one time he and the master carver worked on a sculpture the size of a large house. After spending two years in France, Rivera returned home in 1988. For a time Rivera found it difficult to create artworks that were not influenced by European styles. It took about two years of going to pueblo dances, sketching, and working with other pueblo artists before he was able to

George Rivera, 1997. Photograph © by Marcia Keegan.

create work that looked like anything other than Greek, Roman, or Picassoesque.

While traveling abroad and studying the evolution of great artists, such as Michelangelo and Leonardo da Vinci, Rivera was influenced by their need to create meaningful art for the people of their homelands. These masters portrayed their deepest beliefs in religious and public centers for all to experience. As a result, Rivera began to consider ways of giving art to his community, of establishing something he could leave behind as an expression of Tewa culture. When he returned home, he came up with an idea that has become significant in promoting art and culture of the northern New Mexico region—the idea of a Tewa arts center.

Rivera began to talk to other pueblo artists who had similar ideas about promoting Tewa art and culture and together they developed a Tewa arts center to be named Poeh Center. *Poeh* is the Tewa word for "pathway" or path to be taken in life. Pojoaque was chosen as the location of the center because it is situated along a major traffic route. The Poeh Center, which opened in November 1991, represents Tewa people from Nambé, - Pojoaque, San Ildefonso, San Juan, Santa Clara, and Tesuque. Upon completion, the center is to be a veritable showcase of Tewa culture and history, with replicas of ancient structures ranging from multistoried towers to pit houses. Besides the museum, gallery, and shopping center, there are future plans for an amphitheater, working studios, a research center, an artist demonstration space, and a traditional cooking area.

Rivera is married to Kyu-hee of Korea, who is also an artist. They have two children, a son, Kwang Tsireh, and a daughter, Kwang Po Queen. The home they built includes a studio-workshop made from adobe. Since the studio was completed, Rivera has begun creating monumental clay and stone sculpture. For the first piece, he had friends help him dig and process about two tons of clay from the mountains.

Although Rivera is a serious artist, he also finds time to serve his pueblo and the arts community. He is lieutenant governor of Pojoaque Pueblo. He also served as president of the Board of Directors of Pojoaque Economic Development. As executive director for the Poeh Center, he oversees construction of additional buildings and the operation of business activities, including crafts sales and the museum. Even though Rivera sometimes thinks of retiring from all work not related to his art so that he can devote all his time to it, community involvement is important to him, and he wants to oversee projects until they are completed. One such project is the kiva now under construction at Pojoaque. Tribal members have talked about rebuilding the kiva ever since Pojoaque was reestablished, but actual construction did not begin until recently. Although the kiva is not yet completely finished, the pueblo was able to use it on their feast day in 1993.

Rivera says that he developed leadership skills by applying what he learned as a teenager in Santa Fe. He worked at the Santa Fe Boys' Club from the age of thirteen and by age eighteen was managing the club. His duties included serving as a lifeguard and art teacher. As a Boy Scout leader, he also took children on week-long camping trips.

Rivera also learned skills from many friends and mentors such as artists, musicians, politicians, and a priest. Someone once gave him some advice about advice, which he remembers and practices: "When someone gives you advice, you don't need to practice all of it, but you should take and use what is relevant for you."

One of the main objectives Rivera is striving for is to encourage pueblo people to build their homes with adobe. He thinks that building with adobe gives people self-esteem and allows them to learn that they are capable of building their own homes in their traditional way. Rivera also believes that the cultural preservation of buildings, Indian dances, and other native arts and culture is very important—an understandable belief considering how close the people of Pojoaque Pueblo came to losing their aboriginal land and culture.

Talking about taking a leadership role in community life, Rivera said, "No matter what it is we do, whether it is to dance, or create art, or demonstrate how we handle business relations, we need to believe strongly in ourselves, to be confident in what we do so our people will have confidence, too."

When I first met Rivera, he was much younger. As I sat talking with him at the Poeh Center, I was pleased to see how far he has traveled and how much he has learned since he was in my ethnohistory class at IAIA. Now a great leader and a well-known sculptor, he continues to contribute in unique ways to the betterment of Pojoaque Pueblo and the neighboring Tewa people.

NOTE

1. Malcom Ebright, "Advocates for the Oppressed Indians: Genizaros and Their Spanish Advocates in New Mexico, 1700–1786," *New Mexico Historical Review* 71, no. 4 (October 1996); 312.

CHAPTER 28

Gregory Cajete
Santa Clara Pueblo

Santa Clara Pueblo is located twenty-four miles north of Santa Fe and borders the town of Española. Historically, members of a Santa Clara family played key parts in the Pueblo Revolt of 1680 and the later uprising of 1696. A man by the name of Domingo Naranjo is described by the Spaniards as playing a leading role in the first revolt while his son, Joseph Naranjo, acted as an interpreter, guide, and leader of the pueblo warriors who helped the Spaniards. Joseph's brother Lucas, on the other hand, is cited as the war captain who led the last uprising in 1696.

In modern times Santa Clara Pueblo has become well known in the art world. It is recognized particularly for the families of prize-winning potters who have earned international fame. Sarafina Tafoya and her daughter Margaret were among the first Indians to gain individual recognition for their art.

Although the younger generations have benefited from the recognition accorded the elders of the community, they continue to face discrimination based on the stereotyping of minorities. There are numerous stories about young American Indians who, when they began their education in the public schools, were automatically placed with the slow learners because of preconceived notions about their abilities. Such was the case of Gregory Cajete, Ph.D., of Santa Clara Pueblo.

I interviewed Cajete, an outstanding Indian educator, artist, consultant, and writer, in his office at the Institute of American Indian Arts in Santa Fe, where he teaches. He had just edited the second volume of *Visions and Life Journeys,* which depicts the memories and thoughts of contemporary Indian people of New Mexico. This publication was produced under the auspices of the New Mexico Indian Education Association. The following is Cajete's short written account of his life; it reflects issues faced by Native Americans today.

Telling the story of one's life journey is tracing your footsteps backward through the people, events and places that have formed you. And, as we pause at each special memory we realize that we have indeed been formed by our encounters with the stories of others. Telling one's own story is a way to "remember to remember" who we are and to honor the special life that we have been given.

To remember is also a way to reknow and reclaim a part of our life. My personal recollections of my childhood and growing up in the context of my family and community are rich with warm memories, images, and sensations.

I was born at the Santa Fe Indian Hospital, September 23, 1952. My mother's name is Clara, and my grandmother's name was Maria. My first memories are of growing up in our family home on the Santa Clara Pueblo Reservation. I was raised in my grandmother's household, which included my aunts and uncles Alex, Frank, Pauline, and Manuel. My mother worked in Los Alamos, New Mexico, so I spent much of my time with my grandmother. My grandmother's frame of reference and values were deeply rooted in traditional pueblo life. It is these values along with Mother's caring thoughts that I now find deeply embedded in my perspective of. . . life and work. It is true that we are first shaped by the caring hands of our mothers!

. . .What I remember most about that time was always being with people, hearing talking, singing, and laughing. These are my first memories of family and community; just sounds, images, and the feeling of being safe and warm. I remember it was a good feeling!

. . .When I was about five, I remember going with my grandmother to visit with her friends and relatives in the pueblo. I remember those days vividly because each visit was an adventure. . . . I seem to remember everything and every place we visited during that year. It was the year before I started the first grade. I learned so much with my grandmother during that time before going to school. My grandmother was in every sense a matriarch, well known and respected in the pueblo as well as in nearby Hispanic villages. She was of a generation born before the turn of the century. Her world and frame of reference were therefore of old New Mexico, a time when pueblos seem to reflect a deeper expression of community. I remember helping old people of our pueblo plant and hoe their gardens. I remember sitting with the old ones during hot summer afternoons eating Indian cookies and listening to all their stories.

I remember gathering plants with my grandmother and other older women around the foothills near the pueblo. I remember playing with other children who came along with their grandmas and grandpas. I remember eating lots of watermelon and trout baked in a firepit with wild peppermint in Santa Clara canyon. Afterward, all the children would jump into the stream to play and try to catch tadpoles, and the old ones laughed and laughed.

I remember my grandmother telling me that all older people were my aunts and uncles and their children were my cousins and that I should always greet them as relatives and treat them kindly. I remember that everyone, young and old, shared food with one another. When we went to visit older people, we would take food, clothing, or some gift to give to them. We would return with fruit, vegetables, or other gifts. It was a form of reciprocal giving; that is how things got spread around. But that wasn't all—tools, shiny marbles, comic books, baseball cards, and hundreds of other things got spread around, too.

I remember always walking or riding somewhere. When my grandmother and I would attend a feast day at a neighboring pueblo, I remember the kindness with which we were received, especially by the other grandmas. In these visitations, I came to know the differences between the pueblos and other Indian people. I also gained a sense of the relationships within the greater pueblo world. I felt that, indeed, we were all related. I remember times sitting with my grandmother and other people in the "saints' house," a small cottonwood leaf-lined shelter set up in the main plaza especially for pueblo feast days. In the shelter many people, old and young, sat praying the rosary to the saints, visiting, talking about the news and of the "old days." In this way they reaffirmed their faith in a Christian god and simultaneously, the traditional sense of pueblo community, values and way of life. Pueblo life has always revolved around tradition and age-old practices.

I remember watching my grandma and other women and men of the pueblo replastering their houses with adobe mud, laughing and working as one body. I remember my grandmother and other aunts baking bread in pueblo ovens, and my cousin and I would sneak about trying to be the first to taste the fresh bread, pies, and cookies they left cooling near the oven. I remember those special feasts when all my family and relatives would gather at my grandmother's home or those times she and my mother would go to other homes to help them prepare for weddings, baptisms, or some other occasion.

These things still happen in pueblo communities today. But it is my earliest memories that still have the greatest vividness and remain within my heart. These memories are similar to those other pueblo people mention about growing up at that time. Our sense of community evolves over time in sync with the changes in our lives. Yet it is *our earliest memories that seem to form the foundation for our personal story. These early memories provide me with my sense of rootedness to place and community. There are, of course, memories of sadness and frustration with regard to my community. But, in all, I cannot remember a time when I didn't see things differently as a result of some communal activity or when I was not learning in some way. This is what impressed me about the strength and continuity of pueblo communities. The grandmas and grandpas still remind us today, as they did then, to celebrate our life, be happy with what we have, care for one another, be of good thoughts and words, help each other, and share the life that we have been given. They continually remind us to be happy that we are pueblo. In this way pueblo people continue to live, in our memories and in our personal stories.*

I received a good and very well-rounded education while attending public school in the Española Valley. Due to the return of lands to Santa Clara Pueblo as the result of the 1934 Indian Lands Bill, my grandmother was assigned land adjacent to the boundary with the city of Española. It was therefore more convenient to attend the public school, which was only a quarter of a mile away. I remember the first day my mother took me to school. I cried and cried because it was such a strange place, and I knew no one there. It took me a very long time to get used to school. I probably didn't say one word throughout the first grade. I really wasn't connected to education from first through the fourth grade. I was shy and quiet and usually ended up getting grouped with other Indian and Hispanic kids in the lowest academic group. This was fine with me since these kids were mostly my neighborhood playmates.

In spite of my disconnection at school, my mother was very supportive of my learning and helped me in many ways to keep up with my schoolwork. It wasn't until fourth grade that I somehow realized that school was a kind of game. I became connected to school once I learned the "rules of the game." I made the connection between the value placed on each student based on their achievement in school. In other words, I learned how to "compete," and I learned that I could be good at it. I excelled as a student from then on. I also had some excellent teachers who followed me from elementary through high school and cultivated my interest in art and science. By the time I was in high school, I was an honor roll student, in the college prep program, involved with athletics, science clubs, and art. I was especially interested in art and science, which I saw as being intimately related, although in school these disciplines were widely separated. My experiences through family and community had left me with an apprecia-

tion for art and nature. So, it was quite natural for me to maintain and cultivate these interests in school. In addition, my interest in art was encouraged by an art teacher named Florencio Montoya. He introduced me to . . . forms and concepts of art. I learned very early that art is a creative process that trains mind, spirit, and perception.

The summer after I graduated from high school I was selected to attend a summer college prep program at Phillips-Exeter Academy, a prep school that placed students at Harvard, Dartmouth, Princeton, Yale, and other Ivy League schools. This experience taught me several things which would later play a major role in my decision to become a teacher and greatly influence my work in Indian education. At Exeter I was introduced to a very self-absorbed Eurocentric social environment that did not understand or know how to honor who I was as a Pueblo Indian. I was faced with stereotypical, romanticized type casting typical of eastern educational efforts of that time to help "the poor Indian." Intellectually, I was the equal of any student there, but I felt alienated and lonely. Several Ivy League schools offered me scholarships in an attempt to recruit me to come to their school. However, because of my feeling of cultural disconnection, I decided to attend New Mexico Highlands University in Las Vegas, New Mexico. Highlands was close enough to allow me to return home often and maintain close ties to my family and community. Highlands also had an excellent reputation in the area of biology. I ended up taking a double major in biology and sociology and a double minor in art and secondary education.

I graduated from Highlands in 1974 and began teaching biology immediately thereafter at Las Vegas Robertson High School. My first year of teaching at Robertson gave me firm grounding in cross-cultural understanding and perspective. It was important for me to make learning about biology culturally meaningful for the students I was teaching. I tried lots of different things in my classes, looking for points of cultural connection with my students. I knew that many of the students had a rural background similar to mine, so I used stories about the land, plants, and animals of northern New Mexico as the foundations for my lessons in biology. I used northern New Mexico folklore about plants for experiential lessons related to ecology. I invited local ranch people into my classes to talk about plants and tell stories of their lives and experiences. Through this process of community-based science education, I gained a deep appreciation for the "groundedness" of New Mexico rural people in their traditions and the strength they derive from their relationship to the land. These first teaching experiences also increased my appreciation for the fact that everyone has a deeply embedded cultural base and frame of reference through which they learn, live, and gain meaning.

The following year, I began teaching at the Institute of American Indian Arts in Santa Fe, New Mexico. At IAIA, *I was given many opportunities to creatively explore my deepening interest in culturally based science education. During my many years of teaching at* IAIA, *I have been able to bring many of my ideas about teaching Indian students into being. In addition, I have been able to fine tune my thoughts regarding the integration of culture, science, and art. The exploration of these thoughts led me to the completion of my master's degree in secondary and adult education from the University of New Mexico in 1982 and my Ph.D. from International College University without Walls in 1986.*

My doctoral program under the auspices of International College was a true collaboration between myself and many excellent educators and creative thinkers. The way in which this experience enriched my understanding of art, science, culturally based education, and indigenous philosophy is beyond description. It went far beyond anything that I could have done or experienced within a traditional Ph.D. program at a mainstream university because the program honored who I was, my life experience, and the extensive creative work in the field that I had already done. My work in this program led to my writing a creative dissertation entitled "Science—A Native American Perspective: A Culturally Based Science Education Curriculum." This work has, in turn, formed the foundation for my most recent work, Look to the Mountain: An Ecology of Indigenous Education, *published by Kivaki Press, Durango, Colorado.*

Today, I do a variety of things. I am an Indian educator, artist, consultant, and writer. I continue to listen to and learn from the stories of the ways people come to know the natural world. And in listening, I hear the echoes of my own story. I continue to recognize the importance of honoring the fact that there is a unique story and process for learning for each person and each culture. This is why I continue to advocate for indigenous people and their stories, which are a meaningful foundation for their educational empowerment and self-determination. And my family and community of friends continue to be great resources of strength and support for me.

My story outlines a way of perception and creative orientation as it relates to education. In my teaching, I hope to plant seeds of thought and reflection as it relates to indigenous education and its groundedness in the basics of human nature. I believe it is a way of education that is pregnant with potential, not only for the transfor-

mation of contemporary Indian education, but for its profound possibilities for changing modern education as a whole. I believe that we, as Indian people, must develop the openness and courage to make creative leaps to find in our lives and our stories a transforming vision for our future and that of our children. My story expresses some of the experiences of being pueblo that I have come to know. My story is written as an Indian person to other Indian persons, and an educator to other educators. My story is written in support of Indian children, people, and communities. I hope my story will reaffirm their identity as native people and empower their strength, courage, creativity, and the contributions they have made and will make in the future. For me, education is an art of process, participation, making and nurturing life-giving relationships. Learning is a growth and life process. It is good to share one's life with good thought and intention. Be with Life!

In 1990, Cajete created Tewa Educational Consulting, a firm through which he offers workshops in art and science education, multiculturally based curriculum development, strategic planning, the creative process, and program development. He is also often called upon to discuss indigenous science as practiced historically by American Indians. In October 1994, he was one of the main speakers at a conference in Albuquerque on native plants, sponsored by the American Indian Science and Engineering Society of Boulder, Colorado, for American Indians from all areas of the United States and Canada.

Cajete is married to the former Meriam Patricia Trujillo of Taos Pueblo, and they have a teenage son, James. To honor his commitment to his pueblo community, Cajete served on the Tribal Council for one term in 1993. Currently, he is teaching at the University of New Mexico. As a change of pace from his many scholarly activities Cajete relaxes by painting and making ceramic sculptures and jewelry. Cajete, the young student who was once placed with the slow learners, has become an outstanding educator, artist, writer, and role model for Indian students.

REFERENCES

Gregory Cajete, *Visions and Life Journeys: Contemporary Indian People of New Mexico*, Vol. 1. Santa Fe, N.M.: New Mexico Indian Education Association, 1992.

Joe S. Sando, *Pueblo Nations: Eight Centuries of Pueblo Indian History.* Santa Fe, N.M.: Clear Light Publishers, 1992.

PART VI

The New Leadership: Innovation and Continuity

CHAPTER 29

George Blue Spruce, Jr.
San Juan and Laguna Pueblos

A member of the San Juan and Laguna tribes, George Blue Spruce, Jr. was born in Santa Fe, New Mexico, on January 16, 1931. His father was George Blue Spruce, Sr., a Laguna from Paguate, and his mother is Juanita Cruz of San Juan Pueblo.

In his formative years, Blue Spruce's world was shaped by activities at the Santa Fe Indian School campus, where his father taught woodworking, cabinet making, and drafting to Indian secondary school students. The Blue Spruce home was behind the woodworking shop and near the boys' dormitory. This writer can remember young Blue Spruce in those early days as a student in his father's shop. At the end of the school year, when the students were leaving the campus, they would put their room decorations, knickknacks, and trip memorabilia in the dormitory incinerator, and young Blue Spruce would be the first of the "campus brats" to "rescue" certain keepsakes for his room. When World War II began, young Blue Spruce was in his preteens. He would come into the workshop and build airplanes and tanks with scraps of wood.

Although his grandparents could neither read nor write, Blue Spruce went on to become an outstanding medical professional, inspired by his ambitious parents. As his mother stated in 1975, "We wanted more for our son than the government boarding school education that George, Sr., and I received." Fortunately for young George, his parents enrolled him in a local parochial school, St. Michael's College, which offered first through twelfth grade education. Locally it had the reputation of a college since it was one of the first schools in frontier New Mexico to offer classes beyond the eighth grade.

Blue Spruce's reservation-born parents were highly elated with his scholastic achievements; from the third grade and all through high school Blue Spruce never missed the honor roll. His parents had innocently accepted the common belief that Indian students were only capable of competing at a lower standard, and only at an Indian school.

Blue Spruce stated, "The fact that I was an Indian in a non-Indian school has presented moments of hardships." However, his high school years were filled with honors as he was elected class president in both his junior and senior years. In addition to his other successes, he was named the valedictorian of his senior class.

Along with his focus on academics, Blue Spruce participated in soapbox derbies and made his high school as well as his college tennis teams. In the 1970s, as a successful professional man, he continued to play whenever he could find a court available in the tennis-conscious Washington, D.C.-Maryland area. As a result, in 1977 he won the National Indian Tennis Championship; and more recently he won the Arizona Senior Olympics Gold Medal in 1987 in Phoenix, Arizona.

Reminiscing in his office in Bethesda, Maryland, where I first interviewed him in 1975, he stated that his interest in a medical profession came about midway through the ninth grade when he had a painful experience while being treated by a non-Indian dentist in one of the early Indian Health clinics and told his parents that as an Indian he would do a better job.

One of the civic leaders who caught Blue Spruce's attention during this period was a man whom the boys called Dr. Renfro. Renfro was involved in most of the teenage events sponsored by the Optimist Club of Santa Fe. Blue Spruce admired Renfro and wondered what his job was when he was not working with teenagers. When Blue Spruce learned that Renfro was a dentist Renfro became Blue Spruce's role model since he projected that a nice man could be a dentist. Blue Spruce decided then on a dental career for the purpose of improving the dental health care and treatment of Indian people.

During Blue Spruce's senior year in high school, the New Mexico Elks Club sponsored a scholastic achievement competition. Aware of his scholastic successes, the brothers who taught Blue Spruce at St. Michael's mailed his records to the Elks Club. George was one of two top competitors and was invited to attend the state Elks convention held at Carlsbad, New Mexico, that year. There Blue Spruce gave an acceptance speech for winning a 300 dollar scholarship, explaining his background and discussing his aspiration to become a dentist. His speech made a deep impression on the Elks. During the evening the Grand Exalted Ruler of the Elks made a plea for donations and the various lodges throughout the state pledged financial support for Blue Spruce's education.

That night Blue Spruce and his mother, who had accompanied him, were so excited they could hardly sleep. The Elks had pledged to finance tuition and books for his entire seven years of higher education. Blue Spruce and his parents now only needed to finance his room and board, travel, and daily living expenses. To cover these expenses, Blue Spruce worked that summer in Santa Fe.

With a good part of his education financed, Blue Spruce began to look for a college. He was soon accepted by Creighton University in Omaha, Nebraska. When young George arrived at Creighton, he was greeted by great fanfare. No doubt the proud sponsors, the Elks, had announced Blue Spruce's arrival to the Omaha newspaper since the paper proclaimed that an outstanding Indian scholar had enrolled at Creighton. It was a terrifying challenge for a young Indian student to try to live up to such expectations.

"I attended school in a fish bowl," Blue Spruce said. "No doubt everyone who read the paper was thinking of me and what I might do. At the end of the year I had to write a narrative of my progress and grades to the Elks. Now when I think of it, if all this kind of pressure were taken off, I might have given up. I was determined to succeed so the pressure may have helped. This pressure also instilled in me that I could not be ordinary. I had to excel and in order to be excellent, I had to work extra hard."

As a result, Blue Spruce worked hard for his grades, not only to prove he was a good scholar but to prove he was a good Indian scholar. In order to relax from the heavy pressures of classwork, Blue Spruce played varsity tennis with the Creighton University team.

Blue Spruce was a pioneer in higher education. His grandparents could neither read nor write. Many students at the college approached him out of curiosity because he was an Indian, and he had to convince them that he was a human being first and an Indian second. When things were difficult he would sometimes consult a college counselor, who was not always encouraging. At one point, a counselor advised Blue Spruce that dentistry was a poor choice—that it was difficult to get into dental school and only rich white boys could afford an education in dentistry.

Despite such discouragement, Blue Spruce received his bachelor of science degree from Creighton in June 1953 and was accepted by the dental school that fall. He began his last three years of concentrated study in his chosen field. "Dental school was difficult, but I enjoyed the three years of hard work because I knew I was soon going to be a dentist," Blue Spruce said. Finally, on a fine June day in 1956, Blue Spruce joined a line with many other young men to receive a diploma, which bore the name George Blue Spruce, Jr., and the three letters D.D.S. after his name.

Blue Spruce's parents were present in the auditorium for his graduation. And as Blue Spruce reached the stage to receive his diploma, the university president, who was handing out the diplomas, stopped all proceedings to announce that the first American Indian was receiving a diploma in dentistry at Creighton University; his parents were also introduced and asked to stand. In addition to this special acknowledgment, the *Omaha World Herald* ran a story about Blue Spruce's graduation.

After graduation Blue Spruce returned to Santa Fe with his parents. That summer he served as a resident dentist at the New Mexico State

Penitentiary in Santa Fe. In the fall George entered the United States Navy to fulfill his commitment to his country. During his two years in the Navy, he served as a dentist at the Naval Training Station at Great Lakes, Illinois. Later, he was transferred to Mare Island in California, where he was honorably discharged in 1958.

After returning to Santa Fe, Blue Spruce started a private practice but gave it up when he was offered a job in the Public Health Service (PHS). He was assigned the position of staff dental officer at the Indian Health Center at Taos Pueblo, New Mexico. Soon he was transferred to Fort Belknap, Montana, again as a staff dental officer. Here a nurse once mistook Blue Spruce for a local Indian when she saw him entering the hospital through the front door and told him to use the back door. He remained in Montana for two years at the Health Service Outpatient Clinic. A few years later he became deputy chief at this station. In 1963, he was transferred to King's Point in New York as a chief dental officer with the United States Merchant Marine Academy. He remained there until 1966, when he accepted an assignment to the Dental Health Center in San Francisco.

Later that year Blue Spruce enrolled at the School of Public Health at the University of California at Berkeley and received his master's degree in public health in 1967. Following this additional education, Blue Spruce became a dental public health resident at the Materials and Technology branch of the Dental Health Center in San Francisco.

Blue Spruce continued to gain experience and recognition. In 1968, he was appointed a consultant in dental health by the Pan American Health Organization with an office in Washington, D.C., and remained with this organization until early in 1970. Then he became director of the Division of Dental Health, the National Institutes of Health of the Manpower Development Branch, with an office at Bethesda, Maryland. In this position, he recruited minority students into the dental and other medical professions.

Along with his regular duties, Blue Spruce was frequently called upon over the years to speak before clubs as a dentist, as an Indian, and as an Indian dentist. He also found time to do considerable professional writing in his field. In April 1961, he received a cash award for the best dental paper presented at a United States Public Health Service Clinical Society meeting in Lexington, Kentucky.

In 1963, Blue Spruce spoke on a panel at the National Convention of the American Dental Association. Also on the panel were the surgeon general of the United States, the director of the Indian Health Service, and the director of the dental program for the Indian Health Service. Before this nationally televised program, Blue Spruce expressed his views about changes that needed to occur to improve dental health care for Indian children and adults. His opinions carried great authority since they were based both on his position as the only Indian dentist in the PHS and on his experience as a working dentist on several Indian reservations. Following this panel discussion, the surgeon general encouraged Blue Spruce to pursue a career as an administrator in the Indian Health Program so he could be part of planning and decision making and put his ideas into practice. After some thought Blue Spruce enrolled at the University of California School of Public Health in Berkeley.

Blue Spruce's special professional interests are public health administration; dental manpower development, especially young Indian boys and girls; work simplification practices; and simplified dental equipment. As an Indian he is interested in the progress of Indian people, the National Indian Education Association, and the National Congress of American Indians and their activities.

"It is hard to be a lone Indian in a white men's world," Blue Spruce said. "Many eastern 'whites' have never seen Indians or a reservation, and they pour their questions on me," he continued. "The whites have their ideas of middle-class, mainstream American life, and I have to argue for the Indians—that they are mentally healthier for their existence in a culture that is meaningful to them. I may have been away from my fellow tribesmen all these years, but I have spoken for them, defended them, and hope to do more for them indirectly from my position in the manpower development branch of the National Institutes of Health. My ultimate goal now is to return to New Mexico one day after I retire from the Public Health Service and open up a private practice in Albuquerque or Santa Fe and serve my people.

With his experience and character, it is clear that Blue Spruce had excellent rapport with his patients and fellow workers in the vast Public Health Service. According to one story, at one of the Indian clinics he had been working on the teeth of a young Indian girl, and one day after several months of appointments, Blue Spruce informed the young girl that the work on her teeth was completed. The girl began to cry, and when Blue Spruce asked her why she was crying she said that she was sad because she could no longer come to see the pleasant and understanding Indian doctor. Blue Spruce had clearly achieved his goal of "doing a better job" with Indian patients.

During my first interview with Blue Spruce, he told me that when the Public Health Service took over Indian health care in 1955 from the BIA, a majority of American Indians had never been to a dentist and many more had never had any kind of restorative dental treatment. Under the BIA, due to limited facilities and lack of professional personnel it was not uncommon for good medical and dental care to be lacking. Where a dental clinic could be found, it was usually very limited in terms of its office, equipment, and services—often run by one dentist whose services were limited to emergency treatment only. It was not unusual for one dentist to treat not one but several reservations. Portable equipment was set up at Indian day schools in any available place (sometimes even a restroom) to treat all students in a school. In those days this writer witnessed many young boys fleeing the school when they saw a dentist arriving because dental work was often done without benefit of anesthesia.

Since dental care was considered relatively unimportant, such conditions were the rule rather than the exception as late as 1950.

Blue Spruce stressed that regardless of the working environment, the dentist's attitude can make a tremendous difference in one's feelings about dental care and dentists. He said that often the few dentists treating Indians on the reservations in earlier times were irritable, uncaring, and sloppy. Blue Spruce continued: ". . . The memories of such treatment are still clear in the minds of our patients on the reservation today. From such treatment have grown strongly held impressions that dental care means pain and consists of no more than the pulling of teeth. During World War II, Indian servicemen were introduced to better dentistry, and when they returned home they created demands on the reservation dentists . . .

"Apart from the physical problems, dental officers have had to cope with the attitudes toward dental care that the Indians have developed over many years. It is my feeling that, in the short period, the Indian has gone far in his acceptance of dental care, in consideration of the obstacles he has had to overcome," he said.

I then asked him if as a dentist on Indian reservations he had noticed anything else among Indian patients which had molded their attitudes, like their past history.

To this, Blue Spruce replied, "Through lack of exposure to many aspects of the life most other Americans know, the American Indian can behave in a way that is extremely hard to understand at times. This is more characteristic of certain tribes than of others. Their past histories explain a great deal of this. For example, the warlike tribes have passed their belligerence down through the generations. Also, in areas where integration has been very limited, a show of rudeness to outsiders is more evident. The Indian in such areas has lived within a confining environment, and through fear of the unknown and the scarring effects of being pushed around, he is quick to become angry when regimented."

As we ended the interview in Blue Spruce's office, I noticed a sign on his desk that read "George Blue Spruce, Jr. D.D.S., M.P.H." It should also read, I thought, "The first Pueblo Indian dentist."

While Blue Spruce was in the Washington, D.C., area, the Indian Self-Determination Bill was passed and in a 1970 message to Congress, President Lyndon Johnson stated that the bill would become reality when an era is initiated in which the Indian future is determined by Indian actions and Indian decisions. Congress responded to this challenge with the Native American Programs Act (Title VIII of the Headstart, Economic Opportunity and Community Partnership Act of 1974). This act established the Office of Native American Programs to support self-help programs designed and operated by Native Americans.

Blue Spruce was appointed director of the Office of Native American Programs. He accepted the position with enthusiasm and served until 1978 when he resigned to continue his commitment to public health and the Indian community as the director of the Phoenix area Indian Health Service. He served in this position until 1986 when he retired following a thirty-year career.

Blue Spruce's career has brought many rewarding experiences. He was the first and only Indian dentist to hold the highest rank of assistant surgeon general (equivalent to a navy admiral). He has received many honors, including Indian of the Year in 1972 and again in 1974; and the most outstanding alumnus of his university in 1984. Other honors have come from the Association of American Medical Colleges, the American Indian Science and Engineering Society, the Association of American Indian Physicians, and the regional director of the Department of Health and Human Services, for his contribution to Indian people.

In 1988, the United Way honored him as the Outstanding Volunteer for his services to Indian people of Phoenix. He has been on the board of directors for the Phoenix Indian Center; on the Arizona Governor's Advisory Council on Indian Health; and on the Community Services Commission for the Phoenix City Council.

Another great honor came to George Blue Spruce on May 4, 1996, when he was enshrined in the American Indian Athletic Hall of Fame, in Lawrence Kansas, for his numerous championship tournament wins on the tennis courts. He joins such Indian athletic icons as the great James Thorpe, an all-sports professional athlete; Allie Reynolds of the New York Yankees; and Billy Mills, a gold-medalist in the 1964 Tokyo Olympic games. In 1997 he was selected Outstanding Leadership winner in the Arizona Governor's Council on Health, Physical Fitness and Sport Award Program.

Blue Spruce spends most of his time now as a consultant, encouraging American Indian youngsters to go to college and assisting them to enroll in professional schools. He was also asked by Creighton College to be a visiting professor at his old dental school. Blue Spruce continues to make his home in Phoenix, but he returns to New Mexico to visit his mother and to celebrate the major feast days at San Juan Pueblo. It is at such events that I continue to visit with Blue Spruce.

George Washington and Abraham Lincoln are American icons, but it is leaders like George Blue Spruce who are genuine role models for American Indian youth.

CHAPTER 30

Alfonso Ortiz
San Juan Pueblo

A lfonso Ortiz of San Juan Pueblo was a person I learned to know well and to respect—in part because of his struggle to educate himself. He will remain a great role model for Indian youngsters who believe they did not get a fair start in life.

Ortiz was born at San Juan Pueblo on April 30, 1939. Ortiz's parents were Sam Ortiz of San Juan and Lupe Naranjo Ortiz of nearby Santa Cruz. However, like many Indian children, he was raised by his paternal grandmother, along with two older sisters. His grandmother Saya had to struggle to clothe and feed him, but he took advantage of his opportunities and achieved much in his life.

In his youthful ignorance, Ortiz begged his grandmother to let him start school at age five at the San Juan Day School. In those days Head Start programs were unknown, and first-year Indian students learned very slowly. Everything was strange, the teachers' complexion, the color of their hair, their clothes, and their language. But in time, Ortiz and the other Indian children began to develop a common vocabulary.

After the sixth grade, Ortiz enrolled at the Santa Fe Indian School but stayed for only one semester. He returned home after school to help Saya cut wood, irrigate and hoe the garden, and do other chores. The second semester he enrolled at the San Juan Public School, where he graduated from the eighth grade. He went on to Española High School for a semester.

Ortiz, who was a student during the Korean War, often dreamed of volunteering for the navy. And because many of his peers left San Juan Pueblo after high school, he also contemplated moving to Los Angeles, San Francisco, or another large city to learn a trade. The Bureau of Indian Affairs had just begun a program of sending Indian high school graduates to urban areas to learn trades and to find employment. Either of Ortiz's two ambitions might have become a reality if he had stayed at the Santa Fe Indian School until graduation; however his transfer to Española High School completely altered his future.

Many factors helped determine Ortiz's future. First, there was the principal of the Española High School, Robert MacNeely. MacNeely had a genuine interest in Indian students at the school and understood that they needed a special kind of counseling. He encouraged new avenues of thought, plans, and aspirations for Ortiz and other Indian students. As a result, Ortiz set his sights on a college education, hoping to become a teacher or a lawyer.

"In retrospect," Ortiz said, "I especially value the chance to have attended a large public high school. The diverse student body brought out the best in me, in a way that I don't think staying on at the Santa Fe Indian School would ever have."

After spending one semester in a dormitory at the Santa Fe Indian School Ortiz felt that he was too dependent on schedules, and too much time spent with his peers kept him from reading and studying. He spent the next four years living at home under the strong influence of his grandmother while attending the public high school. He says, "Somehow she sensed the value of education and encouraged me to study." Although Ortiz's grandmother had had only three days of American education, she kept Ortiz at home at great personal sacrifice to allow him to get a better education. "We were so poor that studying hard and surpassing all my non-Indian classmates in school was one of the few things that gave me any feeling of self-worth in those years. They might have had the clothes and the cars, but I got the grades," Ortiz said.

In an interview Ortiz discussed the impact of early poverty and his grandmother's sacrifices:

> One thing that has remained with me through the years is the memory of having to work for Spanish farmers around San Juan for ten to twelve hours a day, hoeing corn or chile for as little as three dollars a day. And of picking apples for as little as eight to ten cents a bushel. I remember knowing as early as when I was nine years old that I was not going to always let myself be exploited like that. A more poignant memory is of Saya, already blind and in her sixties, working her hands raw pulling burrs out of sheep and goat pelts using a wooden stick with metal claws. She would get twenty-five to fifty cents each for cleaning them, depending on how wooly they were and how many burrs they had. She never made more than fifty cents per hour, however good she got at it. All this she did just so we kids could have enough to eat, and sometimes, when the dealer did not have enough pelts, it almost became a losing proposition. Yes, when the subject turns to heroics and self-sacrifice, a special chapter will have to be set aside for Saya. As you can see, I did not want for inspiration, a model for motivation, or a living symbol of the indomitable Indian spirit.

Two of Ortiz's friends helped him in other important ways. Tony Garcia of San Juan encouraged Ortiz when he was on the verge of deciding that a college education was not worth all the red tape required for admission. In addition, Charley Minton from Santa Fe, who had been to college himself, and was the executive director of the New Mexico Commission of Indian Affairs, helped Ortiz in applying for scholarships.

In the end, these positive influences and strong encouragement brought rewards. During his senior year in high school, Ortiz was awarded the Principal's Scholarship for Outstanding Citizenship. He also won a National Merit Scholarship for his first four years of college.

For his college study Ortiz enrolled at St. Michael's College, now called the College of Santa Fe. As a freshman he was highly motivated and showed strong leadership qualities. His classmates noted this, and he was elected president of the freshman class in 1957–1958. As president of his class, he was also a member of the student council.

Because St. Michael's was a small college, in order to take the courses of study he desired, Ortiz transferred to the University of New Mexico in Albuquerque. At UNM he majored in sociology, receiving his bachelor of arts degree.

After graduation, in July 1961, Ortiz married Margaret D. Davisson. They had three children. Currently, thirty-three year old Julianna is employed as an accountant in southern California. Elena, who is twenty-nine, works for the Eldorado Hotel in Santa Fe as a tour planner. Twenty-five year-old Nico, a graduate of Brown University, worked exclusively with Native American Tours of which he was president and co-owner along with his sister Elena. The tour business has since been sold, and Nico is working on a degree at the Kellogg School of Business at Northwestern University.

As a student Ortiz was involved in many campus activities. He was president of the Kiva Club, a club for Indian students that annually sponsors the Nizhoni dances and raises funds for Indian scholarships. During his sophomore and junior years, he also served as president of the San Juan Pueblo Youth Council. During his junior and senior years, Ortiz was a member of the UNM student senate, and as a senior he served as a member of the Resident Standards Council of the Men's Residence Halls and president of the Southwestern Regional Indian Youth Council.

During the summers following his sophomore and junior years, in 1959 and 1960, Ortiz participated in the UNM field session in anthropology, as a teaching assistant. This experience led him to apply for a job as a seasonal park archaeologist at Bandelier National Monument near Los Alamos after graduating from UNM. In the fall he enrolled at Arizona State University to study Indian education.

As a student at UNM Ortiz had interviewed Indians in higher education in the Southwest as part of a study conducted by the Center for Indian Education at Arizona State University. Later, as a student at Arizona State, he was a field researcher for the Pima-Maricopa tribal land claims.

By this time Ortiz had decided that anthropology would be his field of study and research. Of his career choice, he said:

> *After discovering that I enjoyed teaching very much, as well as scholarly research, I decided to go into anthropology because here was a field in which I could read about Indians all the time and teach, and further Indian opportunity, especially in education. This is what I am doing. I have also been able to work in the field of promoting Indian scholarships, and in other areas of educational opportunity.*
>
> *Anthropology was a field in which I could read about and deal with Indians all of the time and still make a living. . . . Imagine, if you will, a rather provincial fellow with a graduate fellowship and a fresh degree in sociology from the University of New Mexico in hand, and imagine, too, the difficulty anyone who is culturally Indian has in trying to find something to do in graduate school which is relevant to his background, something which would permit him to keep his own pride and identity. This was my predicament. I had contemplated entering law school, but all of the lawyers I spoke with in those days seemed to be completely preoccupied with Kiwanis Club luncheons, making money, and running for public office—though not necessarily in that order. I have never been much concerned with the first two preoccupations, while any Indian running for public office in my part of New Mexico [Rio Arriba County] had about as much chance of success as a snowball in hell. The selfless orientation toward public service and avenues in which to exercise it were just not there in 1961, whether in law or in any other field. Nor had any other currently fashionable field of endeavor yet proven relevant to Indian concerns and aspirations. My interests were rural sociology, or race and ethnic relations. Only in anthropology could these interests be treated as a central concern.*

During a recognition dinner held by the Association of American Indian Affairs in New York City, of which Ortiz was president, I introduced him as the only Indian for whom the Ford Motor Company had named a car, the Taurus, and some people believed the story. In the fall of 1962, Alfonso was awarded the highly coveted John Hay Whitney Opportunity Fellowship to study anthropology at the University of Chicago. He was awarded a University of Chicago Fellowship during his second year of graduate work, 1963–1964, at which time he also received his master's degree in anthropology. That summer he served as assistant field director for the Field Institute in Social Anthropology, co-sponsored by Harvard and Columbia universities.

Ortiz was awarded the John Hay Whitney Fellowship a second time for the year 1964–1965. During his last year of study when he was working on his Ph.D. (1965–1966), he was the recipient of the National Institute of General Medical Sciences Fellowship. He received his Ph.D. in June 1967. In 1969, he was awarded a post-doctoral fellowship by the Center for Advanced Study at the University of Illinois. He deferred acceptance until a future date.

During the year 1975–1976 Ortiz was awarded the John Simon Guggenheim Memorial Foundation Postdoctoral Fellowship. This was followed by a similar fellowship at the Center for Advanced Study in the Behavioral Sciences at Stanford University during 1977–1978. Another invitation which he postponed accepting was membership in the Institute for Advanced Study at Princeton. In 1982–1987 he was awarded his last fellowship, by the prestigious John D. and Catherine T. MacArthur Foundation.

Ortiz held the position of assistant professor of anthropology at Pitzer College in Claremont, California, in 1966 and 1967, and assistant professor and later associate professor of anthropology at Princeton University for six years, ending in 1974. Following this he returned home to New Mexico to become a professor of anthropology at the University of New Mexico, where he taught until the year before his death. He took time off to teach as a visiting professor at the University of California at Los Angeles (1978) and Colorado College (1981).

Ortiz talked about his reasons for concentrating on teaching:

I settled on teaching because that was one way that I could interest some of the most talented young people in the nation to devote some of their energies, if not their lives, to working unselfishly for the people. The battleground in the quest for justice is and always will be in the minds and hearts of people, especially young people because they are still eager to learn and to change. I have never stopped believing that time and reasonable people working together and trusting one another will solve any problem.

I do not like to look back on past accomplishments or efforts because I see that as giving in to the temptation to rest on one's laurels . . . Also, when there is so much more to be done one can only be impressed by how little he has accomplished. Nevertheless, a few things stand out from the past few years. First, I have prevailed upon a few brilliant and humane students to become interested in working for the Indian people, in fields as diverse as medicine, law, and education. One, whom I sent out to the Rough Rock Demonstration

School in Arizona, in 1968, helped found a national program of medical aid services by medical students, to serve Indians in the Southwest. Others are in law school and planning careers serving Indians, partly as a result of having worked on the Navajo Reservation, where I have been sending student volunteers for four summers. After having taught at Princeton, one of the nation's finest and most select universities, for six years, I have little doubt that I have had some future senators, congressmen, or cabinet members—perhaps even a future president—in my classes. If one of these future leaders comes out of my course with a deep appreciation of the beauty of the Indian heritage and a sensitivity to the needs and problems of the Indian people, then something will have been accomplished.

Ortiz also spoke about the success of his efforts at Princeton in actively recruiting and offering scholarships to Indian students.

As is common for American Indian scholars, Ortiz served on many boards and councils. For instance, he was a member of the Editorial Council of *The Indian Historian,* a quarterly publication of the National Indian Historical Society. He was also the Southwest editor of the *Handbook of American Indians North of Mexico,* volumes nine and ten, sponsored by the Smithsonian Institution and published in 1979 and 1983. He was an educational consultant to the Xerox Corporation, the Ford Foundation, and the National Endowment for the Humanities. He was also a member of the Executive and Education committees and Board of Directors of the Association on American Indian Affairs, a delegate to the White House Conference on Youth as a member of the National Advisory Council, and a member of the Advisory Board of the Native American Rights Fund in 1971–1972.

"In working with the large private foundations," Ortiz said, "I have also been guided by the same quest: to help make their officials more sensitive to the special problems and needs of Indian people, and to convince them of the need to consult local Indian leaders when formulating their programs. These kinds of contacts will, I hope, have good long-term consequences for all Indian people."

As an Indian anthropologist, Ortiz is vitally interested in the religion and society of the North American Indians and their revitalization movements, as well as the ritual drama as symbolic action. He has written on these topics in his book *The Tewa World,* published by the University of Chicago Press in 1969. In this book he also considers the themes of space, time, being, and becoming as they relate to pueblo society.

On space and time, Dr. Ortiz has written,

There is no Indian language of which I am aware that has abstract terms for the notions of space and time. Space is only meaningful as

*the interval between places. Yet, there are profound differences in the
way these simple and basic notions are applied. So basic are they in
fact that they underlie all reality for all peoples. The general American
view seems to be that empty space is intolerable. It must be filled with
objects. It never ceases to amaze me how white Americans can never
gaze upon a landscape without wanting to fill it with sheep, barns,
plowed fields, or something else. They just can't seem to let it be, to
just look at it and enjoy it for what it is. Most Indian people can still
let an "empty" landscape be, and enjoy it. Most of them can still in-
fuse it with meaning and order without infusing it with objects. There
is no compulsive need to make it useful. And the examples are legion.*

*The next notion is time. Again, the general American view seems to
be that if it is empty, it must be filled with activity, even if it is busy
work, or even if it becomes compulsive or neurotic. We seem to have
lost the ability to just be. This orientation, as you know, this attitude
toward time has been one of the most enduring sources of misunderstanding between Indians and non-Indians in this country from the
beginning.*

Ortiz wrote about other areas of misunderstanding between Indians
and non-Indians: "Even doctors have long believed that Indians are
impervious to pain because Indian children just sit and look straight
ahead when they are being vaccinated, or when they undergo other
painful treatment. The question is, why jump up and down and scream
about it? Sure it hurts, but yelling is not going to make it feel any better.
Indians recognize this, but those who would presume to understand
Indians attribute it all too often to racial differences."

With his understanding and knowledge of Indian culture, Ortiz was
able to make the American public more aware of Indian perspectives and
philosophy by interpreting them for non-Indians. It is the Indian way that
regardless of one's background a person can succeed and become useful
to his people as Ortiz did. His teaching, writing, and speeches will no
doubt help many young Indian Americans to be better understood as they
join non-Indians in various sectors of society.

Ortiz was the author of numerous articles, books, and book reviews
on American Indian education, federal policy, history, oral narratives, religion, and the Tewa worldview. He gave keynote speeches at the Second
National Indian Education Conference in Minneapolis in 1970 and the
Eighth Annual California Indian Education Conference in 1974. Further,
Ortiz was a visiting professor at many universities, including Distinguished Lecturer in Religious Studies at the University of Oregon, 1973;
Distinguished Bicentennial Professor, University of Utah, 1976; Weather-
head Scholar in Residence at the Navajo Community College, 1976;

Charles Charropin Visiting Scholar Lecturer, Rockhurst College, 1977; Distinguished Visiting Professor, Southern Methodist University at Fort Burquin, 1978; and George A. Miller Distinguished Visiting Professor, University of Illinois, 1979.

Professional memberships and listings include *Who's Who in America; Who's Who in the World; Community Leaders and Outstanding Americans; Dictionary of International Biography; Who's Who in Education; Personalities in America;* Fellow, American Anthropological Association; and Fellow, Royal Anthropological Institute of Great Britain and Ireland.

Other memberships include Board of Directors, Institute for the Development of Indian Law, 1974–1978; American Indian Art and Culture Review Panel, United States Department of the Interior, 1979–1980; Board of Trustees, National Museum of the American Indian, 1989–1990 and Chamiza Foundation, 1989 to 1997.

Knowing that Ortiz had a busy life, I asked him if he had time for fields of special research with reference to North American Indians. He replied that he was interested in Indian religion and society, the ritual drama and cultural performances by the tribes, their worldviews, and revitalization movements that seem to be occurring as the tribes reviewed the value of Indian life. Ortiz also was concerned with oral traditions, the traditional Indian histories in contrast to written histories of Indian-white relations in the United States; stereotypes of Indians in American culture; and contemporary Indian affairs. It is easy to understand why he was a popular professor at the University of New Mexico.

As a professional person Ortiz was involved with numerous committees and advisory groups, including the Social Science Research Council for various studies; the Native American Advisory Group for the Performing Arts; the Selection Committee of American Indians and Minorities for Ford Foundation Grants; the Advisory Council for the Danforth Graduate Fellowship Program; the Sun Valley Center for the Arts and Humanities; the Council for Higher Education for Minorities under the Ford Foundation; the Advocacy Council D'Arcy McNickle Center for History of American Indians; and the Advocacy Committee for Petroglyph National Monument.

The following are some of the research grants and professional prizes that were awarded to Ortiz:

Ray D. Albert Prize for outstanding master's thesis in anthropology at the University of Chicago, (1964); Research grant from Project Head Start, Office of Economic Opportunity, to evaluate the programs as they affect the Pueblo Indian programs with his graduate professor, Fred Eggan of the University of Chicago faculty (1965); Summer research grant, Committee for Foreign and International Affairs, Princeton University (1967); Field research grant from the American

Philosophy Society (1968); Summer research grant from the University of Arizona's Indian Oral History Doris Duke Foundation Project (1969); National Science Foundation grant (summer 1970); Ford Foundation travel and study grant (1971–1972); Indian Achievement Award Chicago Council Fire of American Indians (1982); Research travel in Siberia, Russia, for the National Geographic Society (summer 1990).

Ortiz's publications include *The Tewa World: Space, Time, Being, and Becoming in a Pueblo Society* (Chicago: University of Chicago Press, 1969); *New Perspectives on the Pueblos* (editor), (Albuquerque: University of New Mexico Press, 1972); *Myths and Legends of North American Indians,* with Richard Erdoes (New York: Pantheon Press, 1984); *The Ethnohistory and Social Anthropology of Native North American Peoples,* with Raymond J. DeMallie (Norman: University of Oklahoma Press, 1996).

Ortiz was an example of a successful pueblo man who had a very humble beginning. Among other accomplishments, he contributed greatly to the knowledge and understanding of the Pueblo Indians, bridging the gulf between their cultures and those of non-Indians.

The Pueblo people have a saying that often a person is born to accomplish many good deeds quickly and then is called to return to the place of origin. On the evening of January 27, 1997, Alfonso Ortiz passed on to the next world. He would have been fifty-eight years old in April. Although he had taken medical leave during the first semester of 1996 due to a heart problem, his death was totally unexpected.

Tributes poured in. Dr. Ted Jojola, a fellow professor at the University of New Mexico, said, "Alfonso always had an enormous presence here." Dr. Marta Weigle, chair of the UNM anthropology department said, "It's hard to imagine how we shall replace him." The governor of San Juan Pueblo, Joe Garcia, said, "This is a great loss to the Indian community. There was a lot of knowledge and wisdom in that man." The *Albuquerque Journal* summed it all in the headline, "A Great Scholar Has Passed Away." This feeling and a sense of great personal loss were shared by his numerous friends, colleagues, and many students and former students. The most noted Pueblo Indian scholar of our time will be greatly missed.

The early sacrifices of Alfonso Ortiz's grandmother were rewarded when he became able to help other Indian Americans. Tangible material assets have less meaning and less value for Indians than for non-Indians; however, to be able to help your fellow man is considered by Indians to be a manifestation of an abundance of *pinan* from the Great Spirit. Pinan is spiritual power or strength; in Ortiz's Tewa tongue, it literally means, "there is heart." His own life exemplified that ideal.

CHAPTER 31

Conroy Chino
Acoma Pueblo

Located fifty-two miles west of Albuquerque on Interstate 40 then twelve miles south, Sky City of Acoma claims to be one of the two oldest continuously occupied villages in the nation. But most of the Acoma people, who speak the Keresan language, do not live year-round at Sky City as there are no modern facilities on the mesa 430 feet above the valley floor. Instead, the people live at two farming communities a few miles from there, Acomita and McCarty. Atop the mesa is San Estevan del Rey Mission Church, which was built between 1629 and 1642 and repaired in 1799. Still in use, it is one of the oldest churches in the United States and among the first Spanish colonial mission churches in New Mexico. Many tourists come year-round to see historic Acoma, where there is also a museum at the base of the mesa featuring Indian pottery and history exhibits. From here a small bus takes visitors on a guided tour of the pueblo.

For many years there were numerous occupations that pueblo people, as minorities, were not considered for; if they qualified, they were not hired. Indian employees working for the government were mainly janitors, cooks, and maintenance personnel. Many of the veterans of World War II who were the first to graduate from colleges could not be employed because the white power establishment did not accept competition. However, eventually, Indians made a breakthrough and began to work in professions in which no Indian had ever been employed. This was mainly due to the diplomas they earned from prestigious universities, in addition to their capabilities and reliability as employees.

Then the second generation of students began to attend colleges and become professionals in many fields undreamed of earlier. One such pacesetter was Conroy Chino of Acoma Pueblo. Today, he is an investigative reporter and anchor for television station KOB-TV in Albuquerque.

Chino was born at Acoma Pueblo on August 21, 1949. His parents are Wilbert Chino of the Eagle clan and Velma Cerno of the Antelope clan. The Antelope clan at Acoma is the ruling clan which through tribal tradition selects the officials for the coming year at Acoma. The rulers are usually called caciques. At some pueblos one person is the cacique while at others there may be a Cacique Society. At Acoma it is the Antelope clan that bears this title and duties.

The word cacique was brought to the pueblo country by the conquistadors when they first arrived and asked who the cacique was at the various villages they reached. The Spaniards had learned this word in the Caribbean Islands from the Taino Indians. In fact, the cacique that the Spaniards wrote about was called *Hata-way,* a name still used today. It is a Keresan word; Keresan is Chino's first language.

Chino began his education at St. Joseph Mission School located at San Fidel, near the Acoma Reservation. After Chino finished there with respectable grades, another parochial school was recommended to his parents by the local priest. Although he wanted to go on to St. Catherine's in Santa Fe with his cousins, Chino had to abide by the wishes of his parents who had high expectations for their son

Chino arrived at the Santa Barbara, California, parochial school that had been recommended and soon learned that he was different. First, he was handicapped since he came from an environment where he had spoken his native language, and his English vocabulary was limited. It took a few weeks before he could adjust to the non-Indian world of daily life and rules of a boarding school. Most of the students were from wealthy families, and Chino was aware that his own family was not affluent. The boys, most of whom were blond and blue-eyed, began to single Chino out because of his differences. In one California history book the class read about a California tribe that dug roots for their food and were called "digger Indians." Some of the roughnecks had already learned that Chino was an Indian so they began to call him "digger Indian." And because he was not as light complected as the other students, one called him a "nigger Indian." This incident was the cause of Chino's first fight. Such problems during his formative years strengthened him since he learned while young to deal with the fact that life could be difficult—especially for minorities in American society. Because he came from a strong, stable family, Chino persevered through these adversities, and found satisfaction by studying hard and getting good grades, which pleased his parents. In addition, he excelled in sports, competing in football, basketball, and track. Chino graduated from high school in the spring of 1967.

Returning to Acoma, Chino enrolled as a freshman at the University of New Mexico in Albuquerque. At UNM there were fewer students from affluent families. Among the students were many Hispanics and a few American Indians. This was the time of student protests against the Viet-

Conroy Chino, at Acoma Pueblo, 1997. Photograph © by Marcia Keegan.

nam War, and Chino participated in demonstrations on the UNM campus as a member of the National Youth Council based in Albuquerque. This youth council was telling the world that it was all right to be Indian; they demanded recognition as equal citizens to participate in all phases of American society, including employment opportunities and scholarships.

Along with other minority students, Chino became involved in the civil rights movement, protesting treatment of Indians as second-class citizens by American society. Consequently, Chino became an admirer of Mahatma Gandhi and the Reverend Martin Luther King, and read many of their writings. Since Chino had developed good study habits at prep school, he was able to keep up with his classwork while involved with extracurricular activities at UNM. Besides being active in political protests, he was a disc jockey with the campus radio station KUNM. During the summer months he fought forest fires with the Acoma Fire Fighters.

Chino received his bachelor of arts degree in 1972 from UNM with a major in American literature. Since Chino's motivation for higher education was strong and his grades were promising, he applied and was accepted for graduate work at Princeton University. There he met a fellow Pueblo Indian Keresan speaker who was an undergraduate—Regis Pecos, who is featured in Chapter 33. Both had to work and study diligently to keep up their grades, but during spare time they got together to reminisce about their homes and sing pueblo songs. Although the graduate school at Princeton had much to offer, Chino did not seem to fit in; for him it was too structured and demanding. At UNM he had had time to participate more in extracurricular activities. Finally, a counselor suggested he transfer to a less demanding school and he returned home.

Back in New Mexico in 1974, Chino began looking for a job. The All Indian Pueblo Council had just started a radio station, and with his experience at KUNM, Chino began investigating work in communications. He was referred to KQEO, where he began as a trainee reporter. After two months he went to another radio station, KDEF, where he worked for two months before hearing about a possible television job. Following an interview with Dick Knipfing at Channel 7, KOAT-TV, Chino was hired as a weekend reporter-photographer; during the weekdays he continued with his radio work.

Chino was beginning to feel at ease with television work when his clan at Acoma selected him to be an official with the secular government of his tribe. Beginning in January 1975 Chino spent three years at his pueblo assisting the officials in the day-to-day operations of tribal government. His educational experience was useful in addressing crucial concerns such as the case of Acoma's land claims. The federal government had offered the tribe monetary remuneration for aboriginal land, but Chino spoke for the side that demanded their land back instead of cash. Those three years

Chino spent with his tribe were valuable in terms of his education and personal identity. He learned much about the daily life, the traditions, and the problems of the Acoma tribe and their relationship with the state and federal governments, and corporate world.

Following his three years with the tribal officials he returned to work at KOAT-TV in November 1978. As a reporter he was responsible for writing, researching, and producing investigative stories. After three years in this position he was awarded the prestigious Nieman Fellowship to Harvard University for the academic year 1983-1984.

Following his return to New Mexico, Chino once again worked at KOAT-TV, where he remained until May 1991 when he accepted another position in Los Angeles, California, with KCOP-TV. There he was responsible for writing and reporting on breaking news stories, as well as assigned and "enterprise" stories. During this time he covered the Los Angeles riots, and the flooding and the earthquakes in southern California in 1991 and 1992.

It was about this time that Chino became involved in narrating and assisting in the production of the Public Broadcasting System documentary about the Pueblo Indians titled "Surviving Columbus." The production was a joint venture between the Institute of American Indian Arts National Center for Production of Native Images and KNME-TV, Channel 5 in Albuquerque. This program, which was aired nationally on October 12, 1992, to commemorate the Columbian Quincentennial, later won the George F. Peabody Award for the best documentary of the year. The characters were all Pueblo Indian men and women who told their version of tribal history and their relationship with the three foreign powers— Spain, Mexico, and the United States—that had ruled their land.

In August 1992, Chino began to work for KOB-TV, where he is an investigative reporter and, an anchor on the early evening news. He has developed a good following both among Indians and non-Indians. One of the major stories Chino uncovered involved allegations of sexual abuse by priests in the Archdiocese of Santa Fe, including that of former Archbishop Robert Sanchez. Other stories he has investigated are the alcohol problem in Gallup, New Mexico, Medicaid fraud, elderly abuse, prostitution, dog fighting, organized crime, and misuse of tax dollars by the Indian Health Service and other public agencies. Other stories that he has covered include problems in the Bernalillo County sheriff's department, sexual harassment in the State Highway Department and allegations of embezzlement in the Isleta Women, Infant, and Children Program.

Chino married Darva Randolph of Acoma in 1976, and they have three boys, Joseph, Daaron, and Conlin. Darva is Director of Indian Education for the Albuquerque Public School System.

CHAPTER 32

Peter M. Pino
Zia Pueblo

Located eighteen miles northwest of Bernalillo on NM 44, Zia Pueblo is a small community with most houses clustered on a hilltop, near where the Rio Jemez flows. The people speak the Keresan language.

The 1990 United States census reported a population of only 613 for the Pueblo of Zia, but it was soon discovered that the population of most pueblos was either undercounted or overcounted. By its own count the population of Zia is 650.

However, despite its relatively small size, this hilltop pueblo played a large role in history during the early confrontation with the European invaders. This was partly due to the significant actions of a man during the colonization by the Spaniards in the pueblo world—Bartolome de Ojeda.[1] When Governor Antonio de Otermín returned to New Mexico a year following the Pueblo Revolt of 1680 his army ransacked and burned Zia Pueblo. During the battle, Ojeda was wounded and was taken by Otermín to El Paso del Norte (present-day El Paso) with the army. There Ojeda learned to speak, read, and write Spanish. Consequently, when Don Diego de Vargas arrived in New Mexico in 1692, Ojeda was on his side and paved the way for the Spaniards' return.

Today, Zia Pueblo is the only place where one can see a duplicate of the original crosses planted by Gaspar Castaño de Sosa during 1590–1591 on the various pueblo plazas. Zia has changed a great deal since that time. Considerable economic development is taking place for the benefit of its people. Spearheading these efforts are the annually selected secular tribal officials, the governor and his staff. But since most pueblo governors are selected for only a year, the tribal administrator must take responsibility for the continuity of development programs.

The tribal administrator is Peter Matthew Pino, the son of James Pino and Reyes Gachupin of the Sagebrush clan.

Peter Matthew Pino was born at Zia Pueblo on January 1, 1949. He began his education at the BIA Day School located below the hilltop village to the west. After the sixth grade, he attended the Jemez Valley High School, from which he graduated in 1967. As a senior he took a battery of tests to determine what his aptitudes might be for a future career. His counselor told him what was often said to Indian students—that he was "not college material" but that he would do well in the trades, especially in the electrical or electronics fields. Since Highlands University in Las Vegas, New Mexico, offered a two-year trades course, he enrolled there.

After two years in this program, Pino was still three hours short of the necessary credits so he returned and decided to also take other courses—to prove his high school counselor wrong. Thus, not only did he receive his associate in arts degree in 1970, but he received his bachelor of arts degree in 1972, with a major in industrial education and minor in secondary education. In addition to his formal education, Pino attended numerous workshops where he received certificates of satisfactory completion of study. Some of these were in planning, administration and management of contracts, program implementation, and proposal writing. In 1980, he received a certificate in energy resource exploration, development and reclamation from a Denver-based corporation known as the Council of Energy Resource Tribes. He later was placed on the Board of Directors of a subsidiary known as Education Fund, Inc. In 1989 Pino was made chairman of this subsidiary, a position he still holds. Since 1985 Pino has been a member of the New Mexico State Board of Commissioners of the Office of Indian Affairs.

While Pino was attending Highlands University, he worked for the Bureau of Indian Affairs at the Southern Pueblos Agency as an engineering draftsman. There he prepared working drawings for heating systems needed in areas under the agency, including offices and day schools in the pueblos. He also drafted layouts, topography cross sections and ground lines for new and old roads in the same areas. Following his return from school after a midterm graduation, Pino continued to work at his BIA job for six more months. At this time he was designated bonded treasurer of Zia Pueblo by the Tribal Council. In this capacity he worked part time while attending graduate school at the University of New Mexico and full time during the summer. This job required him to keep records of tribal and federal funds, prepare payment vouchers for tribal employees, and in general, assist the various governors in managing tribal programs and projects.

Then one day Pino saw a flyer advertising the Anderson School of Business Administration. He applied and to his surprise was accepted. At this school he studied business administration, the same kind of work he was doing at Zia. This study enabled him to take on even more responsibilities at the pueblo. Pino was the bonded treasurer for Zia Pueblo until December 1976 and the following year he was appointed administrative

Peter M. Pino, at Zia Pueblo, 1997. Photograph © by Marcia Keegan.

assistant and treasurer. In this position he had considerably more responsibilities, preparing program proposals and later directing the funded
projects. These were usually federal programs that involved preparation
of detailed reports. He also became the liaison between his pueblo and the
state and federal government agencies, as well as private firms. At the
same time he continued to manage the tribal and various program funds.

Pino served as assistant administrator in 1977. Since he was doing all
the work anyway, in January 1978 his title was changed to administrator.
Today, Pino continues this work—preparing and directing projects at the
pueblo. As an example, he directed the preparation of a four-phase comprehensive plan for the pueblo. Some of the programs are the BIA 93–638
programs and grants, Social Services, Tribal Courts, Johnson-O'Malley,
Adult Education and the Zia Scholarship program. Pino has been instrumental in securing much needed funding for community and tribal office
buildings, a Headstart addition, and a fire station, all of which were
funded by the Economic Development Administration. Other developments included drainage improvement, a Zia Lake recreation area, and
fire protection improvement, as well as water and sewer improvements—
all funded by the Department of Housing and Urban Development
through a Community Development block grant. For the pueblo offices
and employees Pino established and implemented personnel policies,
accounting, procurement, and property and records management.

Also, Pino and the Zia officials have successfully negotiated numerous
leases, rights-of-way, easements and contracts with private businesses
such as electric utilities and gas and oil companies.

In addition to all these activities here is another aspect of Pino's contribution to his tribe. One of the most important positions in a Pueblo
Indian society is the song leader, which is considered a position of great
honor. The song leader is central to feast day dances. Pino has been a song
leader at Zia Pueblo since 1985. As many people know, the time-honored
Corn Dance is the traditional feast day dance, especially among the
pueblos in Sandoval County. Usually there are at least seven dances on a
feast day, depending on the time of year, with the two moieties, or kiva
groups, alternating after each thirty-minute dance. The song leader is
crucial for coordinating the singers and dancers of the two moities during
dance performances. The song leader sets the tempo of the song while the
drummer takes his cue from this tempo and the dancers listen to the beat
of the drum. If the drum beat is too fast or too slow, it is hard for the
dancers to maintain the rhythm.

Zia Pueblo's feast day is August 15 annually in honor of their patron
saint, Our Lady of the Ascension. Perhaps limited by the size of the plaza,
only about 120 to 125 corn dancers at a time may participate on one side,
along with about thirty singers. The rest of the plaza is filled to capacity

by visitors. The dancers at Zia are paired perfectly, with each male dancer having a female partner. Most noticeable is that every woman has on a headpiece, or *tablita*. Teenagers, who dance along with the adults, are at the rear of the dance column. Because of the discipline and dedication of the people of Zia Pueblo, their feast is one of the best among the pueblos.

After nearly twenty years of working and living in two worlds, Pino has had time to reflect on his life both on and off the reservation. He told me that if he had worked only outside his reservation he would have just put on his business hat, devoted all his energy to his job, and when quitting time came, set aside his business hat and on the way home started thinking about being a tribal member—whether it was practicing a song or considering ditch work. In this scenario he wouldn't have had to worry about tribal business projects, and it would have been easier to control the pressures of both worlds. However, despite the fact that dealing with both the business world and working at his pueblo has made his life a bit more difficult, it has been more in line with pueblo philosophy—which teaches people to put the needs of the community first, then one's family, and last, oneself.

As a change of pace from his responsibilities, Pino loves to garden and to hunt. He also appreciates his deepening relationships with family and friends.

And he says, "The longer I am here and I grow older, I find that I have family ties . . . to most members of the pueblo. This is because . . . my wife Stella and I have been *padrinos,* or sponsors, to four marriages, which makes us second parents to the couples and grandparents to the couples' children, as well as [having] my own children—Morris, my son and Reina, my daughter."

NOTES

1. Joe S. Sando, *Pueblo Nations: Eight Centuries of Pueblo Indian History* (Santa Fe, N.M.: Clear Light Publishers, 1992), 237.

CHAPTER 33

Regis Pecos
Cochiti Pueblo

American education has been available to the Pueblo Indians since 1880, when the Albuquerque and Santa Fe Indian schools were established. However, education had little meaning at that time, since there was a barrier between the Anglo-American teachers and the Indians. The teachers rarely explained the value of education or that higher education was also a possibility for Indian students.

It was not until after World War II that real education became available to Indians. This writer's peers, who were supervisors and veterans of World War II, finally had an opportunity to attend the colleges of their choice through the GI Bill. Most of these veterans majored in education since teaching was considered an honorable profession. When Indian veterans began to teach, it had an enormous impact on Indian high school students. They began to see real role models they could relate to.

One of the young pueblo students who was motivated by Indian teachers and professionals was Regis Pecos of Cochiti Pueblo. Pecos was born at Cochiti Pueblo on June 18, 1953. His parents are Caroline Melchoir of the Sun clan and José Delores Pecos. His three older brothers provided examples for Pecos. His brother Richard attended Denver's Technical Institute, once designed computers for IBM, and is now the administrator for Cochiti Pueblo. His brother Carlos graduated from New Mexico Highlands University in Las Vegas and received his master's degree from the University of New Mexico. Before Carlos's unfortunate death, he was the associate superintendent of the Bernalillo Public Schools. Pecos's third brother, Matthew, was educated at UNM and has been tribal treasurer for the pueblo for the last ten years while also teaching at the Santa Fe Indian School.

During an interview Pecos often reiterated his grandfather's advice: As Indian people we must give value to those things that make us Indian people—our language, our culture, the values and traditions that perpetuate our cultural survival; at the same time, we must give equal value to educating and developing those skills necessary to deal with the external community to protect our community internally, creating a balance in our lives.

With this advice in mind, at the tender age of fourteen, Pecos applied on his own to Phillips Exeter Academy in Exeter, New Hampshire, having heard that this was one of the best prep schools in the country. Receiving high recommendations from his teachers in Bernalillo, he was accepted in the prep school's summer program. His family could not afford the airfare to New Hampshire so Pecos traveled by bus for three days to Phillips Academy. There he spent eight weeks among the elite young people from around the country and the world. Aside from attending classes from 7 A.M. to 4 P.M., he also worked in the kitchen to support himself financially. With a slight smile, he recalled the smell of diesel fumes from the Greyhound bus as he looked out to see his family waving good-bye. Those were among the loneliest days of his life, he said, but admitted that the experience impressed on him what he must do the rest of his high school years—compete among the best educationally. It was also that summer that he first heard of Princeton University and became interested in applying.

During his junior and senior years in high school, because of his athletic ability, Pecos was sought for baseball teams of prestigious universities such as Stanford and Arizona State. To this day many of his achievements in baseball still stand as unbroken records. He is listed and pictured in the Sports Hall of Fame at his high school. At this time in his life Pecos again turned to his grandfather for advice. "What is it that you wish to do with your life?" his grandfather asked. Regis responded that he wanted most to help his people. His grandfather replied, "How will baseball do that for you?" Consequently, Pecos made a decision to attend Princeton following his graduation from high school in 1972.

At Princeton Pecos majored in political science and history. He graduated in 1976, with honors, becoming the second Pueblo Indian, one of only ten American Indians, to graduate from Princeton. His senior dissertation, titled "The Changing Concepts of Pueblo Sovereignty," won him honors. Although the regular courses were demanding, he took an additional course which earned him a teaching certificate in American history. With this certification, he taught during part of his senior year at the Lawrenceville Academy in New Jersey. Remaining at Princeton for another year, he took classes at the world famous Woodrow Wilson School of International and Public Affairs. At this school, Pecos studied with world class scholars in history and public policy.

With renewed confidence and assurance of a place in the business world, Pecos returned home to New Mexico in June of 1977. In July he began working for Americans for Indian Opportunity, an Albuquerque

-based Indian advocate organization founded by LaDonna Harris, Comanche, in 1970.

Pecos became an economic development specialist, under contract with the United States Economic Development Administration. In this capacity he directed and administered the project to train tribal decision makers in basic commercial problems and solutions involved in economic and resource development. He also conducted a series of regional seminars and studied three diverse tribes to evaluate tribal structures and forms of government, law and order codes, barriers and opportunities for economic resource development, inventories of human resources, and assessment of tribal priorities. The result was published in a report on a self-evaluation process for Indian governments.

It was in January 1978 that the Tribal Council of Cochiti first appointed Pecos to the Tribal Code of Law and Order Committee. From October 1978 to March 1984, Pecos was director of research for the same organization. In this position he served as assistant to the project director responsible for the administration and reporting of a precedent-setting multi-agency contract with the Departments of the Interior; Commerce; Labor; Health, Education and Welfare; Energy; the Indian Health Service; and the Environmental Protection Agency. He directed a staff of ten research assistants, and over a period of four years, over twenty college interns on this extensive nationwide study.

The project had the following objectives: (1) To increase the awareness of Indian tribal decision makers concerning the environmental health impacts of development activities; (2) to develop information and documentation to assist Indian communities in their efforts to protect their own health and environment; (3) to develop alternate methods and options for organizing Indian community environmental health production systems; (4) to increase awareness of government agencies with responsibility for various aspects of environmental protection, health research, health care delivery, and occupational safety of Indian concerns; and (5) to establish communications among tribal governments and federal, state, and local governments on environmental and other mutual concerns.

Approximately a dozen federal agencies participated at some time during the project. And as director, Pecos maintained a flow of information to all participants, tribal and federal agencies. Six regional seminars were conducted as part of the project. Participating were approximately 200 tribal representatives from throughout the country, 140 federal officials, 25 state officials, and 85 interested private individuals.

As in 1978, in 1980 Pecos was again appointed to the Economic Development and Environmental Review Committee at Cochiti. This combined committee began a long laborious process of piecing together the chronology of events leading up to the forced construction of Cochiti

Lake, which had devastated the pueblo's traditional farmlands. Pecos gives a history of the lake construction and its aftermath:

Cochiti, as long as I remember, as the stories go with my grandfather, has always engaged in farming, and farming has always been central in our lives and central to the binding and the cohesion of the people of our community. But . . . in the early 50s an incredible effort was made by the U.S. government to develop and construct one of the largest man-made lakes in this country on Cochiti land. The older members of this community fought and fought and prevailed in those fights to prohibit the construction of the tenth largest reservoir in the United States. But then came the pressure in the late 60s from external forces, and Congress appropriated dollars to construct Cochiti Lake. In the construction of Cochiti Lake, it devastated and completely destroyed 50 percent of all the traditional farmlands and traditional homelands. Our people fought to stand up against the United States Corps of Engineers [which planned] to build Cochiti Lake, but we lost in that effort, and since the time I was in high school, for more than ten years on a twenty-four hour basis, machinery moved earth. In the early 70s construction was completed and public access was made available to Cochiti Lake. Two years following the opening of Cochiti Lake, we began to experience seepage from Cochiti Lake so that in a matter of two years the remaining 50 percent of agricultural lands were completely under water and in five to ten years there was at least a foot of water standing in all the remaining agricultural fields. As a result of the damage from Cochiti Lake, the lifestyle of our people was completely taken away. But to add insult to injury, as we began to examine how we were going to hold the United States of America liable for its destruction in the construction of Cochiti Lake because of the alluvial nature of the area, there was only one significant area that was referenced as a geological structure, and its purpose as a geological structure was defined by the engineers. That geologic structure represented one of the most holy places for pueblo people . . . even for people as far away as our brothers and sisters from Hopi. That was the only place our people wanted protected, and they were willing to forego compensation when it was imminent that it was going to be condemned, whether they liked it or not; that the lake would be built. And we discovered during the deposition phase that as they agreed to protect that area that is one of the holiest places to pueblo people, that was in fact one of the only feasible places that the mouth of Cochiti Lake could be built. So although they promised the people of Cochiti that they would protect that holy place, that was one of the first places dynamited, and that became the mouth of Co-

chiti Lake. Because of the force and power of the water channeled back into the Rio Grande and the devastation, I need not say more when you see older men and women shed tears because of the pain that they feel that one of the holiest places was completely desecrated. The holy place and agriculture were taken away, and it was that which engaged and sustained the native religion; they are inseparable and interdependent.

But as if that was not enough, associated with the development of this major reservoir was one of the first efforts by the Economic Development Administration to open up reservations for private investment under a new economic policy in the early 70s. This resulted in one of the first private investments for residential development. First there was the desecration of one of the most holy places, then the construction and interference of Cochiti Lake, and then a master lease for ninety-nine years to build a residential retirement town known now as the Town of Cochiti Lake. The projection for this residential retirement town was for 40,000 people by the end of this decade; there were less than 1,000 people in our community.

At about the time I finished my work at Princeton University, I came home to fulfill a responsibility that my grandfather talked about as individual responsibility to the community. He would often talk to us about education and the maintenance of language and culture as a dual responsibility, and he often used the word ske'wa, which represents a duality. He often said it was important to travel this road of dual existence in order to develop the necessary skills to provide service to the community in protecting those internal things that define who we are as a people; thus began my twenty years of work in this effort. Those first years were spent forcing the United States government to accept liability for its devastation, and through the course of litigation over eight years, we prevailed against the United States. The federal court ordered the Corps, the Congress, and Cochiti to work together on a settlement agreement that had three parts to it. One, that the government would pay past damages for the devastation; two, that it would restore lands by reducing the water table; and three, that there would be a settlement to provide operation and maintenance to sustain the system that would reduce the water level of the lake so that we could once again reengage in farming. [The settlement brought approximately $11.5 million, according to Pecos.] During the course of this litigation and the energy crisis, Los Alamos wanted access to cheaper energy, and then came forth the fight to build a major hydroelectric power plant at the mouth of that sacred area. Some people believed that that was clean economic development, clean energy production and that incredible revenue would be derived *from the power plant. In those longer council sessions when some community members were eager to jump at this hydroelectric development, my granduncle, who passed away in his early 90s, said to me in the course of one discussion, "Why have we engaged in this fight and prevailed when with the other hand we are going to take money from an activity that is going to be an ongoing desecration of one of the most holy places?" So our effort to stop hydroelectric power began. Our native religion is bound by secrecy as one of its fundamental principles; the members take a sacred vow. As we went through the process to prevent hydroelectric power, we went before the Federal Energy Regulatory Commission to prevent their issuance of a permit to a private developer to build the hydroelectric power plant at that site. We prevailed through all those administrative levels, but then we came to the point where someone had to answer why we hold this place so deeply religious and holy. In order to respond to that question, a member of our community would have to break their religious vows and sever their relationship to the community; we decided not to respond to that question so that no member of our community would be sacrificed. In the 1989 session of Congress, Congressman Bill Richardson carried a bill that two minutes before adjournment, two minutes before midnight, Congress passed, legislation specifically prohibiting hydroelectric power at that site. So once again we prevailed. . . .[1]*

In the summer of 1994, phase one of the restoration project began. Congressional staff and tribal attorneys gave Pecos the authority to orchestrate a hearing at Cochiti Pueblo which resulted in securing the political support of Senator Daniel K. Inouye of Hawaii, chairman of the Senate Select Committee on Indian Affairs. The New Mexico congressional delegation also championed this long struggle for Cochiti.

We now had the fight of how we could reduce the town of Cochiti Lake to something we could control so we wouldn't be a minority on our own reservation. Thus began another lawsuit to minimize the growth and recapture control. The private investors had their home base in Texas, and we literally, on some days, would fly from Albuquerque to Dallas in the bankruptcy proceedings to force them to reduce the development, come back the same day, and go again the following day for several weeks at a time. Once again, our lawsuit prevailed, which resulted in proceedings which reduced the core of the development to what is now the town of Cochiti Lake; it will never grow beyond 300 homes. We have to live with the compromise, but nonetheless we have regained control and are not a minority on our own reservation.[2]

During the struggle to regain control over development, Pecos was simultaneously serving on another committee that was working to regain a 25,000-acre tract known as the Santa Cruz Spring Tract. The tribe had previously exhausted all legal means to convince the Indian Court of Claims that this tract had been fraudulently taken from the Pueblo. However, the committee's research efforts brought to light a missing document, found in a Guadalajara, Mexico archive, which pertained to the tract. This document, uncovered by a local attorney working on a water rights case and later translated by a former Princeton professor, bolstered the claim of pueblo ownership of the 25,000-acre tract.

Consequently, the tribe began an all-out lobbying effort locally and nationally to have the tract returned. In 1984, largely through the efforts of the New Mexico congressional delegation, particularly Congressman Bill Richardson, Congress finally passed a bill that returned the tract to Cochiti Pueblo.

Beginning in 1978, Pecos played a key role, spearheading important committees involved in the fight to reclaim Cochiti land. He describes the progress that has been made in restoring agriculture, but notes that other changes in the community cannot so readily be reversed:

Through all of these efforts, the fight was about how we could sustain our little community of Cochiti. In the course of all these years, many of the people who greatly influenced my life never saw the day that we prevailed in our fight to sustain the community through all these efforts. But the story that directly has been a lesson is that as a result of all of these twenty years of legal battles, when we drive on our way to work in the morning, we can see the harvest of the first produce of those lands in the last twenty-three years. The proposed cost of the system which reduced the water table, enabling us to farm, ranged from a low of $4.3 million to a high of $99 million in excess of the construction of Cochiti Lake. We chose the lowest point maintenance system and reduced the water table, which resulted in amendments to the soil. Last spring four hundred acres of those lands were put back into production using alfalfa as a way of stabilizing this first year. Two hundred and fifty more acres are now ready for planting next spring, and the remaining two hundred and fifty acres closest to our community are going to be reserved to reengage individual members of our community in farming. We have to do something consciously about it because what happened in that twenty year loss of farming included a loss of lifestyle, which has resulted in an incredible drop in the maintenance and use of our native language. With the lack of agriculture, a wide gap was created between the older members of our community and our younger ones. Language loss among our community mem-

bers can be directly related to the developments within our community over the past twenty-five years.

Through this whole process we have gone through an internal reassessment concerning what our most important priorities are to pass along to our children. We are not immune to all the influences we have been subject to, and so this has been a difficult time for them to be growing up. We did not want to have won all of the court battles over the last twenty years and then lose the war here at home. We have to consciously engage our people in farming again by creating opportunities for them to reengage, and reengage both young and old people in the beautiful way of life that we once had. When I was growing up, I worked on a farm with my father, and we walked three or four miles a day to the fields. As kids growing up in Cochiti, we worked side by side with our brothers and other extended family members, and the sharing and developing of family and extended relationships was one of the most beautiful things in terms of an expression and reflection of a community's compassion and respect for one another. I would give anything to re-create the same opportunity for our young people so they can appreciate the value and meaning that comes with that engagement. There is a certain value that comes from sharing and that sense of interdependence. I remember how much satisfaction we received at harvest time when we would take corn, chilies and melons to an old lady who lived along the road and how appreciative she was that someone in the community would do this for her. It was a kind of binding and cohesion that farming brought into our lives. It brought a relationship with man and nature of the highest order in terms of the maintenance and responsibility and also in our sense of spirituality and feeling for the environment around us. It was an incredible classroom of sorts for the entire community.[3]

Pecos goes on to describe the process of community rebuilding:

I hope that our struggle over the last twenty-five years and the backdrop of the last one hundred years might be a testament of the perseverance of an entire community of people. There is nothing as beautiful as life in a rural community and the closeness that community brings into our lives, providing the maximum realization for one of the most beautiful human gifts to be shared—the feeling of satisfaction when I can extend my hand to you for no other reason than that we are at a level of mutual respect of caring and loving for one another. What we are consciously doing now at Cochiti is creating a community-based education program at the Santa Fe Indian School where we have the largest number of students at the secondary level.

This community-based education program results in using our community as another classroom. In our community the kind of people who give value and meaning to our lives are not carrying the credentials of formalized education, but nonetheless, their credentials in terms of humanity and the compassion in their hearts are second to none. We make it clear that those things are important and that we give value to those members of our community as teachers equal to those of formal institutions. We are using our community as a place to engage young people to become consciously involved with whatever challenges confront our community so that there might be a natural motivation to commit to their individual responsibilities and obligations early in their lives—a realization that they have a place in the community. We are consciously engaging them in using language as a focal point in this reengagement, and in this process we are creating what we are calling an environmental conservation and preservation youth corps. We are actively engaging young people in the community to have a sense of value and commitment to those things that are a priority to members of our community, and in this way are collectively and visibly reengaging everyone in something that has given value and meaning in my life and the lives of the other people in the community. Our hope is that the discussion and dialogue through this process is simply the beginning of planting those seeds to eventually become the beneficiaries of what we harvest, because we are willing to cultivate and nurture those principles fundamental to the well-being of all of us as individuals, as families and as a community. No, it is not too late, because as long as there are seeds to plant . . . our way of life can be sustained.[4]

Pecos was involved in state government during this hectic period. In the fall of 1984, Governor Toney Anaya appointed Pecos deputy director of the State Office of Indian Affairs. A year later he became the youngest executive director of that office. In 1986, Governor Garey Carruthers reappointed him to the same position; and Governor Bruce King in 1990 called on Pecos to continue as part of his administration. In this position, Pecos directed the investigation, study, and consideration of Indian conditions and relations within the state of New Mexico, including—but not restricted to—the issues of health, economy, education, legislation, and government. He also served as a liaison between state, federal, and private agencies with relation to all Indian matters in the state. As the director, for ten years he has been a registered lobbyist with the state legislature on behalf of tribal governments.

Pecos is a former chairman of the Board of Education of the nationally renowned Santa Fe Indian School. He is also a board member and founder of the New Mexico Indian Education Center for Excellence, an entity serving public schools with a mission for research initiatives, and vice-chairman of the Council of Independent Colleges and Universities of New Mexico.

Statewide, he has been a member of the Southwest Commission on Civil Rights, a member of Governor Bruce King's Council of Policy Advisors on Rural Economic Development, a past board member of the University of New Mexico National Origin Desegregation Assistance Center, as well as past director of the National Bilingual Education Center at the University of New Mexico.

Nationally, he was appointed by Senator Daniel K. Inouye, Chairman of the Senate Select Committee on Indian Affairs, to the Executive Committee of the National Planning Committee on Indian Affairs, appointed by Congress to conduct a feasibility study to establish a National Indian Policy Institute. Pecos is also chairman of the National Task Force on Cultural Resource and Rights Protection and a member of the National Environmental Protection Agency Pollution Prevention and Education Task Force.

Besides spearheading important committees at Cochiti, in 1990 and 1996 Pecos was selected by the Pueblo leaders to serve as lieutenant governor under the traditional form of government. He is now a lifetime member of the Tribal Council at Cochiti.

Other recognition includes the Outstanding Young Man of America Award (1980), the Americans for Indian Opportunity Distinguished Service Award (1981), and the Jefferson Award for significant community contribution (1986).

Since his father is the head of the Pumpkin Kiva, or moiety, at Cochiti, Pecos has been participating in most tribal dancing activities ever since he was able to shake a rattle. Some Anglo purists used to say that when an Indian becomes well educated, like Pecos, the Indian ceases to participate in Indian life. Such a thought has never entered Pecos's mind; he remains a Pueblo Indian through and through.

Reflecting on his involvement in political projects and issues, Pecos once wrote:

> *Someone once remarked that the American Indian is too busy struggling with everyday problems to care about philosophy or abstract questions. I disagree; and with that in mind, I sought to become a member of the state legislature. Philosophy, specifically political philosophy, is unquestionably within the realm of the abstract; yet the application of political beliefs, ideas, values, and attitudes constitutes the brick and mortar from which the systems and institutions which govern people on an everyday basis are built. The type of governments*

we design and adopt will, in a large part, determine the course of our lives. Whether those lives will be productive, healthy, secure, and peaceful or riddled with unemployment, poverty, and despair depends on the ability of governmental structures to provide for the well-being of the people and to create an environment conducive to economic productivity.

Strong, stable tribal governments will produce economic well-being on Indian reservations, and thus contribute to the overall strength of this state in the larger context. What is needed is the conceptual framework with which to proceed. Imposed systems, whether they be social, economic, or governmental, create dissatisfaction, disharmony, and stagnation. Creative approaches, equitable partnership, and an attitude of acceptance and goodwill are needed. The cycle of dependency will be broken; but first, tribal peoples must have the opportunity to review and revitalize their internal, institutional infrastructures, as well as to develop the physical infrastructures necessary for economic well-being.

I strongly believe it to be useful, and even desirable, for the larger society to have some grasp of the complexities and difficulties confronting the tribal peoples of this state. Above all else, however, I wanted to contribute and show my commitment to tribal people to continue to strive for survival as a people, as distinct cultural and governmental entities which can prosper and flourish beside and within the state of New Mexico.[5]

NOTES

1. Cited from the personal papers of Regis Pecos.
2. Ibid.
3. Ibid.
4. Ibid
5. Ibid.

Afterword
by Alfonso Ortiz

Until the generation of scholars that reached maturity in the late 1960s, there was no tradition in American biography of writing about any Indian people who were not artists, colorful war chiefs, or another kind of highly visible leader. It seemed as if both scholars of the American Indian and professional biographers were unable to grasp the modest idea that Indian people had heroes, role models, and other people of importance by their own lights and standards of evaluation who were not artists or war chiefs. At that, such artists as were selected for biographical attention were chosen because they were regarded as important enough by white canons of judgment to merit this kind of attention.

As for the war chiefs, few Americans know that the most familiar war chiefs out of American history, people such as the Lakota leaders Crazy Horse and Sitting Bull, or, closer to the subject of the present volume, the Apaches Geronimo and Cochise, and the Tewa Popé, were spiritual leaders long before they became war leaders. Indeed, if they were not regarded as having powerful spiritual guardians, young men would not have followed them into war. Sadly, it is the war exploits of these and countless other departed patriots of the Indian past that were written about, not their leadership qualities as people of peace.

Forgotten as well is the fact that in every instance it was the European invasion of their lands and the subsequent threat this invasion presented to their people and to their way of life that put them onto a war footing in the first place. War was regarded by Indian people throughout North America north of Mexico as an abnormal and temporary condition, one which must be abandoned as quickly as possible, to avoid as many deaths as possible. That the unrelenting pressure presented by the white advance forced so many leaders to remain on a permanent war footing, until their very deaths, does not invalidate in the least their preference for peace. Nor does the singling out of their war exploits by white historians detract in the least from their status in Native esteem as spiritual leaders, first and foremost.

Indeed the only exceptions to this bleak picture of misguided biographical emphasis and outright neglect are presented by anthropologists who wrote about their favorite Native consultants, and by Indian people who either wrote down their own stories, or dictated them to friendly whites. For whatever reason, these exceptions have not received much attention, although some of them have been available for almost a century.

Beginning in the 1960s, with the publication of Alvin Josephy's *Patriot Chiefs,* the terrible wrongs brought about by the distorted and very incomplete biographical emphasis began to change. In time, full-length biographies of physicians and national activists Carlos Montezuma and Charles Eastman, the Shawnee Prophet, and other people who were not war chiefs or artists began to appear. As well, briefer biographical sketches of modern Indian leaders, including, at last, some women, began to appear as well. Another major development in redressing the problem occurred in the late 1980s, when the University of Nebraska Press founded an "Indian Lives" series, which has emphasized the publication of biographies of Indian people of letters, as well as ordinary people of accomplishment in other walks of life. The list already published includes even a long-term prison inmate.

Today, the publication of biographies of noteworthy Indian people of diverse accomplishments is an established and healthy part of the publishing industry, with presses clear across the United States and even into Europe publishing Indian biographies. The emphasis is still on individuals who have distinguished themselves in ways approved of by the larger society, but at least the net is now cast widely enough to include people other than colorful war chiefs and artists.

It is against this general background that Joe Sando's achievement must be seen for it to be fully appreciated. Sando's profiles are of people who were and are concerned, first and foremost, with serving the Pueblo people, to ensure their survival and well-being. All are people who were and are important in the eyes of Pueblo people; many are even important in the eyes of the national Indian community. Yet, all are important as well by the canons of achievement established by the larger society. As such, this volume of profiles represents a pioneering achievement. On the one hand, Sando demonstrates once and for all that there have always been achievers in the Pueblo world who need not be warriors or artists to stir the imagination by the example of their lives. Most of the people of whom Sando writes overlap several of his part title headings, of course, but he has placed them in those categories in which their lives have had their greatest meaning and focus.

Sando's book also presents the reader with an unexpected bonus—unexpected, at least, for most collections of this kind—for we are treated to unique and valuable glimpses into the Pueblo peoples' remarkable cultural resiliency, tenacity, and sheer will to endure. Because the volume is organized chronologically, we see how different generations have fought the good fight to ensure that the Pueblo people might yet endure with dignity and cultural integrity intact in an increasingly complex and dangerous world. This volume should gain an appreciative audience in the years ahead, both among Pueblo people themselves, and among those who would seek to understand them. Let us also hope that future generations of biographers of Indian people heed its example.

Pueblo Locations

All directions begin at Albuquerque, New Mexico.
Includes telephone numbers of the tribal administration offices.

Acoma	I-40, west 52 miles to exit 108; south 12 miles on County Road 12A. 505-552-6604.
Cochiti	I-25, north 33 miles to exit 259; north 14 miles on N.M. 22. 505-465-2244.
Isleta	I-25, south 12 miles to exit 213; south 2 miles on N.M. 314 to jct. with N.M. 147; 1 mile southeast on N.M. 147. 505-869-3111.
Jemez	I-25, north 16 miles to exit 242; northwest 25 miles on N.M. 44 to jct. with N.M. 4 at San Ysidro; 4 miles northeast on N.M. 4. 505-834-7359.
Laguna	I-40, west 46 miles to exit 114; west 1 mile on N.M. 124. 505-552-6654 or 505-243-7616.
Nambé	I-25 north to Santa Fe; 84/285 north from Santa Fe 16 miles to jct. with N.M. 503 north of Pojoaque; east 2 miles on N.M. 503. Sign on highway. 505-455-7692.
Picuris	I-25 north to Santa Fe; 84/285 north from Santa Fe 24.3 miles to jct. with N.M. 68 in Española; 20 miles north on N.M. 68 to jct. with N.M. 75 vicinity of Dixon; 13 miles east on N.M. 75. Sign on highway. 505-587-2519.
Pojoaque	I-25 north to Santa Fe; 84/285 north from Santa Fe 15 miles. Sign on highway. 505-455-2278.

Sandia	I-25, north 16 miles to exit 234; northwest 2 miles on N.M. 556 to jct. with N.M. 313; north 3 miles on N.M. 313. Sign on highway. 505-867-3317.
San Felipe	I-25, north 26 miles to exit 252; north 2 miles on local road. Sign on highway. 505-867-3381.
San Ildefonso	I-25 north to Santa Fe; 84/285 north from Santa Fe 15 miles, to jct. with N.M. 502 in Pojoaque; 6 miles west on N.M. 502. Sign on highway. 505-455-2273.
San Juan	I-25 north to Santa Fe; 84/285 north from Santa Fe 24.3 miles to jct. with N.M. 68 in Española; 4 miles north on N.M. 68 to jct. with N.M. 74; 1 mile west on N.M. 74. 505-852-4400.
Santa Ana	I-25, north 16 miles to exit 242; northwest 10 miles on N.M. 44. Sign on highway. 505-867-3301.
Santa Clara	I-25 north to Santa Fe; 84/285 north from Santa Fe 24 miles to jct. with N.M. 201 in Española; west 1 mile to jct. with N.M. 30 in Española; 1 mile southwest on N.M. 30. Sign on highway. 505-753-7326.
Santo Domingo	I-25, north 33 miles to exit 259; north 4 miles on N.M. 22; 505-465-2214.
Taos	I-25 north to Santa Fe; 84/285 north of Santa Fe 24.3 miles to jct. with N.M. 68 in Española; 48 miles north on N.M. 68 to jct. with U.S. 64 in Taos; 1 mile north on U.S. 64. Sign on highway. 505-578-9593 or 505-758-4156.
Tesuque	I-25 north to Santa Fe; 84/285 north from Santa Fe 9 miles. Sign on highway. 505-983-2667.
Zia	I-25, north 16 miles to exit 242; northwest 18 miles on N.M. 44. Sign on highway. 505-867-3304.
Zuni (2 routes)	I-40, west 78 miles to exit 81 at Grants; south/south-west 76 miles on N.M. 53.
	I-40, west 138 miles to exit 20 at Gallup; south on N.M. 602; jct. 33 miles on N.M. 53; then 10 miles southwest on N.M. 53. 505-782-4481.

THE NINETEEN NEW MEXICO INDIAN PUEBLOS

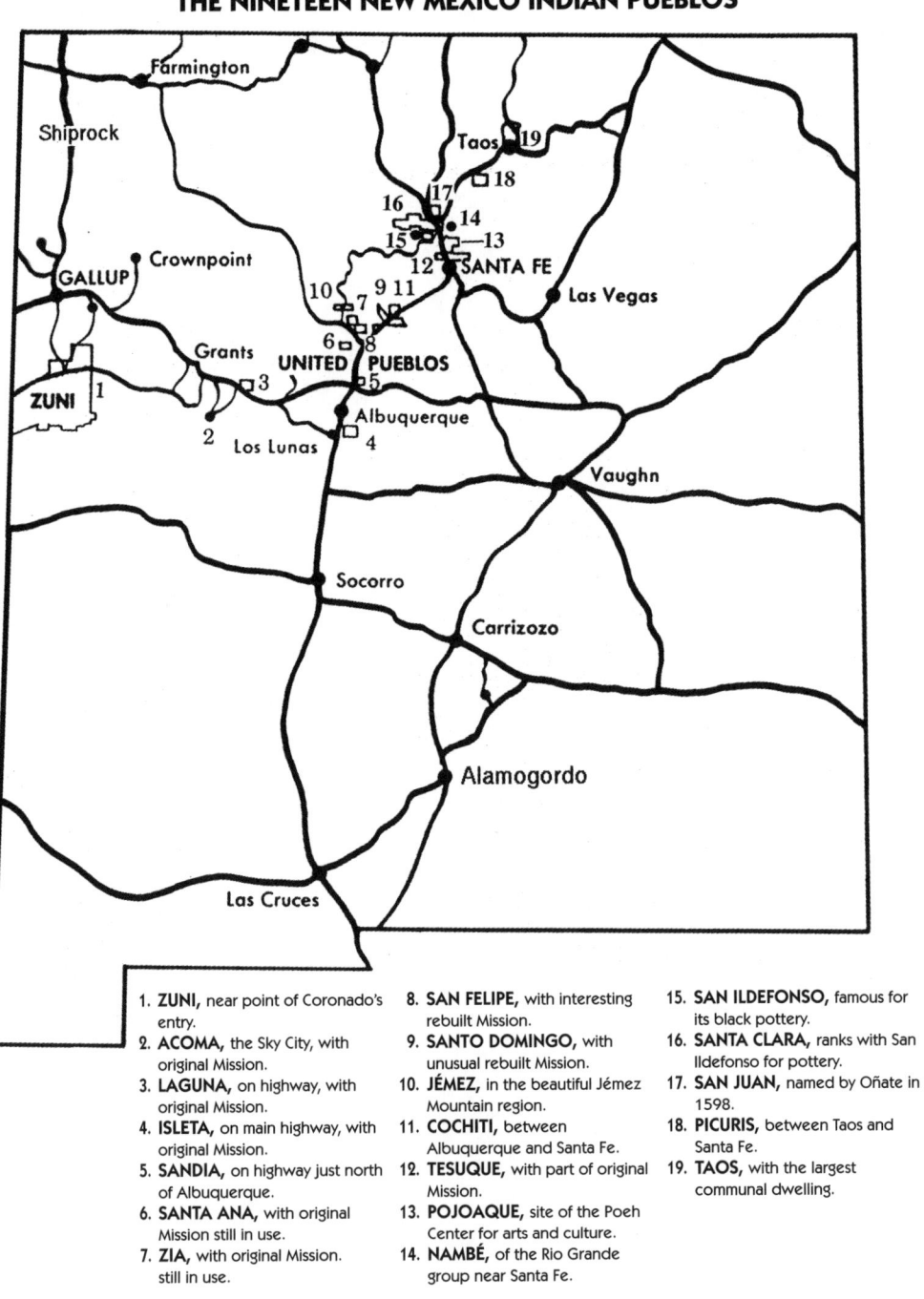

1. **ZUNI,** near point of Coronado's entry.
2. **ACOMA,** the Sky City, with original Mission.
3. **LAGUNA,** on highway, with original Mission.
4. **ISLETA,** on main highway, with original Mission.
5. **SANDIA,** on highway just north of Albuquerque.
6. **SANTA ANA,** with original Mission still in use.
7. **ZIA,** with original Mission. still in use.

8. **SAN FELIPE,** with interesting rebuilt Mission.
9. **SANTO DOMINGO,** with unusual rebuilt Mission.
10. **JÉMEZ,** in the beautiful Jémez Mountain region.
11. **COCHITI,** between Albuquerque and Santa Fe.
12. **TESUQUE,** with part of original Mission.
13. **POJOAQUE,** site of the Poeh Center for arts and culture.
14. **NAMBÉ,** of the Rio Grande group near Santa Fe.

15. **SAN ILDEFONSO,** famous for its black pottery.
16. **SANTA CLARA,** ranks with San Ildefonso for pottery.
17. **SAN JUAN,** named by Oñate in 1598.
18. **PICURIS,** between Taos and Santa Fe.
19. **TAOS,** with the largest communal dwelling.

INDEX

Names appearing in **boldface type** are individuals who have been profiled.
Page references in **boldface type** refer to illustrations.